Praise for

DARK INVASION

"Wonderfully gripping . . . cleverly crafted tension."

—*Washington Post*

"Howard Blum's riveting and perturbing *Dark Invasion* . . . is well researched and written, and it maintains a fairly high level of suspense, which is difficult to bring off in a book about historical events."

—*Wall Street Journal*

"*Dark Invasion* . . . will move you to the edge of your seat with the facts alone, but the author's suspenseful detective-mystery narrative is what keeps you there." —*USA Today*

"History is all about retelling tales that need telling. In *Dark Invasion*, Howard Blum has rescued a batch of compelling ones and woven them into grim, fascinating remembrance." —*Dallas Morning News*

"Howard Blum's story of the sinister and scary German terror attacks on America one hundred years ago reads more like a le Carré novel than a meticulous reconstruction of history. But the fact that it's true makes *Dark Invasion* all the more riveting. This is a terrific spy story." —Cokie Roberts, author of *Founding Mothers*

"*Dark Invasion* is a must-read for lovers of suspense and anyone who wants to understand how the basis of our homeland security system was born. Between 1914 and 1917, a clandestine network of German terrorists orchestrated a campaign of mass destruction and murder on American soil that has never been equaled. The network was made up of brilliant scientists, suave diplomats, and military and civilian operatives at the highest and lowest levels. The one requirement imposed on its members was a willingness to murder Americans on whatever scale necessary, by whatever means necessary. Opposing this juggernaut was Captain Tom Tunney, head of the NYPD's Bomb Squad, who in the process of working with his crack team of operatives would wind up creating the basis of America's Homeland Security System nearly a century before 9/11. Expertly told by Howard Blum with shocking betrayals, surprising heroism, artful cons, and heart-in the-throat chases, *Dark Invasion* grippingly brings to life two sets of equally fascinating antagonists—cops and terrorists—as they contend over a nation's fate."

—Tom Reiss, *New York Times* bestselling author
of *The Black Count* and *The Orientalist*

"A suspense-filled tale, *Dark Invasion* uncovers a fascinating corner of history when courageous New York City police officers fought insurmountable odds to defend America against sophisticated German saboteurs at the start of World War I."

—Ronald Kessler, author of *The Secrets of the FBI*
and *In the President's Secret Service*

"In his gripping and expertly crafted narrative, Blum demonstrates that the best stories are true. Told in the great tradition of spy thrillers, *Dark Invasion* is the startling tale of German secret agents operating in the United States during World War I and the determined effort of a New York detective to stop them. The result is a book that is not only engrossing, but helps explain why America entered the Great War."

—Scott Miller, author of *The President and the
Assassin: McKinley, Terror, and Empire
at the Dawn of the American Century*

"I read *Dark Invasion* without stopping. It is a well-researched and exceedingly well-written account of a pre–World War I series of terroristic attacks on the United States, in this case perpetrated by Germans. It is full of good stories and characters."

—Norman Stone, award-winning author
of *The Eastern Front: 1914-1917*
and *World War One: A Short History*

"Throws light on the war of espionage and terror Germany waged against the U.S. in 1915."
—*Vanity Fair*

"Blum's narrative of America's first exercise in homeland security is a worthwhile page-turner, combining the best features of a police procedural and a spy novel with a firm base in verifiable events."
—*Publishers Weekly*

"Terrifically engaging and pertinent tale of the New York City bomb squad that foiled German terrorist plots against the United States at the outbreak of World War I. *Vanity Fair* contributor Blum masterly retrieves this largely forgotten, haunting history of Germany's subversive attempts to halt the U.S. ability to send munitions to the Allies fighting against it in Europe. The author pursues the key players in an episodic narrative . . . creates some memorable portraits, accompanied by a lively gallery of photos, and keeps the heroic good-versus-evil plot simmering along in a nicely calibrated work of popular narrative history. Instructive, yes, but also as engrossing as good detective fiction."
—*Kirkus Reviews* (starred review)

"A spy thriller of the first order . . . *Dark Invasion* is another page-turner that is compelling to such a degree that one begins to doubt its veracity. Truth is stranger than fiction, however, and no one knows that more than Blum. He has a remarkable talent for both uncovering history's most inexplicably forgotten stories . . . and for writing non-fiction paced like a big-budget thriller."
—*Daily Beast*

"Sounds like a pretty good espionage thriller. . . . In fact, it's nothing less than authentic—albeit long-forgotten—American history, brought to vivid life. . . . *Dark Invasion* reminds us . . . that 'the past is never past.'"
—*Life.com*

Front page of the *Washington Times*, July 4, 1915.

DARK
INVASION

---

*1915: Germany's Secret War
and the Hunt for the
First Terrorist Cell in America*

HOWARD
BLUM

HARPER  PERENNIAL

NEW YORK • LONDON • TORONTO • SYDNEY • NEW DELHI • AUCKLAND

HARPER PERENNIAL

A hardcover edition of this book was published in 2014 by HarperCollins Publishers.

HarperCollins books may be purchased for educational, business, or sales promotional use. For information, please e-mail the Special Markets Department at SPsales@harpercollins.com.

An extension of this copyright page appears on pages 451–453.

Frontispiece: *Chronicling America: Historic American Newspapers*, Library of Congress.

First Harper Perennial edition published 2015.

Designed by Michael Correy

Library of Congress Cataloging-in-Publication Data has been applied for.

ISBN 978-0-06-230756-9 (pbk.)

15 16 17 18 19   OV/RRD   10 9 8 7 6 5 4 3 2 1

Once again, for Ivana

And, as always, with love

And to the memory of Annette Kuhn

"She got everything she needs

She's an artist, she don't look back."

The interest of history lies not in its periods but in its problems.

—HUGH TREVOR-ROPER

The lessons to America are clear as day. We must not again
be caught napping with no national intelligence organization.
The several Federal bureaus should be welded into one, and
that one should be eternally and comprehensively vigilant.

—ARTHUR WOODS, NEW YORK POLICE COMMISSIONER, 1919

The Dark Invader

—TITLE OF THE MEMOIR WRITTEN BY
FRANZ VON RINTELEN, THE GERMAN SPY NETWORK'S
CHIEF OPERATIVE IN 1915 AMERICA

CONTENTS

A NOTE TO THE READER

This is a true story. It was inspired by an article in the Central Intelligence Agency's in-house publication *Studies in Intelligence*. Written by a member of the CIA's history staff and published one year after the 9/11 attacks against America, the article was subtitled "Protecting the Homeland the First Time Around." Reading the piece, I began to realize that Captain Thomas J. Tunney, who led the New York Police Department's Bomb Squad from 1913 to 1917, was for all practical purposes the first head of Homeland Security. Intrigued, I set out to learn more about him and his activities.

In the nonfiction spy tale that follows, I tell how a sophisticated foreign intelligence organization launched a covert campaign of terror—bombs, germ warfare, and murder—against an unsuspecting turn-of-the-century America, and how Tunney and his men, at first overwhelmed and overmatched, rose to the challenge of defending the home front. This book is not an attempt to give the reader a comprehensive history of a reluctant America's entry into World War I. Rather, it shares the mysteries Tunney's team confronted and reveals, in their struggle to solve these, a dark and startling corner of the growing drive toward war.

In writing this account I was greatly assisted by the memoirs, diaries, and letters of the people involved, as well as by government documents, legal papers, and contemporaneous newspaper reports. All the material, including dialogue, in direct quotations comes from one of these sources. A complete chapter-by-chapter sourcing follows at the end of this book.

—HB

CAST OF CHARACTERS

THE SPIES

The Heads of the German Network

WALTER NICOLAI—master spy running Abteilung IIIB (the German secret service) in Berlin

COUNT JOHANN VON BERNSTORFF—German ambassador to the United States and titular head of Abteilung IIIB's operations in America

CAPTAIN FRANZ VON PAPEN—military attaché to the German embassy and desk officer in charge of sabotage operations

CAPTAIN KARL BOY-ED—naval attaché to the German embassy assisting von Papen in directing sabotage operations

DR. HEINRICH ALBERT—commercial attaché to the German embassy, and the American network's paymaster

Field Agents

CAPTAIN FRANZ VON RINTELEN—self-styled "dark invader" overseeing "the Manhattan Front"

HORST VON DER GOLTZ—Abteilung IIIB operative and saboteur

HANS VON WEDELL—agent in charge of false passports

PAUL KOENIG—security officer and enforcer

DR. ANTON DILGER—principal agent coordinating the network's germ-warfare operations

WALTER SCHEELE—longtime undercover agent in America and inventor of the "cigar" bomb

GEORGE FUCHS—sabotage operative recruited by his cousin, Koenig

ERICH VON STEINMETZ—Abteilung IIIB professional working closely with von Rintelen

ROBERT FAY—German soldier and engineer sent to America to assist von Rintelen

PAUL HILKEN—head of operations in Baltimore and involved in both the germ-warfare campaign and the attack on the Black Tom munitions depot

CHARLES VON KLEIST—a former sea captain assisting in the ship-bombing operations

MARTHA HELD—onetime opera singer running the network's safe house, a bordello on West Fifteenth Street in Manhattan

ERICH MUENTER (aka FRANK HOLT)—Harvard professor and wife murderer recruited by the network as an assassin

THE SPYCATCHERS

Officials in Charge

FRANKLIN POLK—intelligence liaison to President Woodrow Wilson

ARTHUR WOODS—New York City police commissioner

GUY SCULL—Deputy commissioner supervising the city's counterintelligence team

GUY GAUNT—head of Section V, the British Secret Intelligence Service's New York station

The Counterintelligence Team

CAPTAIN TOM TUNNEY—relentless head of the New York Police Bomb and Neutrality Squad

SERGEANT GEORGE BARNITZ—Tunney's loyal right-hand man

DETECTIVE AMEDEO POLIGNANI—veteran undercover operative

DETECTIVE PATRICK WALSH—master of disguises

DETECTIVE VALENTINE CORELL—German-speaking officer possessing a Romeo's charm

DETECTIVE HENRY SENFF—German-speaking marksman

DETECTIVE HENRY BARTH—the team's deep thinker

PROLOGUE:
"THE SPELL OF BELIEF"

If Erich Muenter hadn't walked across the Harvard campus to Emerson Hall on that wet February day in 1906 to borrow a book, he would never have seen the student pull the short-barreled black revolver from his pocket, aim, and, just as his arm was grabbed, fire. And then things might have been different.

It had been raining all morning, but as Professor Muenter made his way from the tiny classroom where he taught German to the formidable redbrick building on the opposite side of the muddy Harvard Yard, the storm suddenly became torrential. He tried to hurry, but his condition—"tuberculosis of the bones," the doctor had diagnosed with a helpless finality—made walking even in the best of weather an awkward exercise. By the time he reached the pillared portico of Emerson Hall, he was soaked.

"What is man that Thou art mindful of him?" challenged the inscription carved above the massive entrance doors. Charles Eliot, the pious Harvard president, had personally selected the lines from the book of Psalms only weeks before the building had opened to students the previous year. But Muenter held little countenance for religion or, for that matter, any philosophy that questioned his rightful place in the scheme of things. He bristled with an egotist's combative certainty; humility never had a chance to take root.

This dismal afternoon Professor Muenter's always feisty, self-important attitude—a demeanor that famously filled timid Harvard undergrads struggling through German 101 with fear and anxiety—

was further sharpened by the fact that he was drenched. The best Muenter could do, though, was to slap his damp, center-parted brown hair into place, give his shabby Vandyke a restorative tug or two, wipe his wire-framed glasses dry, and try to fix his customary confident, bemused expression on his sallow face. He might be soaked to the bone, but he'd still make it clear that he was a man of whom anyone, even the Harvard president himself, would be wise to be mindful.

The long trek up the three winding flights to the university's new psychology laboratory was difficult; his spindly legs, the muscles weakened by his degenerative illness, didn't do well on stairs. But Muenter was determined. At an off-campus German Society gathering he'd recently made the acquaintance of the lab's director, the celebrated professor Hugo Munsterberg, and the two men quickly found they had much in common.

It didn't seem to matter that Muenter, thirty-five years old and as thin and boyish as an undergraduate, could easily have passed for the portly forty-three-year-old bald-headed professor's son. Nor was their bond simply that they both had been born in Germany, still savaged their English with a distinct guttural rumble (although the younger man's accent was significantly fainter; after all, he'd been living in America for nearly half his life), and that both proudly held a cherished, even on occasion reverential, allegiance to the Fatherland. Rather, their budding friendship was built on a deeply held common interest in the criminal mind.

Professor Munsterberg had come to Harvard at the urging of William James, the philosopher, to set up the first scientific laboratory in the nation to explore the psychology of crime. And while Muenter's bachelor's degree from the University of Chicago was in German, as a graduate student at Kansas State University he had investigated the motives (or more often rationales, he'd correct with a sly precision) that drove individuals to commit crimes. His research had resulted in a paper entitled "Insanity and Literature." Now at Harvard, although he was pursuing his doctorate in German literature, Muenter retained his fascination with the mental mechanisms that create criminals.

When Muenter explained all this to Munsterberg, the professor immediately invited the younger man to visit his lab and to borrow any books he wanted from his personal library. Today, undeterred by the weather or the climb, a curious and enthusiastic Muenter had come to take advantage of the professor's generosity.

What a world Muenter entered! The top floor of Emerson Hall was a warren of rooms through which wound a snaking trail of electrical wires connected to ingenious machines that, Munsterberg boasted, could do nothing less than "reveal the secrets of the human mind."

As christened by the psychologist, the devices included an "automautograph," to measure arm and finger muscle movements under stress; a "pneumograph," to measure variations in breathing caused by emotional suggestions; and a "sphygmagraph," to record the halts, jumps, and rapid beatings of a guilty heart. These machines, Munsterberg promised, "reduced a knowledge of the truth to an exact science." In fact, in a widely read interview published in the *New York Times*, a resolute Munsterberg had proclaimed that "to deny that the experimental psychologist has the possibilities of determining the truth-telling powers is as absurd as to deny that the chemical expert can find out whether there is arsenic in the stomach."

Months later, when questioned about Muenter's tour of the laboratory on that rainy day, the professor would also be reminded of his bold comment to the newspaper—and his choice of metaphor would come back to haunt him with a chilling prescience. But that afternoon the renowned criminologist had no suspicions. In fact, he invited his young friend to sit in on a class that was about to begin.

Muenter was standing in the back of the lecture hall, listening to the professor with interest, when the outburst occurred.

"I want to throw some light on the matter," a student interrupted, rising to his feet as he spoke.

All at once another student jumped up to challenge him. "I cannot stand that!" he shouted.

"You have insulted me!" the first student angrily replied.

"If you say another word—," the second student warned, clenching his fist.

The first student drew a short black revolver from his coat pocket.

In a fury, the other student charged at him.

At the same moment, Professor Munsterberg hurried from behind his lectern, managed to put himself between the two students, and grasped the gunman's arm.

Suddenly the gun went off. Clutching his stomach, one boy slumped to the floor.

The classroom was pandemonium. Shrieking students jumped from their seats, eager to escape. But Erich Muenter, it was observed, stood rigidly at the back of the room, watching all that went on around him with a calm, unruffled fascination.

Nor did Muenter show any reaction when in the next instant the "wounded" student, grinning broadly, dramatically rose to his feet.

Calling the astonished class to order, Professor Munsterberg instructed the students to write an exact account of what had just happened. Tell me *precisely* what you saw, he reiterated.

As the students wrote, their professor explained that this was an exercise to demonstrate the fallibility of even eyewitness testimony in a criminal case. The search for truth, he lectured, may be well intentioned, but memory is always subjective. The shrewd courtroom defense attorney can use the power of suggestion to defeat most attempts to get at the truth. Similarly, the professor went on, the expert criminal can manipulate people so that they'll believe what he wants them to believe.

When the students read their reconstructions aloud, it was clear that Professor Munsterberg's thesis was correct: no two students offered identical versions of the "shooting." And when the psychologist tried to influence their memories with his own probing questions, their recollections grew further distorted. "Truth," the professor concluded, "exists only as an invention created under the spell of belief."

That evening as Muenter—clutching the borrowed book, its specific title long forgotten—made his way back to the rooms he shared with his pregnant wife and their daughter on Oxford Street, he found himself still thinking about all he'd seen. Time after time he played back in his mind the demonstration he had witnessed, and the students' contradictory and easily manipulated recollections of events. It had been an education.

But there was another reason the demonstration held his thoughts. It confirmed his long-cherished theory that the perfect crime was possible. Cast a "spell of belief," and you could get away with anything. Even murder.

Professor Erich Muenter, circa 1905, before he sported a Vandyke.

IN THE MONTHS THAT FOLLOWED, Muenter was busy. His long days on campus were crowded: a heavy teaching load, the graduate philology seminar required for his doctorate, and research on his thesis. Yet, whenever he could grab a moment, he traipsed to the top floor of Emerson Hall to select another arcane volume from Munsterberg's vast personal collection. As the oppressive Cambridge winter finally gave signs of turning into a welcome spring, despite all the academic demands on his time, the focus of Muenter's attention shifted anxiously to his pregnant wife. Leona was sick, and getting sicker. With her April due date approaching, her pregnancy had grown increasingly problematic.

The birth of their first child had been unmarred by complications; Helen was now a bubbly blond three-year-old who had inherited, admirers were quick to point out, her mother's ready smile. But the final weeks leading to this new baby's scheduled arrival had been an ordeal. Leona suffered bouts of excruciating abdominal pains.

Doctors were summoned, but the best they could do was recommend that Leona be confined to bed. Muenter made sure his wife obeyed. However, when the pains didn't subside, he lost patience. He dismissed one physician, then another. Instead, he decided that, with the help of a pair of hired nurses, he'd look after his wife himself. He'd accomplish more than any of the ineffective quacks who'd been consulted. His love for his wife would do more good, he diagnosed, than any medical degree.

Over the next ten fretful days, the nurses, a Miss Case and a Miss Dietrich, said they had never witnessed such solicitous attention from a husband. The professor was at his wife's bedside day and night. Why, the professor even insisted that he, and he alone, prepare the beef broth that was poor Mrs. Muenter's only source of nourishment, since she couldn't hold down solid food. The professor, they told concerned neighbors, would cook it just so, shooing them out of the kitchen, and then he'd sit on the side of his wife's bed and lovingly spoon-feed her. If Mrs. Muenter protested that she had no appetite, Nurse Case recounted with admiration, the professor would not be deterred. He insisted that his wife swallow every last drop, for her sake and the baby's. Such devotion, the nurses gushed. Such a good husband.

Muenter's ministrations succeeded. On April 6, as the doting professor at last agreed to leave the bedroom and allow the nurses to take charge, Leona gave birth to a healthy baby girl. The child was named Mary after Leona's favorite aunt.

The next three days, the nurses would fondly recall, were joyous. Not only was the infant flourishing, but Mrs. Muenter seemed on the mend. Her appetite had returned. One night she even ate the plate of boiled chicken Miss Case had prepared, and then surprised them further by asking for a second helping.

Yet by the week's end Leona was once again eating nothing but her husband's spoon-fed broth, and, more of a concern, the pains had returned. This time they were worse than ever. She suffered, and the nurses watched with sympathy as her husband suffered along with her. His pain and anguish as his wife's condition deteriorated tugged at their hearts.

When Leona died on the morning of April 16, Muenter was devastated. Neighbors heard him howling like a wounded animal. "I don't know what to do," he sobbed helplessly to Nurse Dietrich.

By late afternoon, though, the professor had pulled himself together and come up with a plan. A Cambridge undertaker had already removed his wife's body, but now Muenter decided that his wife would have wanted to be buried in Chicago with her parents in attendance at the funeral. Would the two nurses accompany him and the children on the train trip to Chicago? he asked. He'd like to leave tomorrow. Better to get this over and done with for the children's sake, he explained through his tears. Of course the nurses agreed, sobbing along with him, their tears as much for the brokenhearted professor as for his poor wife.

That evening when Muenter tried to make arrangements for the body to accompany him on the next day's train, there was a complication. Mr. A. E. Long, the undertaker, said that the body could not be removed from the funeral home until a certificate identifying the cause of death had been signed by a doctor. That meant, Long explained, that there would need to be an autopsy. After the procedure was completed and the certificate duly signed, the body could be shipped wherever the professor desired for burial.

Muenter flew into a rage. He insisted that he be allowed to take his wife home to Chicago so she could be buried in the presence of her grieving family. He shouted that the undertaker had no right to interfere.

Long apologized, but he remained adamant: a rule is a rule.

Muenter considered; and then he broke down in tears. He pleaded that he just wanted to bury his wife. He wanted her to find some peace at last. He cried and cried, his body shaking with grief. He was inconsolable.

Long could not help feeling the unfortunate man's pain. He finally told the professor that he'd have Mrs. Muenter's coffin on the morning train.

But after Muenter left, as Long prepared to embalm the body, he had second thoughts. Perhaps there was a way, the mortician reasoned with a more characteristic prudence, to satisfy both the bereft professor and the authorities. He decided to remove Mrs. Muenter's internal organs. First thing in the morning, he'd send them on to Dr. Whitney Swan, the Cambridge medical examiner. Of course by the time Dr. Swan got around to looking at them, the body would be on the train to Chicago. But it wouldn't matter, Long reassured himself. The autopsy of a Harvard professor's wife was, after all, just a formality.

THE FUNERAL SERVICE WAS HELD in the small living room of Leona's parents' home on Fullerton Avenue in Chicago. Burial followed at Rose

Hill Cemetery. Throughout the service and the internment Muenter was wooden, as if in shock. He seemed incapable of speaking. His gaze was vacant. After he returned from the cemetery, however, Muenter managed to pull himself together sufficiently to talk with Arthur Kremb, Leona's father.

He explained that he needed to get away. He wanted to think about everything that had happened. He asked if the Krembs would mind watching the children for a few days.

Of course, agreed Kremb. He told his grieving son-in-law to take some time for himself, to sort things out.

Muenter promised that he'd be back in two days.

Five days later, when two Chicago detectives came to Kremb's home with a warrant issued by the Cambridge police charging Erich Muenter with the murder of his wife, the professor had still not returned. The detectives explained that the Cambridge medical examiner had become suspicious after examining Leona's internal organs and had delivered them for further analysis to W. F. Whitney, a chemistry professor at the Harvard Medical School. Whitney quickly confirmed the medical examiner's suspicions: the remains were laced with arsenic. Leona Muenter had been slowly and painfully poisoned, he concluded.

Arthur Kremb refused to believe that his daughter's husband had murdered her. "I am sure that when a thorough investigation is made it will be found that everything is all right," he insisted stubbornly.

But as weeks, then months, and then years passed without any word from the professor, as Kremb and his wife were forced to raise their two grandchildren, Kremb began to realize that he had been wrong. Not only was his son-in-law a murderer, but he had gotten away with it. Erich Muenter had vanished.

PART I:
"A TROUBLED HOUR"

CHAPTER 1

Early-morning light beamed through the tall stained-glass windows, scattering a misty, diffuse glow over the nave and the rows of pews in St. Patrick's Cathedral on Fifth Avenue. But on this cold March morning in 1915, New York Police captain Tom Tunney deliberately stuck to the shadows, moving up a narrow side aisle as dark and gloomy as a sepulchre. When he drew closer to the altar, he ducked behind a massive stone pillar. He waited a moment to allow his eyes to get accustomed to the half-light shrouding his hiding place, and then he did a quick reconnaissance.

In the vestibule, three scrubwomen puttered about with pails and mops. The one with long red hair kept her head down as, on hands and knees, she washed the marble floor. She wore a faded blue skirt that reached to her ankles, a white blouse, and, rather oddly, a dark shawl that stretched like a tent across her broad shoulders. She scrubbed with diligence, and as she labored the shawl rose up her back. Tom saw a flash of the revolver in the holster strapped across her chest. But there was no way now to alert detective Patrick Walsh to fix his disguise. Things were moving too quickly.

The New York Police Department detectives, disguised as scrubwomen, who foiled an attempt to blow up St. Patrick's Cathedral. *From left:* Patrick Walsh, Jerome Murphy, and James Sterett.

Tom turned and looked up the aisle toward the front pews. An elderly usher, stooped and white-bearded, directed the stream of worshippers arriving for the seven a.m. Mass to their seats. The usher wore shiny gold spectacles and an absurd double-breasted frock coat that, Tom silently moaned, seemed more suitable for a minor European prince.

Giving him further cause for concern, detective sergeant George Barnitz—Tom's usually dependable right-hand man—was playing his role to a contrived hilt. The usher wheezed up the aisle with a theatrical slowness, his back bent in a pretense of age and humility that was comical. Tom wouldn't have been surprised if Barnitz's snow-white wig fell off his head, with all his bowing and scraping.

But these small worries receded as Bishop Hayes began chanting Mass. As the parishioners prayed, Tom prayed too. He prayed, he would later say, with more fervor than he had ever before evoked in all the years of his long churchgoing life. He prayed that he could prevent this great cathedral, and all who were in it, from being blown to bits. But for now all he could do was wait, and hope a merciful God would answer his prayers.

New York Police Department captain Thomas "Tom" J. Tunney.

TOM WAS THE HEAD OF the New York Police Bomb Squad. He had joined the department seventeen years earlier in 1898, a strapping, broad-shouldered twenty-two-year-old. The reasons for his signing on, he'd concede with a philosophical candor when years later he looked back at his long career, were a mixed and rather murky stew.

There was, for one thing, the example of his uncle John, sainted in family lore, who had proudly served in the Royal Irish Constabulary for more than two decades. Tom, who had been born in county Cork but since his eight birthday had made his home on Manhattan's West Side, nevertheless had the wistful notion that a way of life that had worked for one Tunney might work for another.

A further nudge was the public commitment of police commissioner Teddy Roosevelt to fill the department's ranks with the best and brightest rather than simply the recruits whose journey had begun in the politicized corridors of Tammany Hall. Always competitive, Tom wanted to prove that he could meet the commissioner's high standards.

But most of all, while Tom had only a vague knowledge of the policeman's job, it was the prospect of helping others and acting with honor that sent the young man to the downtown headquarters to file his application.

Honor was crucial. "It's the one thing they can never take from you," his Da, an Irish immigrant who had shuffled from one back-breaking day laborer's job to another until he keeled over dead at forty-eight, had lectured. And what could be more honorable, Tom instinctively felt, than being on the side of law and order? It was a direct, uncomplicated, and unyielding way of moving through the world, and it would serve him well throughout a lifetime of service.

From the start, Tom was gung ho. His first assignment was walking a beat in Brooklyn, and Officer Tunney was quickly known throughout the neighborhood as a dependable presence. There was the time, for example, when without bothering to call for reinforcements he single-handedly charged into a raging Friday-night bar fight and, with only a couple of swings of his nightstick and an intimidating stare, managed to restore order. Or, when he took off in surprisingly rapid pursuit of a purse snatcher and twelve blocks later ran him to ground (a feat that proved not to be a fluke when he won the hundred-yard dash at the Police Field Day that year in an impressive 10.5 seconds). People always felt safer when Officer Tunney in his high-collared gold-buttoned tunic was walking his beat.

At headquarters, Tom's superiors were also quick to notice the young man. From the first, it was recognized that Tunney had a commanding way about him, they would recall in testimonials written toward the end of his career. Although he was a big man, it wasn't so much his hulking size that made him such a dominating presence. Rather, it was his ability, deputy commissioner Guy Scull would remark, "to listen to those around him in thoughtful silence." It was a polite demeanor that earned respect. Tom never said much, Scull noted, but when he did speak, "people would listen."

Over the next decade, Tom's career flourished. "I went through the mill," was how Tom modestly recalled it, "graduating from one duty to another." He moved from patrol to the "shoo-fly squad," the plain-clothes cops who toured high-crime precincts throughout the city to see if officers were at their posts, and then on to the elite Detective Bureau, where he rapidly made a name for himself.

In one celebrated case he went undercover as a garage mechanic to solve the mystery of who had run down an unfortunate Brooklyn doctor as he stepped off a streetcar after a night spent delivering a baby. "Clever Detective Work," lauded the *Times*. Then there was the time he doggedly tracked down the villain who had poisoned an archbishop and thirty other prominent members of the University Club. "His exploits read like detective novels," a fawning press was soon gushing about its new tabloid hero.

As for Tom, while he was embarrassed by the attention he was getting, he had to concede that he had found his calling. He loved what he called "the stern chase" of detective work. "The thrill of starting without a clue, or maybe having just a single thread," he'd write in an account of his life and work, "and then working your way to the end was always an exciting journey."

Then in early 1913, after being promoted to acting captain by police commissioner Arthur Woods, the Harvard graduate and former Groton School English teacher who had been brought in to reorganize the department, Tom was put in command of the newly formed bomb squad.

From left: New York City police commissioner Arthur Hale Woods, New York City mayor John Purroy Mitchel, and General Leonard Wood review the Thirtieth U.S. Infantry as they pass Manhattan's City Hall on January 20, 1915.

New York had become a city of targets. Over the past unruly decade, both anarchists and Black Handers, as the cutthroat gang of Sicilian immigrants who signed their ransom notes with a black ink handprint had become notoriously known, had wantonly hurled bombs and planted explosives. Buildings had been destroyed, and lives lost. And the carnage, Commissioner Woods anticipated with a despairing logic, would only escalate.

The grudge match between the forces of labor and capital was heating up around the country; in Los Angeles twenty-one people had been killed by a bomb planted by union men at the *Los Angeles Times* building. There was no reason to expect this vendetta wouldn't soon zero in on the towering structures that lined the concrete-and-steel canyons of Wall Street.

Also cause for concern, the police department no longer had a formal unit to monitor the Black Handers. The Italian Squad, as it had been known, had been disbanded four years earlier after the police lieutenant who headed it was shot as he walked through the streets of Palermo, Italy, to meet "an informant."

It was Tom's assignment to stop the bombings. He was to arrest the men who mixed the chemicals and procured the sticks of TNT before they planted the devices. If that failed, if he was too late, he was to sift through the wreckage for clues. Then he was to hunt the bombers down. "To the ends of the earth, if need be," the commissioner solemnly ordered.

From the start, Tom was given a free hand. He could recruit any men he wanted for his mob, as special squads were called in the department. The commissioner also offered Tom the abandoned office of the Italian Squad.

It was a narrow, dingy loft above a Centre Street saloon, and it hadn't been cleaned in the years since the Italian Squad had been dissolved. But Tom accepted at once. The opportunity to work in secret, away from the tumult and politics of headquarters, would be, he realized, more important than comfort.

Another blessing: the commissioner made it clear that Tom would report to him, and only to him. No one else in the department, regardless of rank, had the power to question Tom's activities or countermand his orders.

Tom set to work. His first step, as he sardonically put it, was to make "the acquaintance of the bomb itself." He went to prisons and cajoled convicted Black Handers to explain how they had made their devices. He spent long days at the New York offices of the DuPont company, where officials and technicians gave him an extended course in explosives. He pored over Bureau of Mines publications, searching for information about the latest advances in demolition. He even, he said with some surprise, found himself "forced to become something of a student of chemistry."

It was a thorough tutelage, and it paid off. Over the next year Tom had, he'd say, "a good deal of experience in tracing bomb outrages to certain of the anarchistic and Black Hand elements in the population of the city."

Then, the previous summer, he had launched the investigation that eight months later would lead him and his team in the icy predawn darkness to St. Patrick's Cathedral.

CHAPTER 2

———

The first operational steps in Tom's long journey to the imposing cathedral had been taken in the basement of a decrepit tenement far uptown on 106th Street near the New York Central tracks. This was where the Brescia Circle, named in honor of the anarchist who had murdered an Italian king, met on Sundays.

These were uncertain times in the country: people were out of work; families were going to sleep each night hungry. The Circle's public meetings were fired with raw, desperate talk. The speakers raged about the swaggering forces of capital taking advantage of the working class. They railed with a fiery intensity about how the Catholic Church, with its well-fed priests and ornate temples, was ignoring its duties to the tithed and deluded masses. There were demonstrations, too, demanding jobs and fair pay. Last spring, a brash mob led by the Circle had stormed into St. Alphonsus Church in Brooklyn and refused to leave unless they received food.

Tom, who had grown up in a home where on some nights there was only thin soup for supper, could understand the anger and desperation building in the city. He was neither a husband nor a father; his job was his life. Yet he'd experienced enough hard times to feel for those who were out of work, for families who were struggling. And although he had little tolerance for people who charged into churches or wanted to undermine the government, members of his squad had heard him complain, "Some things in this country just aren't right." "Can't blame people for wanting a fair shake," he sympathized when other officers condemned the radicals.

But the Circle didn't merely talk or demonstrate. They also, as Tom put it with a professional's bitter cynicism, "had a fondness for bombs."

On July 4 the year before, a man had been arrested as he climbed over the wall surrounding the John D. Rockefeller estate outside the city in Tarrytown. On that same day, three members of the Circle were blown up in their rooms on Lexington Avenue when the device they were assembling exploded. Searching through the bomb factory debris, the police found evidence that tied together the day's events: the man in Tarrytown had been sent to reconnoiter the estate, and the next day he'd have returned to plant the Circle's bomb beneath a window of the Rockefeller mansion.

Tom gave the Independence Day incidents considerable thought. It was clear that only luck had averted a disaster that would've shaken the nation. Yet Tom was a cautious man, and he waited until he felt certain about how the bomb squad should proceed before sending word to Commissioner Woods that he needed to talk.

At the commissioner's suggestion they met in the Harvard Club; Woods liked to get away from the hubbub of headquarters, and he also liked a whiskey at the end of the day. It was Tom's first time in the university's clubhouse on Forty-Fourth Street, and they sat, drinks in hand, across from one another in a dimly lit high-ceilinged room that to Tom's eye seemed to stretch the length of a city block.

Scattered about the large hall, men had settled into leather chairs, sipping their cocktails and holding decorous, muted conversations. The bustling city with all its tumult and woes might have belonged to another universe. Tom couldn't help wondering what the Circle would have had to say about this cushy patrician sanctuary. For that matter, he found it all uncomfortably grand and ruling-class; at his roots he was still the rough-and-tumble Irish immigrant brought up on the West Side, the lad who'd left high school before graduation to bring home a paycheck.

After a few moments of small talk, though, he shoved any unease from his mind and plunged ahead. He began to explain to the commissioner why he'd asked to meet.

"Unrest is contagious," he declared, according to the account he'd write of the conversation. "The anarchist likes disturbance as well as he dislikes order." Although the botched attack against the Rockefeller family had resulted in the death of the three bomb makers and one arrest, in the minds of the Circle and its supporters, Tom explained, the very fact that the events had made headlines could be counted as success.

Then Tom turned grave. In the low, quiet voice he fell into whenever there was bad news to share, he offered up a prediction that had been troubling him for days.

It's not over, he declared. The notoriety will bring more attacks. More bombs will explode. Only next time, it might not be the bombers who are the victims.

"It's our duty," he said, "to make a careful investigation of the Brescia Circle."

The commissioner was a thoughtful man. He had been a master at the Groton School before joining the police department, and it was his pedagogical instinct to ask questions rather than summarily bark orders. He also respected Tom's knowledge; a decade of policing the sidewalks of New York taught the sort of things not even imagined in the classrooms of Harvard and Groton. He asked Tom what would be the best way to proceed.

Tom had a strategy; it had been clear in his mind before he'd arrived at the club. But he didn't just blurt it out. He believed there was more to be gained by giving the commissioner a glimpse of how he'd come to his plan. He was, after all, well aware that the scope of the operation he was envisioning, one that could go on for costly month after month without producing results, was unprecedented. He needed the commissioner's formal consent. If Tom overplayed his hand, Woods might dismiss the proposal as overly ambitious, at once both too risky and too expensive. Cautiously, Tom backed into his request.

His first instinct, he began, was to recruit an informant from within the Circle. It would be the safest approach, he explained. The department would need to provide bribe money, but, he went on, none of its men would be in any danger.

No sooner had Tom voiced this suggestion, however, than he went on to dismiss it. "I have always tried to avoid using stool pigeons," he explained as if giving a lecture to a novice—which in fact was pretty much the situation. "He's an uncomfortable ally on a case. You cannot be sure that a man who associates with criminals and is giving them away is not giving the case away at the same time."

The commissioner agreed that this seemed reasonable. He asked what alternative Tom was suggesting.

"We insinuate a detective into the Brescia Circle itself," Tom said.

He swiftly outlined the scope of his plan: One man working on his own. Send him in with a new name, new family history. We even get him a place to live. We give him a completely invented identity. And we run the operation long. We let our man slowly work his way into the Circle. Let him take his time, and win their trust. Then, when the next bomb's about to go off, he'll know. And my squad will be able to stop it.

Woods played with the idea in his mind. Tom worried that he'd been too bold, his scheme too grandiose. The New York Police Department had never before sent an officer off on such a deep, open-ended undercover operation.

"Let's do it," the commissioner announced at last.

IT DIDN'T WORK.

The officer went to the Circle's Sunday meetings. He spent long evenings hanging around the 106th Street basement headquarters. But he was never accepted into the group. And he didn't speak Italian; he couldn't eavesdrop when the huddled conversations in dark corners quickly switched from English.

Perhaps, then, it was his frustration that made him try even harder to ingratiate himself. Whatever the reason, the Circle grew suspicious. On two occasions he was accused of spying and brought before a Circle tribunal. Each time he was acquitted. But when he was singled out a third time, Tom grew fearful for the man's safety. He ordered the operation terminated.

CHAPTER 3

Count Johann Heinrich von Bernstorff, German
ambassador to the United States, 1915.

ike Tom's, Count Johann Heinrich Andreas Hermann Albrecht von
Bernstorff's plan had also fallen apart. The imperial German ambassador to America had counted on spending the summer with his
mistress in Newport, Rhode Island. But in the last week of June 1914,
he was ordered without warning back to Germany "for consultation."

And so on July 12 von Bernstorff, black silk top hat on his head and a chestful of medals and jeweled orders glittering on his black tailcoat, sat glumly in the back of an open carriage riding through the stifling streets of Berlin. The ambassador was certain his summons home had been unnecessary, an overreaction to a trivial event. Gottlieb von Jagow, the foreign minister, a silly, gloomy little man with an ungentlemanly stub of a mustache, had simply panicked.

The horses' hooves clip-clopped against the asphalt as the carriage proceeded down Unter den Linden on its way to 76 Wilhelmstrasse, the rambling rococo palace—once the home of the doe-eyed Italian dancer who was Frederick the Great's mistress—that was the headquarters of the Foreign Office. Tall trees lined both sides of the boulevard, spreading a leafy canopy, but the shade could not cool the ambassador's temper. He often quoted Bismarck's dismissive appraisal of Berlin as "a desert of bricks and newspapers," and baking in the hot summer sun, the city appeared even more stolid and gray than usual.

It was certainly empty. No one—at least none of the *hoffähig*, the people suitable to be invited to court—was in town. They would be at Kiel on their yachts or, like the kaiser, who had escaped to his grandiose palace in Potsdam, at their country estates. Von Bernstorff wanted to get his meeting with the irritating von Jagow over and done with as quickly as possible. He'd suffer through the no-doubt perfunctory briefing, and then he too could leave Berlin. He'd take the first liner back to New York, dutifully spend a day or two with his American-born wife at their summer estate on the north shore of Long Island, and then, after inventing a suitable excuse, hurry to Newport, where the season was in full swing, the starry nights were crowded with gay parties, and his mistress was waiting. The order to report "with all deliberate speed" to the Foreign Office, he felt with a simmering resentment, had been damned inconvenient.

Only two weeks ago he had been dining with the Spanish ambassador, a lively, erudite aristocrat who shared his appreciation for a well-turned ankle, in the Metropolitan Club in Washington, D.C., when the news spread through the dining room. The archduke Franz Ferdinand, the Austrian heir apparent, had been assassinated by Serbian nationalists. At once people began gathering around von Bernstorff's table, wanting to know what the German ambassador thought, whether he believed the murder of a royal in some obscure European city would have any larger consequences.

Peace in Europe, he'd explained that night in his faultless English, had been successfully maintained for years by an intricately woven web of diplomatic and military alliances. Treaties committed Germany to stand by Austria-Hungary. Russia, with its colossal army, had vowed to defend its weaker Slavic cousins. France would immediately retaliate for any attack on Russia. And England, although beleaguered by its problems with the rebellious Irish, had vowed to respond to any aggression against France.

It was as if the European rulers had locked themselves into a giant chess game, he went on genially, using one of his favorite metaphors. A move by one player was guaranteed by treaty to provoke a response.

Therefore, he insisted with total certainty, no one would dare move a single pawn. Common sense, as well as self-interest, dictated that the players continue to contemplate the board with pensive concentration, sitting around the table in an apparent stalemate rather than doing anything to risk upending the game and sending all the pieces flying.

The ambassador agreed that the murder of the archduke was a tragic event. But he assured his audience that it would be quickly forgotten, recalled, if at all, as only a small, irrelevant footnote to the larger concerns of the times. And with that the conversation moved on to the club bar, where, over cigars and brandy, the talk focused on the stock market, the grim rumors about the rapidly declining health of President Wilson's wife, and the upcoming weekend's parties.

Von Bernstorff was both surprised and annoyed when the flash cable arrived just three days later instructing him to return to Berlin at once. Nevertheless, a product of his rigid Saxon upbringing, he accepted an order as an order. On July 7 he was on board the *Vaterland*, the newly commissioned jewel of Germany's passenger liner fleet, as it left New York Harbor.

Despite his put-upon mood, it had been a pleasant voyage. His six° successful years as ambassador to the United States had earned him a good deal of acclaim, and the other first-class passengers vied to have the count at their table.

And he never disappointed. He was always charming and amusing, moving effortlessly from English (he had been born in London while his father was serving as ambassador) to German or to French to suit the preferences of his fawning dinner companions. The ladies found him quite dashing—tall, lithe, with a waxed upturned mustache like the kaiser's, deep blue eyes, and an aristocrat's elegant confidence and precise manners. When he waltzed them across the dance floor with a well-practiced grace, they were enthralled. The men, over cigars and the occasional game of poker, found him good company too. He'd almost managed to forget his annoyance at having to interrupt his summer's plans and rush to Germany.

But on this oppressive, hot day, as the carriage stopped in front of the Foreign Office building on Wilhelmstrasse and the liveried footman hurried to open the door, the count's simmering temper had once more taken firm hold. He rushed up the long stone steps, his mood as sharp as a Prussian officer's sword, eager to see von Jagow and then be on his way.

HE WAS KEPT WAITING. A soldier in a scarlet dress uniform had escorted the count to the second floor, where the foreign minister kept his office. But almost at once a frock-coated aide appeared from behind a closed door and asked if the ambassador would be so good as to take a seat. The foreign minister would be with him momentarily.

Directed to a plush settee in a small paneled room, von Bernstorff waited mutely for his summons, back straight as a cavalryman's, his white-gloved hands folded in front of him. Yet each passing moment ratcheted up his impatience another notch. Finally, when an official entered the salon to greet him, it was not the foreign minister, but rather the undersecretary, Arthur Zimmermann.

From left: Chancellor Theobald von Bethmann-Hollweg, undersecretary of state Arthur Zimmermann, and secretary of state Gottlieb von Jagow in front of the Reichstag in Berlin, circa 1915.

The count bristled. Over the years he had come to the conclusion that von Jagow was an annoyance, a narrow-minded, jumpy bureaucrat. But Zimmermann, he deeply felt, was a much more dangerous sort. The fat, red-faced bachelor with his hearty, back-slapping gemütlichkeit was the grinning embodiment of a precedent that could, he had little doubt, undermine both the distinction and the effectiveness of the German foreign service.

For generation after generation, the highest diplomatic positions had gone to the Junker class, the ruling elite who by breeding and instinct knew what was best for the Fatherland. Yet Zimmermann, a son of the middle class who had started in the lowly consular service, had somehow bounded up the foreign service ladder all the way to the second-highest rung. It was most inappropriate. Worse, the count feared for his country if its burghers, a crass and unsophisticated lot, would soon be strutting through ministry hallways and seated at fashionable dinner tables.

Zimmermann, effusive, offered apologies for the delay, but the count brushed them off. According to an account of the testy exchange that would become Foreign Office lore, he insisted that he see the foreign minister at once.

His tone flat and direct, Zimmermann said that would not be possible.

Von Bernstorff insisted that he had been instructed to come all the way from America to meet with Herr von Jagow.

The instructions, Zimmermann agreed, were to return home at once. But not, he said pointedly, to meet with the foreign minister.

Von Bernstorff said he did not understand.

But Zimmermann did not explain. He simply gave the count an address on Königsplatz. They are expecting you, he said.

Von Bernstorff began to protest feebly.

Zimmermann repeated that the count was expected. *At once.* Then he walked off, leaving the bewildered von Bernstorff standing alone in the room.

CHAPTER 4

The building on Königsplatz was squat and dingy, and there was neither a footman to open the count's carriage door nor a uniformed doorman at the entrance.

Once inside, though, von Bernstorff had to pass through a series of locked doors, each guarded by an armed soldier in field gray battle dress. This was, he decided, some sort of military command post, and clearly a most secret one.

He had known that clandestine government offices were hidden throughout Berlin, but these were small, discreet salons where the kaiser or the privy councillor could hold meetings in utmost secrecy, without even the comings and goings of the participants observed by curious glances. This building was a fortress, however, and a very busy one. Soldiers streamed through the long corridors and disappeared behind guarded doors. It was all very efficient, and very mysterious.

But for now, all the ambassador's racing mind could do was wonder what happened behind all the closed doors, and about the identity of the person in charge, an individual so powerful that even the Foreign Office had bowed to his authority. And wonder why this man had summoned him so urgently from America.

Before he could say a word, a soldier approached and instructed Herr Count von Bernstorff to follow him. A door opened onto a long hallway. Midway, a narrow, twisting staircase curved down and down, finally ending in the basement. Von Bernstorff couldn't help having the whimsical feeling that he was being taken to the wine cellar. But that lighthearted moment passed in an instant. He knew only too well that he hadn't been brought to this heavily guarded basement deep beneath the streets of Berlin to discuss vintages.

ONLY A SINGLE OVERHEAD LAMP lit the windowless subterranean room, yet its glare illuminated the man sitting behind the desk as effectively as a spotlight. He was short, compact, middle-aged, with a head of close-cropped dark hair and a hard, unforgiving face. He sat confidently, staring directly at the count, as unsmiling and purposeful as any interrogator. He wore a major's uniform, and that only added to von Bernstorff's growing unease. It seemed most irregular that a mere major would be in command, or that an officer of such rank could summon an imperial German ambassador.

But as soon as the officer introduced himself, von Bernstorff understood.

"I am Major Walter Nicolai," he said.

The count had heard of Nicolai, but until that moment he had seriously wondered whether the celebrated officer was a living, breathing person or simply a myth. Berlin was in many ways a small city, but no one in von Bernstorff's circle, people who lived with an intimate connection to power and privilege, had ever seen Nicolai. He remained a shadow, a mystery.

According to the legend that had become attached to Nicolai's name, for years he had directed the penetration of Russia by the Oberste Heeresleitung (OHL), the Supreme Army Command. From an army outpost in Königsberg, he'd recruited and then run a network of agents who infiltrated deep into the czar's army and government.

Yet Nicolai, who commanded an infantry regiment early in his career, had not been a cloistered deskman. Admiring stories had him serving side by side with his agents on the front line inside Russia as their guide, their confidant, their protector, sharing their constant terror, their gnawing anxiety that they'd been uncovered and the czarist police were about to pound down the door. And the plunder, if the accounts could be believed, had been extraordinary. The German general staff, it was whispered, now had copies of many of the czarist army mobilization plans as well as certain Russian diplomatic codebooks.

With the success of his Russian operations, the OHL had two years ago brought Nicolai back to Berlin. He was made head of the Sektion Politik des Generalstabes.

The name was misleading. This command did not primarily concern itself with politics. It was an intelligence agency. Its purpose was to conduct espionage: to learn by any means necessary what was happening around the world. And to conduct covert operations: to launch secret missions in foreign lands that would undermine the enemies of imperial Germany.

It was a vast organization; its ranks included more than a thousand agents and support personnel. Its power was immense. It answered to the kaiser, and he demanded only results; methods did not concern him. It worked in secret, yet, no doubt by shrewd design, tales about its shadowy activities and valuable accomplishments had swirled through the highest circles of government and Berlin society. Its name summoned respect and, in no less measure, suspicion, even fear.

It was known as Abteilung IIIB. It was the kaiser's secret intelligence service. And Walter Nicolai was its supreme commander.

Now that Nicolai had the count's attention, he went on without further prelude. Quickly, he made two pronouncements. The first came as a shock. But it was the second that left von Bernstorff completely undone.

There will be war, Nicolai said flatly. He added that it would be soon, before this summer was over.

As von Bernstorff struggled to come to terms with this grim news, Nicolai declared that the ambassador's help was required. He had been selected to perform an important service for the kaiser and for the Fatherland. He would direct Abteilung IIIB's operations in America.

IT WAS OTTO VON BISMARCK, Germany's farseeing chancellor, who in his prudent and ruthlessly practical way first understood the need for a centralized organization to gather intelligence on his country's foreign enemies. In 1861 he appointed Wilhelm Stieber, a former Berlin criminal investigator, to head the Central Intelligence Division, as it was originally known. Stieber, who had policed the streets of Berlin by establishing a network of informants, people in all walks of life who, for cash or a favor, would pass on information, brought a cop's mentality to the task.

Knowledge, Stieber's years in law enforcement had convinced him, was the key to power. As Germany's first spymaster, he sent out a string of agents recruited from the police and military academies to cultivate informants all across Europe.

A half century later, when Nicolai took control, the methods had grown more sophisticated, but the service's guiding principle had not changed: Know the enemy.

At a training school outside Berlin, novice agents went through two years of rigorous education. In addition to weapons instruction, sabotage techniques, and code writing, they studied topography, trigonometry, and draftsmanship so that the precise details of a military fortification, or a harbor, or a munitions factory could be accurately sketched. They became experts in European army and naval equipment, trained to identify at a glance whether the stockpiled shells were, say, for a 75-mm cannon, a 105-mm howitzer, or just a Stokes mortar, or whether the ship steaming off to sea was a destroyer or a light cruiser.

After graduation, Abteilung IIIB agents—and there were a fair number of women in each class—were sent abroad with the orders to find jobs at once. Good cover, Nicolai believed with a field man's hard-won knowledge, was essential if you were to live in enemy territory and not arouse suspicions.

In small garrison towns, in waterfront neighborhoods surrounding naval bases, and along gilded thoroughfares of capital cities, agents opened tobacco shops, or grocery stores, or boardinghouses, or brothels. They worked as waiters, or teachers, or governesses, or whores. Whatever they saw or heard, hard facts and tantalizing rumors, was written down. They collected the names of journalists, of soldiers, of statesmen whose vices might allow their loyalty to be compromised. They made lists of immigrants whose family ties to Germany made them potential recruits.

All this information was stored in the long rows of files that filled the basement beneath the Königsplatz headquarters. It was a cave of secrets. By the summer of 1914, Nicolai controlled the largest and most efficient intelligence organization in the world. When war broke out, his operatives would already be in place, ready to move against the enemy.

Except that Nicolai, usually so meticulous, had made one miscalculation.

It was a dangerous error. In fact, it could, he had come to realize, cost Germany the war.

Germany had deployed all its operatives in Europe. It had buried agents deep in England, France, and Russia. It had focused on Germany's traditional enemies—and it had ignored America.

In July 1914 Germany had only a single part-time agent in the entire United States—Dr. Walter Scheele, a timid, elderly New Jersey chemist who lacked the energy to poke about the factory where he worked, let alone fulfill his grandiose assignment of monitoring the entire American munitions and explosives industry.

Yet in the increasingly tense days following the archduke's assassination, as the high command's battle plans were taken from safes, as guns were loaded and the order to open fire drew closer, Nicolai reached a terrible conclusion: he had gotten it wrong. As head of the secret service, he was better able than most to evaluate Germany's chances—and now, with an unnerving jolt, he suddenly understood the folly of his narrow view of the world.

Although separated from Europe by a wide ocean, a maturing, industrialized America had the power to change the course of the war.

It was vital that the United States stay out of the fight. With its potentially large army and vast resources, America could lead Germany's enemies to victory.

Still, even if the U.S. government remained officially neutral, once war was declared, it was inevitable that Britain would blockade the Atlantic. Its mighty navy would very effectively prevent Germany from trading with the United States. It was crucial that the Allies also be prevented from receiving shipments of American munitions, arms, and food. The enemy armies must not be restocked by American supplies.

There were only two ways for Germany to cripple Atlantic shipping coming from America—U-boats and sabotage. The German navy, Nicolai knew, didn't command enough submarines to patrol the shipping lanes effectively. Sabotage was the only alternative.

There was no time, however, for squads of trained operatives to infiltrate the United States; getting agents in place, constructing believable covers, was a long and delicate process. And when the wartime travel restrictions went into effect, the smuggling of even a single Abteilung IIIB spy into the country would owe as much to luck as to tradecraft.

Nicolai had survived by not being impulsive. He had built his career on his measured, reflective habits, mulling all the facets of a problem before deciding on a course of action. Yet the proximity of war forced him to act with uncharacteristic swiftness. There were no other realistic options, he soberly concluded; and then he had von Bernstorff summoned. The ambassador to America would have to do.

SITTING NOW IN HIS BASEMENT office across from the count, Nicolai, understandably, didn't share the mental journey that had led to this meeting. He was not a man to offer confidences. He simply gave von Bernstorff his instructions.

The count, while pursuing his normal and very public diplomatic duties as ambassador, would in total secrecy also direct and develop a network of intelligence agents in America.

Their mission was twofold: first, to keep America out of the war; and second, to prevent munitions and other goods from leaving America and reaching the enemy. Von Bernstorff was to return to the United States as soon as possible to begin his assignment.

There was one further thing, Nicolai added before the meeting ended. He wanted to make sure the count fully understood the importance of his clandestine mission. Von Bernstorff and his agents were to use any means necessary to accomplish their objectives.

CHAPTER 5

———

A s Tom Tunney, meanwhile, struggled to find a way to get his stalled investigation of the Brescia Circle back on track, the bombings continued. A device placed in the aisle of a Queens church exploded in the middle of services. The worshippers fled in panic, but injuries were only minor. The next day a bomb went off at midnight outside a priest's home in Brooklyn. The blast shattered all the windows in the house, as well as those of the building next door. But once again luck held: no one was hurt.

Tom, however, knew the odds were piling up against the city. It would be only a matter of time before someone was killed. He decided he'd no choice but to try again. He'd place another man inside the Circle.

The blame for the failure the first go-around, Tom confessed in a rare display of feelings to Commissioner Woods, was all his. He had picked the wrong man.

The subtle craft of running an agent—being his only lifeline to the world he'd left behind—was new to Tom. Like the commissioner, he too would need to get his education while on the job. But Tom was determined to learn from his previous mistakes.

He sent word to precinct houses throughout the city that the bomb squad was looking for an Italian-speaking volunteer. It would be a special operation. It would be dangerous. No officer should apply unless he was willing to accept the risk.

Tom received the names of eighteen candidates. After reviewing their service records, he "reached out," as the department euphemistically referred to a summons by a superior officer, to six of them. They appeared for interviews at the squad's second-floor office across from headquarters on Centre Street.

New York Police Department headquarters at 240 Centre Street
in Lower Manhattan. The offices of Tunney's bomb squad
were located in a loft across from the building.

The sessions were one-on-one, Tom interrogating a single candidate at a time; and the questions he posed were, he'd admit, as irrelevant as the answers. He was searching for a type, and Tom let his instincts guide him.

He finally decided on Amedeo Polignani. He was a darkly handsome detective, just twenty-seven, with a high pompadour of jet-black hair, a weightlifter's burly physique, and a warm, ready smile so bright it nearly glowed. What Tom liked best about Polignani, though, was the way the detective carried himself—quiet, confident, and unassertive. He was the sort of good-natured young man whom people found easy to like—even those, Tom was gambling, who were angry enough to want to blow up the city.

His instructions to his new operative were succinct.

"Your name from now on is Frank Baldo," Tom said with the authority of a magician waving his wand. "Forget you're a detective. You can get a job over in Long Island City. You are an anarchist. Join the Brescia Circle and any other affiliated group, and report to me every day."

Tom would be his sole handler. There would be no cutouts; he was to call Tom directly. A special telephone line was installed in Tom's office, and Polignani—or was it now Baldo? Tom wondered—was instructed to call this number at specific hours. Make sure, Tom told his operative, to call from a pay phone. Choose a store with only one phone booth; someone in an adjoining booth might overhear. The older members of the group will be suspicious, he warned; they'll follow you. He insisted that Polignani should not call unless he was certain he was alone or not being watched.

There was one final bit of advice, and Tom, the novice agent runner, repeated it like a mantra. "Keep your eyes and ears open, and your mouth shut," he said firmly. "Eyes open. Mouth shut."

Then it was time. Tom was as anxious as if he were the one going off behind enemy lines, yet he did his best to act as if this were not an extraordinary occasion for both of them. He knew there would be emergencies, situations they hadn't planned for, hadn't discussed. All he could do, though, was trust that the man he'd chosen would find the ingenuity to deal with them.

Tom shook his hand. Polignani responded with a sharp salute, a flash of his hundred-watt smile; and then Frank Baldo went off to start his new life.

CHAPTER 6

Kaiser Wilhelm II of Germany, shown here circa 1910–1915.

In Europe events unfolded with an increasingly bleak and bellicose momentum. In the shadows, a tense von Bernstorff hurried about Berlin, making the final preparations for his own war.

On July 27 Kaiser Wilhelm abandoned his summer holiday in Potsdam and returned to the steamy streets of Berlin to confer with his generals and ministers. He strode about meetings in the royal palace in military uniform, saber dangling from his belt, as though he expected at any moment to give the order to charge. The prospect of leading the nation into war, of crushing the enemies who encircled the Fatherland, thrilled him.

The following day, Austria, having been reassured of Germany's "faithful support" even if her actions were to provoke the great Russian Bear, declared war on hapless Serbia. Its booming guns bombarded Belgrade with impunity. In outraged response, armies throughout Europe began mobilizing. The kaiser's envoys in London, Paris, and St. Petersburg delivered earnest ultimatums, demanding that forces stand down. These pleas for restraint, however, were ignored.

Orders went out for two million German soldiers to begin making preparations for war. "Let your hearts beat for God, and your fists on the enemy," the kaiser, now a warlord, thundered to his troops. In Berlin crowds swelled the streets, their fervent patriotic voices rising up to sing "Deutschland über Alles."

Across the map of Europe, the row of dominoes leaned precariously. A wanton push would send them all crashing into one another.

On August 1 a German infantry company crossed the border into neutral Luxembourg. The troops occupied a small cobblestoned town on the slopes of the Ardennes, Troisvierges. In the chagrined parliaments of Europe it seemed clear that the choice of this village was an implicit warning, and that the next two virgins to be violated by German troops would be Belgium and France. The dominoes tottered, and war was a certainty.

VON BERNSTORFF'S WORLD WAS ALSO tottering. He was having difficulty coming to terms with his mission. He was no stranger to deceit; he was a diplomat, after all. But he could not contemplate the treachery demanded by his new clandestine role without feeling soiled.

Gentlemen were not spies. They did not slink about trying to learn other gentlemen's secrets. They did not betray friends, and in his six pleasant years in America he had made many friends. He was being ordered to trample over his own Junker concept of honor.

Yet this was war. The Fatherland had asked for his help. In his agonized mind, class and country struggled for his loyalty. He remained unsure which would ultimately win.

On August 2, the same day that German troops completed their occupation of Luxembourg, von Bernstorff left for America on the *Noordam,* a Dutch liner. This voyage would not at all resemble the trip that had brought him to Germany.

The *Noordam* was a creaking relic, old and tarnished, and soon to be retired. Yet von Bernstorff hardly noticed. He traveled furtively and anonymously, having conspired to keep his name off the passenger list. He ate his meals in the seclusion of his tiny stateroom. When he ventured on deck, he scrupulously avoided conversations. And everywhere he went, day or night, he clutched the handle of a black briefcase in his right hand as firmly as if his life depended on it.

Inside was a fortune—$150 million in German treasury notes.

It was the initial funding for his secret mission in America.

A German Empire banknote with a value of twenty
marks (*Reichsbanknote Zwanzig Mark*), 1915.

On the count's last day in Berlin, Nicolai had handed him the package containing the money without ceremony. It might have been a letter he was asking the count to post. His terse instructions, however, left no doubt about its importance.

Under no circumstances, Nicolai lectured, was von Bernstorff to let the package out of his sight. In the event that war was declared before the ship reached New York and British sailors came on board to seize the vessel, von Bernstorff was to toss the package into the Atlantic. It would be better, the spymaster said, to have the treasury notes on the ocean floor than for the British to begin asking questions about why the imperial German ambassador was transporting $150 million to America.

On board the *Noordam*, von Bernstorff remained vigilant. His manner stiffened, and he stayed alert. The briefcase in his clenched hand was a constant reminder of his mission. The habit of caution was taking hold. Apprehension filled his thoughts. As the long days at sea passed, he began to learn what it was to lead a secret life.

ON THE FOURTH DAY OF August 700,000 German troops, their spiked helmets glistening in the sun, marched in smart, orderly column after column into Belgium. That same morning the kaiser, hand resting on his sword hilt as if he were already posing for a victory statue, stood in front of his throne at the palace and addressed the assembled deputies. "We draw the sword with a clear conscience and with clean hands," he declared with all the self-righteous piety of a man who had neither.

Hours later, his chancellor, Theobald von Bethmann-Hollweg, spoke to a cheering Reichstag, giving a more candid, but equally guiltless, rationale for Germany's firing the first shots: "Our invasion of Belgium is contrary to international law but the wrong—I speak openly—that we are committing we will make good as soon as our military goal has been reached."

Europe was at war.

IN WASHINGTON, PRESIDENT WOODROW WILSON was informed of the outbreak of fighting as he sat at his dying wife's bedside. Already in mourning, this emotionally battered, deep-thinking man with a pacifist's heart and a statesman's optimistic vision heard the news and offered his help. He quickly wrote out an ardent message and asked that it be sent to the leaders of the warring nations: "I should welcome an opportunity to act in the interest of European peace, either now or any other time that might be more suitable, as an occasion to serve you all and all concerned in a way that would afford me lasting cause for gratitude and happiness."

Two days later, his wife died. He was bereft. "What am I going to do? What am I going to do?" he cried out to the heavens as he turned in anguish from her inert body—his heartfelt words an eerie echo of the master actor Muenter's contrived grief.

A week after his wife's burial, Wilson reined in his emotions and, wearing a black armband, addressed the American people. It was important, he felt, that the country understand the opportunity that existed, the "great permanent glory" that could be gained if America acted wisely. It was vital that the country not allow itself to be pulled into the fighting. He had come to the podium to preach neutrality.

His neutrality, however, was not a detached isolationism but something more vigorous and, he deeply believed, decidedly more moral. It was an evangelical strategy. America must assume its rightful place in the center of the world stage as arbiter, the one country that could apply the "standards of righteousness and humanity" to the European nations whose ambitions and greed had led them astray. Neutrality was the path to a benevolent destiny—an American-negotiated world peace.

"Every man who truly loves America," he implored, "will act and speak in the true spirit of neutrality, which is the spirit of impartiality and fairness and friendliness to all concerned." He begged his countrymen to be "neutral in fact as well as name, impartial in thought as well as action." The days ahead, he warned, will "try men's souls." But a neutral America would give humanity "the gift of peace."

CHAPTER 7

―――――――

For months Frank Baldo had been attending meetings, listening with attention to one fervent speech after another either urging the overthrow of the government or denouncing the rapacious greed of the Catholic Church. He'd found a job doing manual labor in a Long Island City factory. He'd rented a sparse room with peeling paint in a building on Third Avenue where the hallways smelled of cat piss, and tried to pretend that it was home. He'd not seen his wife and infant son in the Bronx for so long that their absence tugged at him constantly. Each day in this strange, unnatural world was a lonely struggle.

No less dispiriting, as his daily calls to Tom made clear, was that there was nothing to show for all his painstaking efforts. Only a few members of the Circle had bothered to say more than hello, while the leaders blatantly ignored him. They'd gather in corners whispering intently, and all he could do was keep a respectful distance and fix a disinterested smile on his face.

Be patient, Tom advised, hoping he'd found a steady, reassuring tone. The truth was, though, that Tom was inwardly growing more and more concerned. He was beginning to suspect that this operation too would fail. It was as if he could hear a clock ticking ominously inside his head: *It is getting late. Time is running out.*

In November a bomb wedged against the door of the Bronx County

Courthouse exploded. Was it the work of the Brescia Circle? Tom had no idea, and neither did his agent. The racing clock in his mind ticked louder and louder.

At last, though, Baldo got his opportunity. One Sunday night, as the more important members of the group huddled secretively, someone, bored and in high spirits, suggested a wrestling match. The men went at it. It was all good fun. But Frank Baldo, the new recruit who was built like Hercules, fought like a champion. He tossed one man after another to the floor as effortlessly as if he were handing out flyers announcing the next demonstration.

Baldo, who'd thoroughly enjoyed the chance to channel some of his frustration, was smoothing his ruffled hair back into place when he felt a tap on his back. He turned to see Carmine "Charlie" Carbone, the short, grim-faced shoemaker—a nasty piece of work, Frank had decided when he'd first spotted him months earlier—who was one of the group's leaders.

"You're a strong fellow," Carbone said, and gave the new recruit a long, appraising look. "I'm glad to see you're a member of the Brescia Circle."

Frank smiled, and did his best not to confide how much pleasure it had given him to hurl those men across the room. In other circumstances he'd have gladly broken an arm or two, and could have done it easily and without compunction. They continued talking as they left the basement and walked up Third Avenue.

"The trouble with those fellows," said Carbone, "is that they talk too much and don't act enough. They don't accomplish anything."

"That's right," Baldo agreed, restrained but still playing along.

"What they ought to do is throw a few bombs and show the police something," Carbone went on. "Wake them up!"

Carbone waved his right hand in front of Baldo's face. The fingers were short stumps. "I got that making a bomb," he explained proudly. "Some day I'll show you how to make 'em."

AND SO THEIR FRIENDSHIP BEGAN. They marched shoulder to shoulder at demonstrations, sat together at meetings, and went off for a few beers most Friday nights, and Carbone introduced him to his buddy, Frank Abarno. They became an inseparable trio.

Baldo courted both men carefully. He listened attentively, smiled, but did not talk much. He never asked questions. And in time, Carbone kept his promise and showed him how to make a bomb.

On a wintry Sunday in January when the basement meeting room seemed as frosty as an icebox, Carbone waited until the speeches were finished and then drew Baldo aside. "Come on up to the 125th Street Station," he said quietly. "It's warm up there, and we won't be bothered. I'll tell you something about making bombs."

In the comforting heat of the subway station, the steady churning and high-pitched screeching of the trains making it difficult for bystanders to overhear, Carbone talked freely. He boasted that he could get all the dynamite he needed from his uncle, a contractor. He just needed some ignition caps, each one, say, about two inches long.

"We'll get some dynamite, and then you and Frank and me will blow up some churches, see?"

"Sure," Baldo answered evenly. "What church?"

"St. Patrick's is the best. This time it'll be a good one too. I'll make a bomb that will destroy the cathedral down to the ground."

In the days that followed, they set to work making two bombs. Abarno and Carbone carefully measured the proportions of sulfur, sugar, chlorate of potash, and antimony. Next the mixture was poured into two tin soap cans. A length of strong cord bound strips of iron rod to the can, and this was further reinforced by wrapping copper wire repeatedly around the entire device.

Baldo's heart galloped as he watched the two men; the memory of the three Circle members who'd been blown to bits while working in a bomb factory on Independence Day never left his mind. But when Carbone picked up a hammer and began firmly banging the fuses into the tops of the devices, his courage abandoned him. He scrambled behind the bed on the other side of the small room, and then, for further protection, dropped to the floor.

"No use to hide there, Baldo!" Carbone teased. "If she goes off, she'll blow the whole house down."

The house did not blow up. The two lethal devices were completed, and Carbone gently placed them in the bottom of a steamer trunk. The swirls of copper wire had given them an orangish tint, and they looked like small, very spooky pumpkins. Carbone closed the trunk, and then took a key from his pocket and locked it. As soon as the bombs were out of sight, Abarno shared his plan to destroy St. Patrick's.

"We'll meet here in two days, on Tuesday morning at six o'clock to the minute," he said. "We will get to the cathedral just at 6:20. Then we light the bombs, and the fuses will burn slow for twenty minutes. We can get over to Madison Avenue and then we can all get to work on time. We'll have a good alibi, all right. Then we'll get together Tuesday night and go some place and have a good time."

In high spirits, the men left the bomb factory. Baldo walked with Carbone for a while down Third Avenue and then said he was exhausted. The day's activity, he confessed, had him still shaking. He wanted to go back to his room and get some rest.

Carbone laughed. He told his friend to get a good night's sleep. Baldo, he said, needed to be ready for Tuesday.

Baldo went off alone. He walked slowly. But when at last he was certain he was not being followed, he rushed through the early-evening darkness to find a phone booth. He needed to call a private line on Centre Street at once.

WHERE WERE THEY? TOM WONDERED.

He stood in the cathedral, pressed tight against the stone pillar in the semidarkness, and continued his vigil. The Tuesday-morning

Mass had begun, yet there was still no sign of the bombers. Had they opened the cathedral door, looked up the aisle, and at once seen through his detectives' disguises? Had they bolted?

In the next uneasy moment, another thought jumped into his mind: What if they had made Polignani? He would never forgive himself if something had happened to that brave young man. Should he risk summoning one of his men parked in an unmarked car on Fifth Avenue? Should he have the officer rush down to Centre Street in case Polignani was trying to contact him? Six months of exacting, painstaking work was on the line, but Tom was getting very close to putting the entire operation in jeopardy. He owed it to Polignani, to the detective's wife and baby, to get him out of this alive.

Yet Tom, his stomach twisting into tighter and tighter knots, waited. Just one more minute, he decided.

At last he saw them. There were just two men, Abarno and Baldo, and they were walking up the north aisle of the cathedral. Later, Tom would learn that Carbone had had a last-minute case of nerves. At this moment, though, Tom centered all his attention on Abarno and the ominous object protruding from the pocket of his topcoat.

Abarno led the way. Both men held lit cigars by their sides. It was as if they were holstered weapons.

On the altar, a bell rang. The bishop was about to begin the consecration.

At the tenth pew, Abarno gestured to Baldo to stop. He obeyed, and dropped to his knees in prayer.

Abarno continued on. He walked up another four rows, then took a seat. His head and body bent forward as if he too were in prayer.

The scrubwoman had already put down her mop. She moved up the aisle, a rag in her hand. But she made no pretense of dusting as she hurried forward.

Abarno suddenly rose. He darted to a pillar near the north end of the altar.

"Sanctus, sanctus, sanctus," the bishop chanted.

Abarno crouched by the pillar. Swiftly, he removed the bomb from his coat pocket with one hand and placed it against the base of the stone column. With his other hand, he flicked the ashes from the coal of his cigar and used the glowing end to ignite the fuse. The fuse started to burn, and he fled quickly down the aisle.

By his third step, the charwoman had grabbed him in an iron grip.

In the same moment, the elderly usher suddenly could not only walk upright but run. He sprinted to the pillar, found the bomb, and pinched out the burning fuse with his fingers.

Tom came out of the shadows to arrest Baldo. It was important to maintain Polignani's cover until all the conspirators—Carbone and other members of the Circle—were in custody. Tom did his best not to say anything other than a terse "You're under arrest." He tried not to betray his pure joy at his realization that with those words, he knew his agent had returned from a very dangerous mission. But as Tom put the cuffs on Baldo and led him out to the waiting police car on Fifth Avenue, he couldn't help feeling that never before in his long career had he been so happy to make a collar.

CHAPTER 8

————

The British sailors boarded the *Noordam* as it approached Dover. Europe was at war, and the British navy ruled the sea. Von Bernstorff had no choice but to join the other passengers when the order was given to line up on deck. He went topside with the briefcase that held $150 million in treasury notes in his hand.

On deck, he slowly edged closer and closer to the rail. He moved without apparent purpose, a restless passenger absently stretching his legs. To his surprise, he felt calm, almost at peace. Ever since his meeting with Nicolai he had wondered what he would do, how he would act under stress. Now he knew.

Summoning up a deliberate nonchalance, he leaned absently on the rail. The sharp, crisp smell of the ocean filled the air. If he was challenged, he would toss the briefcase into the water before the sailors could reach him. One hundred and fifty million dollars' worth of notes were as heavy as a brick; the briefcase would sink in an instant to the bottom of the sea. He was prepared.

Von Bernstorff waited. A British sailor fixed his gaze on him from across the deck. The count did not smile; instinct told him that little would be gained by appearing eager to ingratiate himself. Yet at the same time, he tightened his grip on the briefcase. With the sailor's first step toward him, it would fly into the Atlantic.

The sailor moved on. No one said a word to von Bernstorff; he was ignored. And within the hour the *Noordam* was steaming on to New York Harbor.

There had been no drama, no crisis. But a lesson had been learned. Von Bernstorff discovered not only that he could play his secret role but also that he enjoyed its sharp edge of danger. From that moment on he no longer had any qualms, any doubts, about his double life. He would be Germany's spymaster in America. He would lead his country's attack in an undeclared war.

WHEN TOM WANTED TO THINK, or simply escape from the pressures of his job, he'd take off on long, solitary runs. He'd begun running when he first joined the force to train for the annual Police Field Day; in his twenties, he was unbeatable in the hundred-yard dash, and then, older, he won medals in long-distance races. These days, though, he ran only to get his thoughts in order.

With his captain's salary, he'd recently bought a newly built two-story brick house on the corner of Fuller Place in Brooklyn. It had a bay window and a narrow front porch, and both, with a craning of the neck, offered grassy views of Prospect Park.

It was not long after the conclusion of the Circle case that Tom took a loping jog through the park. He had long legs, and he ran easily, without effort or, it seemed, exhaustion.

As he ran that afternoon, he recalled the lengthy, tense operation that had just been put to rest. He felt a sense of pride in what he and his squad had accomplished. Both Abarno and Carbone had been convicted, and would be off the streets for at least the next six years. The Brescia Circle had slowly disbanded; its members had begun to suspect each other of being police spies. Other radical groups throughout the city were also in disarray, their anxious leaders slinking off, wondering if Tunney and his men were on to them, too. Most gratifying of all, as soon as the chiefs fled, the bombings stopped. Months had passed without an incident.

A terrifying threat had been, he wanted to believe, extinguished. And with its end, he told himself, his short-lived career as a handler, mentor, shepherd, friend, and even father to the men he'd dispatch on dangerous covert missions was also, thankfully, over. His harried squad could look forward to a well-deserved rest. His secret life could at last be given a proper burial. The city, he decided, was safe.

Frank Abarno, twenty-two, and Carmine Carbone, eighteen, who were accused and convicted of an anarchist plot to blow up St. Patrick's Cathedral, appear in court on March 20, 1915.

CHAPTER 9

———

Erich Muenter was on the run. The Harvard professor and wife murderer had boarded a train to California in the aftermath of the somber burial service in Chicago. He had left behind his two children, the two doting nurses he'd cajoled into accompanying him on the tearful journey from Cambridge, his grieving and still supportive in-laws, and any encumbering pangs of guilt.

A steady barrage of headlines in the *New York Times* trumpeted "Harvard Teacher Still at Large" and "Muenter Not Yet Found," but Muenter traveled west like a man without a concern in the world and, in his own mind, a blameless one too. He'd only done what he felt he needed to do. His motive for poisoning his wife, he explained in a rambling letter to a Cambridge friend written on his way to Los Angeles, had its roots in revenge. Therefore, he insisted, with a logic that was purely his own tautological invention, the act was quite legal.

What was he avenging? Here the teacher turned perplexingly vague. He hinted that his anger at his spouse was grounded in sexual dissatisfaction; neither harmony nor pleasure existed in their shared intimate moments, he suggested, without providing any of the raw and apparently gnawing details. But a torrent of even more fiercely vituperative paragraphs raged on about the unfairness of his being burdened with a wife and children. Her pregnancies, he implied, were all his cunning wife's mischief. Perhaps this was why Muenter felt he had a legal right to condemn her to a slow and painful death.

Above all, though, the letter worked hard in its sputtering way to make the fantastic case that specific reasons were unnecessary. Leona Muenter had been executed—that was how her husband saw it—for the crimes she had committed. She deserved to die. Erich Muenter, a man who understood the unarticulated laws that governed the universe, had the right—no, the duty—to end her life.

Once in sunny Los Angeles, Muenter, with the discipline of a veteran secret agent, set about reinventing himself. With a pang of regret, he shaved off his mustache and his artfully cultivated Vandyke, but took appreciative measure of the suddenly youthful face staring back at him in the mirror.

The frayed tweed suit that had served as his Harvard uniform was packed into a suitcase, and he bought a pair of shiny khaki pants, a blue shirt, and a deep-pocketed rust-colored jacket at a haberdashery that did a brisk business in secondhand clothes. His gentleman's black derby was discarded too, and replaced by a more plebeian brown felt hat that he set at a rakish angle.

He couldn't disguise, however, his distinctive tubercular gait, and that was a concern; the description widely circulated by the Cambridge police described the fugitive murderer as a "loose-jointed walker." Prudence, he decided, required that he leave the country.

MUENTER TRAVELED SOUTH ON A vagabond route through Mexico. It was an aimless yearlong journey, but it gave him the time to fit a cover story snugly around his incriminating past. He christened himself Frank Holt, born in Wisconsin, parents long dead and without any siblings. Anyone who asked was told he'd picked up his knowledge of German—and perhaps, he'd concede pleasantly, some foreign mannerisms—during years employed as tutor to the children of a wealthy midwestern family as they traveled in high style through Europe.

After much disciplined effort, he even managed to disguise the lingering traces of his German accent. Now when he spoke, it was with the hesitant sibilance of a lisp.

There were gaps and obscurities in his new autobiography, but these were deliberate; nothing should be made too easy or too clear for new acquaintances. If he appeared to be trying too hard, that in itself could provoke suspicions.

Reinvented, he decided the time had come to settle down. Early in 1907 he made his way to El Oro, a dusty town about a hundred miles northwest of Mexico City; walked into the local mining company; and asked for work. His qualifications, he stated with for once not an iota of invention, were that he could read, write, and speak several languages fluently. He was hired as a stenographer.

James Dean, who had a desk across the room, would later recall that Muenter had "proved an excellent stenographer, but kept aloof from everyone in the company." "He had a worried look and frequently gazed abstractedly into space for a long time."

Still, his demeanor, however odd, didn't attract much comment. Most Americans who wound up south of the border in the remote hills of El Oro were running away from something. It was a community of expatriates who knew better than to ask too many questions, and their own rough experiences had tempered their tendency to judge.

For the next two years Muenter seemed to settle with a monklike devotion into his quiet new life. All the while, though, he was waiting, biding his time.

PART II:
THE NETWORK

CHAPTER 10

There are men who never take to the secret life, but von Bernstorff, in many impressive ways, was a natural. From the start he understood that deniability is a primary rule of the covert world and that he was the beneficiary of a bit of beginner's luck: his job gave him the perfect cover.

Upon his return to Washington, the count threw himself into his public role as ambassador. He rushed about the corridors of federal power, urging that America remain neutral. He went out of his way to meet with reporters and editors to share an ardent plea—off the record, of course—that President Wilson must be encouraged to broker a peace settlement. And with a happy-go-lucky energy that surpassed even his own previous immersion in the city's social whirl, he made it a point to be seen out and about at cocktails, dinners, or weekend house parties, always the elegant and charming aristocrat with the mischievous roving eye. As the professionals at Abteilung IIIB would have said with admiration, von Bernstorff lived his cover.

Yet all the while he was also, with no less admirable Prussian efficiency, building his network. He established an organization structured as rigidly as a military unit to recruit and run the agents who'd fight on the front lines. From his wood-paneled office in the German embassy, he'd issue the orders and approve the battle plans. But when the attacks began, when the foundations of bridges shook or factories were rocked by mysterious blasts, von Bernstorff would be another shocked, although not very innocent, bystander.

To insulate himself—and the Washington embassy—further, he gave orders that the network's operational base be established in New York. New York had always been a good city to be German, and with the outbreak of war it became an even better place for German spies. There was the busy Upper East Side neighborhood of Yorkville, where an agent could disappear into the beery gemütlichkeit; private associations like the German Club on Central Park South, where, in cozy smoke-filled rooms decorated with stags' heads, secrets could be whispered without fear of who else was listening; and crowded restaurants like Luchow's on Fourteenth Street, where, as brimming steins were raised and hearty platters of sauerbraten were devoured, all sorts of plots could be gaily hatched. Working behind the lines in New York City was a stroll through friendly territory. And in a collection of offices in high towers grouped in lower Manhattan, in convenient proximity to both Wall Street and New York Harbor, von Bernstorff's handpicked senior field officers set up shop.

Heinrich Albert, the embassy's commercial attaché, served as paymaster. For three years as Germany's chief fiscal officer in America, he had wined, dined, and developed mutually beneficial working relationships with a long and impressive list of bankers. In this cutthroat world of backslappers and blatantly ambitious financiers, people were struck by Dr. Albert's relative youth—he was in his late thirties and looked a boyish decade younger—and a reserve that bordered on diffidence. He'd arrive in a somber frock coat, bow low in greeting, listen with deferential attentiveness, and offer up a terse yet unfailingly polite comment only if asked a direct question. The single clue to a hidden, more aggressive nature was the dueling scar that cut across his cheek like a lightning bolt.

Heinrich Friedrich Albert served as commercial attaché to Ambassador von Bernstorff and acted as the chief fiscal officer for German espionage and sabotage operations in the United States.

In Albert, the network had a shrewd and dedicated man who quickly became familiar with the exacting ways to fund a secret army. He opened accounts in banks all over the country, transferred money in a bewildering succession of deposits, and then, for good measure, further washed the money through legitimate companies run by German American businessmen. From his office high above Broadway, he looked out across the harbor toward the Statue of Liberty, and efficiently dispensed a fortune of nearly untraceable funds. It would later be estimated that in the first year alone of this secret war he distributed $30 million to ragtag cells of agents to fuel their clandestine operations.

A short stroll downtown from Albert's office in the Hamburg-American Building, in a tower at 11 Broadway high above Bowling Green and the Custom House, Karl Boy-Ed established his new offices. Captain Boy-Ed had been the naval attaché at the Washington embassy, and on von Bernstorff's instructions he too had promptly relocated to New York.

Boy-Ed was the son of a German mother and a Turkish father, but he was every inch a Prussian naval officer. Tall, broad-shouldered, with a neck like a fence post, a booming voice, and the rigid, stiff-backed demeanor of a man who'd just jumped to attention, he wore his blue uniform and its chestful of medals with an intimidating authority.

Captain Karl Boy-Ed, naval attaché to Ambassador von Bernstorff.

While assigned to the embassy, he had studied the American navy, becoming familiar with its ship power, its personnel, its strategies, and its coastal defenses. In his new covert wartime role, he was determined to put all the intelligence that his obliging American hosts had so freely offered to operational use.

Franz von Papen was the network's third senior field officer, and, since boldness and audacity can become virtues in wartime, the most dangerous. In 1913, when he was assigned as the military attaché to the embassy, Captain von Papen had been sorely disappointed. The United States was a backwater posting, a position so minor to the German general staff that it had cavalierly been expanded to include Mexico.

Yet in von Papen's own mind, he was a man suited for a brilliant military career. Through his wife, the daughter of a fabulously wealthy Alsatian pottery manufacturer, he had the necessary funds; and through his parents, descendants of a long, if somewhat tattered, strand of Westphalian nobility, he had the social standing needed to climb to the top ranks of the German army. And he certainly had the look—a cavalry officer's confident, deliberately insouciant slouch; a firmness of features further distinguished by a hawk's nose; and a snappy military mustache. He also possessed—and this might explain his exile to such an insignificant post—an intolerable, overbearing personality. His arrogance crackled through even the most desultory conversations. He was a man who was always right, and who never hesitated to share his unflinching certainty.

When the ambassador assigned him to recruit and direct an army of spies and saboteurs in a clandestine attack against both America and Canada, von Papen saw the path to his future glory. He set up offices for this War Intelligence Center, as he grandly christened the operation, on the twenty-fifth floor of 60 Wall Street, and at once began plotting.

Captain Franz Joseph Hermann Michael Maria von Papen—military attaché to Ambassador von Bernstorff—who would go on to become chancellor of Germany in 1932 and vice chancellor under Adolf Hitler in 1933–1934.

THE FIRST TASK, THOUGH, FOR any head of station is to recruit agents to send off into the field. From the start, these three men were emboldened by their shared conviction that this would be easy work. They fervently believed in the rightness of Germany's cause, and felt they were surrounded by battalions of potential recruits whose loyalties also bound them to the kaiser.

Over eight million people—nearly a tenth of America's entire population—had been born in Germany or had a German parent. Even more promisingly, their allegiance to the ancestral homeland, to their German identity, remained strong. Why, von Papen was constantly pointing out, the National German-American Alliance, a fraternal organization that lovingly embraced the Fatherland, had three million members.

Across the country in cities like New York, Chicago, Milwaukee, St. Louis, and Cincinnati were neighborhoods so proudly and visibly Germanic that they were known as Kleines Deutschland. And there were about five hundred German-language newspapers published throughout the United States, with a combined circulation of 1.75 million. In New York alone the *Staats-Zeitung*, an impressively produced and edited paper that vociferously cheered for Germany's victory in the war, sold about seventy thousand copies each day.

In addition to these sympathetic citizens, a large number of German military reservists had found themselves stranded in America when the war broke out. Many of them were eager to fight for the kaiser, but they were soldiers without an army. In their frustration, all they could do was march in boisterous parades, waving their flags with frantic enthusiasm, their hoarse voices singing "Deutschland über Alles." The German foreign secretary, Gottlieb von Jagow, went so far as to challenge the American ambassador in Berlin, James Gerard, with a provocative threat: "You will find there are five hundred thousand German reservists in your country ready to take up arms for their mother country. . . . The United States will be engaged in a civil war."

Gerard, a wealthy New Yorker whose instincts were more combative than diplomatic, shot back, "There are five hundred thousand lampposts in my country and . . . every German residing in the United States who undertakes to take up arms against America will swing from one of those five hundred thousand lampposts."

Another source for recruits was America's large Irish population. It's a pragmatic axiom of both life and war that any enemy of my enemy is my friend, and Germany was eager to exploit Irish antipathy to Britain's rule over the Emerald Isle. There were 4.5 million Irish Americans, and the strains of Irish nationalism ran deep. A common enemy, the New York station heads believed, would furnish volunteers for a common cause.

However, it was President Wilson's neutrality policy that, in its unintentional way, serendipitously created the most effective sources of manpower. According to the president's strict interpretation, neutrality meant that any ship docked in the United States at the outbreak of the war would not be allowed to join the hostilities. As a result, East Coast ports were filled with German vessels—merchant ships, luxury liners, steamers—for the duration of the war.

And more kept coming. From all corners of the Atlantic, German ships at sea raced away from the guns of the mighty British navy and rushed to the safety of American harbors—where they were promptly interned. Within weeks, more than eighty German ships were lined up in an orderly row along the Hudson River docks, all tied together by strong ropes and watched by U.S. Navy patrol boats. It quickly got so crowded that newly arriving German vessels had to be towed across the Hudson to New Jersey.

German ocean liners interned during the war in Hoboken Harbor, New Jersey.

Along with this flotilla of interned ships traveled a navy of German sailors. An unsuspecting America put no meaningful restrictions on these foreign sailors; they were free to roam about New York, to enjoy their escape from the war. But many of them remained loyal sons of the Fatherland. They were eager to find any opportunity to get back into the fighting.

AS SUMMER TURNED INTO FALL, the network took operational shape with surprising speed. The senior officers finalized their strategies. The talent spotters went off to make their first tentative approaches to recruits. The covert attack against America was ready to be launched. Yet von Bernstorff, perhaps out of caution, perhaps out of a well-bred reluctance to strike against the hospitable country that had been his home for the past six years, hesitated.

But in the middle of September 1914 an event shook Germany's confidence so severely, so unexpectedly, that it overrode any previous misgivings. In the stunned aftermath, no rationale for delicacy any longer existed, and wariness rooted in fear became irrelevant.

The war had turned. Throughout August, column after column of spit-polished German troops had pounded relentlessly forward, hammering their way across France until they were at the outskirts of Paris. Then in one bloody week, as a monstrous offensive proceeded along the Marne River—when the enormity of the dead and maimed falling in a single savage day added up to a city of thirty thousand men, when the German army alone would mourn a staggering 220,000 casualties over seven days of fighting—the war became something entirely different.

Not only was the vaunted German army pushed into retreat, but it became apparent that the war would not be a short conflict. The fighting would go on and on. The kaiser had sent his troops off to the front in the first week of August with the assurance, "You will be home before the leaves have fallen from the trees." After the defeat at the first Battle of the Marne on September 12, 1914, there were the inevitable cruel whispers that the kaiser was, of course, referring to Germany's pine trees.

Now that a long, protracted conflict was a certainty, now that it was apparent that the German high command's concept of a short war had been little more than wishful pride, America's strategic importance intensified. In a war of attrition, the United States held the key to victory: the side that had access to the American marketplace had a significant advantage.

The warships of the British navy made it impossible for Germany to receive shipments of food, munitions, explosives, and other vital supplies. Von Bernstorff's network would have to make sure that Germany's enemies also could not obtain shipments from America.

A flurry of flash-coded cables, approved by an anxious Nicolai, went out from the Foreign Office to the Washington embassy:

"It is indispensable to recruit agents to organize explosions on ships sailing to enemy countries, in order to cause delays in the loading, the departure, and the unloading of these ships."

Then: "In United States sabotage can reach all kinds of factories for war deliveries . . . under no circumstances compromise Embassy."

And another: "We draw your attention to the possibility of recruiting . . . agents among the anarchist labor organizations."

And still another: "Secret. General staff desires energetic action in regard to proposed destruction of the Canadian Pacific Railroad at several points, with a view to complete and protracted interruption of travel."

With this persistent drumbeat of cables in his heart and mind, von Bernstorff had no choice but to go to war.

CHAPTER 11

————

Determined to make his mark, the ambitious von Papen desperately wanted to mount the sort of derring-do operation that would attract the high command's attention. But the murky pool of available freelance talent gave him little confidence. The military attaché found the man he was looking for in Mexico, on the run from the *federales* after breaking out of a Chihuahua jail.

Horst von der Goltz was a Nicolai-trained professional who had taken to the Great Game as if it were truly just merry sport. In rapid succession there were missions to steal a treaty from the home of a Russian prince, a tense adventure in the back streets of Madrid, and a long-running operation in Paris where he'd blackmailed an army captain with a gambling problem on the French general staff.

His next assignment to Mexico was much less successful. The authorities were on to him from the start, and after a brutal interrogation, he wound up in a Chihuahua penitentiary. He endured two hard months that tested his resolve. When he finally managed to escape, he took with him a lingering resentment against a German secret service that had done nothing to rescue him. Upon arriving in Mexico City, he sent a terse telegram to the headquarters at Königsplatz, announcing his resignation.

Von der Goltz was a freelance soldier of fortune, fighting against the *federales* with whatever Mexican rebel band would pay the highest price for his services, when he was approached in a cantina. A disheveled-looking man in a dingy white suit came to his table and portentously announced that he'd been sent by the German consul in El Paso, Texas.

"The consul wishes to ask you one question, and the answer is yes or no," the man went on with an officiousness that made von der Goltz bristle. "In case your government wanted your services again, could she expect to receive them?"

Von der Goltz, although still bitter, answered without hesitation: "In case of war—yes."

Two weeks later, a telegram arrived from the consul in El Paso. There was only one word: "Come."

In El Paso, von der Goltz was told, "Proceed to New York and place yourself at the disposal of Captain Fritz von Papen."

HE MET WITH VON PAPEN in the offices at 11 Broadway. They sat opposite one another in comfortable leather seats in a white-walled room so devoid of decoration that von der Goltz was convinced the military attaché had just moved in. With customary earnestness, von Papen spent no time on banter but launched straight into a lecture.

"Washington's neutrality is a fraud," he declared. "America allows arms and food to be shipped to the Allies while our ships remain victims of the British blockade. J. P. Morgan and the other Wall Street bankers lend millions to England, France, and Russia. The American heart is with England, and it will be only a matter of time before their soldiers are fighting side by side with the British."

He had a bold plan, one that, he predicted with an ambitious soldier's vanity, would favorably influence the course of the war. A small team led by von der Goltz would dynamite the Welland Canal. The target, he explained, was only a short distance across the border from Buffalo, New York, joining Lakes Ontario and Erie, and was a major waterway for Canadian shipping.

"It is comparatively simple," von Papen said, brimming with a novice controller's irrepressible confidence. "If we blow up the links of their canal, the main railway lines of Canada and the principal grain elevators will be crippled. Immediately we shall destroy one of England's chief sources of food supply as well as hamper the transportation of war matériel."

"It can be done," von der Goltz agreed.

AT FIRST VON DER GOLTZ was gung ho, eager to once again to be serving the Fatherland. The profession of espionage, of living the lies that shape a covert life, was familiar, enjoyable sport. Using the alias Bridgeman H. Taylor, he went on von Papen's instructions to Baltimore to recruit men from the German ships docked in the Patapsco River.

He found three volunteers, but these sailors, he soon came to realize, possessed neither the steady nerves nor the deep-rooted determination of clandestine saboteurs. They were full of bravado, especially after a night's drinking. But with the hard objectivity of a man who had learned his sinister trade in Nicolai's academy, von der Goltz realized that they couldn't be counted on when the time came to put their lives on the line.

He had no choice, though; an agent mounts the operation with the resources available. Resigned, he led the three men back to New York. Von Papen had three more recruits waiting, also bored sailors, volunteers taken off interned German boats in New York Harbor.

Von der Goltz wearily accepted them onto his team without protest. But in his heart he felt the outcome was clear: this would be a suicide mission.

One hundred pounds of dynamite were picked up by motorboat from a DuPont barge lying in the Jersey flats near the Statue of Liberty. There were two cases, each weighing about fifty pounds. The boat made its way across the Hudson to a dock on 146th Street. From there, a waiting car carried the explosives downtown to a three-story brownstone at 123 West Fifteenth Street.

This was the network's safe house. Funded by Albert, it was run by Martha Held, a large, bosomy woman somewhere north of fifty who decades earlier had been married to a count and had sung at opera houses throughout Europe. At Martha's, there'd be mountains of food and rivers of beer, and night after night, the house would be crowded with a raucous assortment of the kaiser's diplomats, covert operatives, army reservists, stranded seamen, and freelance thugs.

And Martha provided the women: the house on West Fifteenth Street was also a bordello. Whorehouses had been a long-running operational cover favored by Abteilung IIIB. Spies and whores, the logic went, were natural accomplices; after all, both practiced professions grounded in lies. And in a world where prudent tradecraft required that every move must be accountable, a house of easy virtue nicely explained late-night comings and goings to any enemy surveillance team.

That night the men stayed at Martha's. The recruits joined the ongoing party; it was as if they were already celebrating their success. But von der Goltz couldn't share their mood. His uneasy mind jumped back and forth between alternative fates, and each sparked a rush of terror: either he'd be blown sky-high when some reveler carelessly tossed a lit cigarette into the basement where the dynamite was cached, or he'd be shot by Canadian troops as his amateur band inched their way toward the canal with all the stealth of an armored division.

In the morning the house was still standing, and von der Goltz's team packed suitcases with guns and dynamite and took the train upstate. They went to ground in Buffalo, renting rooms on Delaware Street.

Over the next several days, von der Goltz's concerns about his feckless team grew. Now that they were closer to the target, the men were more restrained. They talked about the mission as if it were some annoying chore they were hoping to avoid.

Yet he pushed them forward. He led them to Niagara, New York, and a hotel room became their operational base. The next day they scouted the canal. The banks and locks were heavily guarded, armed squads of soldiers at seemingly every juncture.

Nearly in a panic, the recruits complained that it was impossible.

Von der Goltz agreed that the mission would be difficult. But, he insisted—all the time trying to convey the emphatic conviction of a man who believed the lie he was telling—it was not impossible.

His new plan was to hire an airplane. He'd fly along the entire canal until he found an unguarded stretch where they could detonate their dynamite. The men were to wait in the Niagara hotel room until he returned. Might be a day, might be longer, he advised. He told them to lie low until he came back.

He was gone two days, and when he returned, he found that his men had fled. The reality of a dangerous mission against heavy, deadly odds was not the adventure they'd imagined.

Von der Goltz had no choice but to flee to New York, where he met with a furious von Papen. The military attaché raged and raged; if the one hundred pounds of dynamite had gone up all at once, von der Goltz couldn't help thinking, the explosion would have paled in comparison with the captain's booming tirade.

For von Papen, such a pathetic ending for his first wartime mission was unacceptable. This was not how soldiers win medals, build illustrious careers. He stormed out of the room, and went straight to work drafting a cable, requesting that the incompetent von der Goltz be called home.

CHAPTER 12

———

The American network's first attempt had ended in failure. Nevertheless, Nicolai soon ordered von Bernstorff to launch a new operation. He had little choice: the German army needed soldiers.

The long, hot days of the war's opening months had given way to the rain-soaked autumn of 1914, but the conflict's fury charged on unabated. In just the first six months of savage fighting, Germany suffered 800,000 dead and wounded—nearly half the army that had initially marched off into the field. The valiant Prussian officers' corps was a shambles. It had unflinchingly led the way into battle after battle, but its bravery had been proved with blood: 16 percent of the corps was lost or missing.

And these were, the high command keenly understood, only the opening offensives. The merciless machinery of war would need to keep grinding. If the Fatherland were to fight on, and relentlessly on, to victory, it would need soldiers, especially trained officers.

It was a daunting realization. However, as the generals grappled with this grim mathematics, the Foreign Office delivered news that contained a glimmer of a solution. The consulates in North and South America reported that thousands of reserve soldiers had flocked to their doors in the hope of being reunited with their units.

The rush overwhelmed the consulates, and a practical decision was made to assist only the officers. Nearly one thousand members of the reserve officers corps received funds to finance journeys to New York and then on to Europe.

Only now, Foreign Office diplomats announced with embarrassed resignation, there was a problem. Urged on by vociferous protests from the British and the French, the United States had changed its passport requirements. In August, before the fighting had started, obtaining an American passport had been a perfunctory process: ask, and it was yours. But over subsequent months the government had repeatedly added new requirements. Proof of U.S. birth, the names of the countries to be visited, and even a photograph—all these now were required and carefully scrutinized before the document would be forwarded on to the secretary of state for his signature. As a result, the sidewalks of New York were as close to the front lines as the frustrated German officers could get.

Desperate, the high command still grasped at the tantalizing prospect of bringing the stranded officers into the war. Nicolai was promptly summoned, and his orders might just as well have been given to a sorcerer: make the men appear.

The master spy had performed some impressive feats in his years of clandestine service, but he had little hope that this time he could simply wave his operational wand and conjure the soldiers to the battle lines. The hapless Welland Canal operation had undermined his already shaky faith in the von Bernstorff network, but with no alternative, Nicolai reached out to them again.

A cable went on to Washington, outlining the problem at some length. Then, in a single short sentence that betrayed none of the tempest of doubts swirling about the offices in Königsplatz, it demanded a solution.

The day von Bernstorff received the cable, he left straightaway for New York. He met with both von Papen and Boy-Ed in the com-

fortable privacy of the German Club on Central Park South. No record exists of what was said, then or when the trio later made their
way downtown to the never-ending party at Martha Held's. But in
the course of that long evening a plan was set in motion to commit a singular crime on a scale not previously envisioned in American
history—the mass forgery of U.S. passports.

A forged passport given to Horst von der Goltz under
the alias Bridgeman H. Taylor, circa 1914.

THEY SET UP SHOP IN a grimy storefront on a twisting street in lower Manhattan perpetually shaded by the looming ironwork of the Brooklyn Bridge. A large table was placed at one end of the small room like an altar, and it was piled high with a stack of papers. The sheets were all identical—Form 375, the single-page application required for an American passport.

Each day the storefront was jammed. It was very likely the busiest passport bureau in Manhattan. But the long lines had been expected: each applicant was paid to fill out the form.

Hans von Wedell was the agent running this crucial operation. He'd been handpicked by von Papen, and his selection was enthusiastically endorsed by the ambassador. A tall, well-dressed aristocrat, the nephew of a count who held a lofty position in the Foreign Office, von Wedell spoke engagingly. Even his most casual conversations were sprinkled with a lively wit or a scholar's erudition, and when he was intent on persuasion, he was formidable. Still, he was an unfortunate choice.

Hans von Wedell was by profession and instinct a con man, but that was certainly no disqualification from earning his keep as a spy. His real failing was that he wasn't very successful at fraud. Or, for that matter, at anything else he had tried.

At various times in his vagabond life he'd been a reporter, a lawyer, and a small-time thief. When those trades had ended in embarrassed failure, he had gone into "finance," a business that amounted to little more than fleecing widows out of their nest eggs. Over tea or an intimate dinner, the aristocratic seducer solicited investments that, in their convoluted way, all led back to companies that existed only on paper and of which he was the sole beneficiary. The authorities were already breathing down von Wedell's neck when von Papen approached him. He gladly—and quickly—folded up shop and went into the passport business.

From the start, trade was booming. He spread the word to Bowery bums and the residents of fleabag hotels throughout the city: they could earn a munificent $20 for just minutes of easy work. All they'd have to do was allow their photograph to be taken and then sign a document. Von Papen provided the money, and soon the lines were snaking out into the street.

Von Wedell did the rest; and, to his credit, the operation worked smoothly. He'd send off the application and wait three or four days for the official U.S. passport to come in the mail.

The Great Seal of the United States would be impressively stamped on the passport photograph when the document arrived, but this State Department precaution was easily circumvented. One of his cohorts would later breezily explain how it was done:

"We wet the photograph [on the passport] with a damp cloth," he boasted with larcenous pride, "and then we affix the picture of the man who is to use it. The new photograph also is dampened, but when it is fastened to the passport there still remains a sort of vacuum in spots between the new picture and the old because of the ridges made by the seal. So we turn the passport upside down, place it on a soft ground—say a silk handkerchief—and then we take a papercutter with a dull point, and just trace the letters of the seal. The result is that the new photograph dries exactly as if it had been stamped by Uncle Sam. You can't tell the difference."

Hundreds of reserve officers successfully used these phony passports to get on ships leaving New York for Italy, Holland, and Scandinavia. Once they were on the Continent, border crossings, particularly in wartime Europe, were perfunctory affairs, and it was short work to get to Germany.

It was an ingeniously simple operation, and it might have played on for months and months had von Wedell been content to serve only the Fatherland. But—lacking even a spy's provisional integrity—he remained loyal only to himself. Before long his greed did him in, and the entire passport scheme collapsed in the process.

The end came in one swift act of vengeance. It had been well known among the down-and-out clientele of the Mills Hotel No. 3, a transient establishment near Thirty-Sixth Street, that the going rate for signing Form 375 and allowing your photograph to be taken was $20 cash. For anyone whose pockets were empty, this loomed as a fortune. New arrivals at the hotel couldn't believe their luck. But several months into the scam, as a handful of eager applicants from the Mills Hotel appeared at the Bridge Street storefront, von Wedell casually announced that the going rate for their cooperation was now a meager $5.

Expectations were dashed, and for days there was a good deal of brooding about the additional $15 applicants should have received. Once the $5 had been spent, the intensity of the gripes escalated to the fury of a vendetta. An angry rumor started running through the hotel that von Wedell was pocketing the $15 that should have been theirs.

The rumor was true. Von Wedell continued to receive $20 from von Papen to pass on to whoever signed the form, but he had decided to keep three-quarters of the fee for himself.

They're bums. Give them more money, they'll only buy more whiskey, he reasoned with a self-serving logic. What's the harm?

He soon found out. A vindictive contingent from the Mills, their anger rubbed raw by the injustice done to them, went to the authorities. If von Wedell was going to scam them, then they owed him no allegiance. Once they made their bitter report, the entire operation came tumbling down.

Von Wedell escaped to Cuba. The shrewd von Bernstorff, whose many years of dealings with Wilhelmstrasse's frock-coated princelings had taught him volumes about self-preservation, quickly sent off a coded telegram to Berlin. He assured his superiors that while the passport operation had "unfortunately become known," there was no cause for alarm: "There is no reason to fear that the Embassy will be compromised."

CHAPTER 13

S till, despite its two bungled operations, the network didn't have long to wait for its next chance. On November 28, 1914, new marching orders arrived from Berlin. A secret cable instructed: "It is necessary to hire through third parties who stand in no relations to the official representatives of Germany agents for arranging explosions on ships bound for enemy countries."

Von Bernstorff coolly passed the cable on to von Papen with no further instructions; none were necessary. The ambassador's orders were clear: handle this however you think best, but make sure this time the job gets done.

The military attaché was elated. He had been moping since the aborted Welland Canal and passport fiascos; this operation would be his vindication. The high command would take new measure of his talents. He'd make his mark, win medals.

In a repeat of the cautious tradecraft that had led him to Horst von der Goltz, he decided that he'd need a professional to direct the team in the field. Only this go-around, his handpicked operative was another sort of man entirely.

THE MAZE OF NARROW COBBLESTONE streets leading to Manhattan's Hudson River waterfront was a no-man's-land. This was menacing territory, a makeshift community on the fringe of the city crawling with its own shivery dangers. It was home to bullish longshoremen, knife-packing sailors, desperate whores, and a motley assortment of wharf rats who had long ago cast off the small traces of conscience with which they'd been born. On its dank blocks were run-down hotels that rented rooms for the hour and seedy bars where beer and whiskey flowed, and where heroin or opium could be scored in the back room. A shiv driven into the back, brass knuckles slamming into a mouthful of teeth, a straight razor slashing the jugular—blood flowing on the streets was not uncommon. During the day, when ships were loading or docking, the hustle of activity created an illusion of safety. But with the darkness of night, any doubts vanished: this was a savage land.

Paul Koenig ruled this underworld like the prince of darkness. For years he'd been the detective superintendent of the Atlas Line, a shipping subsidiary of the Kaiser's Own, as the Hamburg-American Line, thanks to its intricate ties to the imperial government, was commonly known. He rode roughshod over a dozen burly men, and each day they marched about the waterfront like the emperor's troops in a savage colonial port, getting the goods on sailors, dock-hands, or anybody else foolish enough to think he could put one over on Hamburg-American.

Once Koenig found a suspect, his method of interrogation was direct. He'd methodically beat the daylights out of his victim. He'd always get a confession, and sometimes it was even true.

Regardless, Koenig—or PK, as he was universally known on the waterfront with a respect entirely rooted in abject fear—loved his work. He was a thug and a bully, and he enjoyed hurting people. He was built for the job, too—a thick-bodied, bull-necked man with long, drooping arms and iron fists that could seem as hell-bent as a runaway trolley car when they were pounding away at your skull. He had sleepy, hooded eyes and a weasel's narrow mustache, and he never smiled, since that would indicate weakness. When you saw him coming, guilty or innocent, the instinct was to run.

Paul Koenig, the employee of the Hamburg-American Line who worked as a German operative in the United States, circa 1919.

Von Papen summoned PK to his office in lower Manhattan and, after only the briefest of interviews, offered him a job. If Koenig accepted, the military attaché explained crisply, he would ostensibly continue his work for the Atlas Line, but his real occupation would be to carry out covert assignments for Abteilung IIIB.

Koenig considered. It would be another hostile world, and therefore familiar territory. Even better, he realized, the stakes would be more consequential, and that would make his battles more satisfying. "Yes," he said, "I think that would be very much to my liking."

HE WAS A MAN WITH a mission, and he went to work without delay. From the downtown offices of the Hamburg-American Line, PK set up a squad culled from the toughest men on his security team, grandly dubbing them his *Geheimdienst*, or secret service division. The unit was an all-purpose tough-guy squad, providing bodyguards for von Bernstorff and the other officials; surveillance work at docks, hotels, and Wall Street banks; and muscle whenever a dose of persuasion was needed. However, the *Geheimdienst*'s primary operational role was sabotage.

Through the fall and then on into the uncommonly cold winter of 1914–15, bombs exploded. They were crude devices, rudimentary dynamite bombs. Koenig enlisted stevedores to plant them on ships. He found factory workers who for $25—a week's pay—were willing to leave a satchel underneath a workbench and not ask any questions. It was a loosely organized, haphazard attack. But it was effective. Week after week, the ominous cadence of destruction boomed on.

In New Jersey, the DuPont powder mill at Pompton Lakes blew up mysteriously in the middle of the night. Five days later, three workers died when the Wright Chemical Works was shaken to its foundations by a blast. Next, a fire raced through the Pain Fireworks Display Company, leaving several people dead. Four people died in Jersey City at the Detwiller and Street munitions factory.

It was all a great cause for concern. Workplace safety rules, fire department authorities sternly admonished, would need to be enforced with greater diligence.

Then fires began to break out in ships at sea. The SS *Knutford* had sailed out of New York Harbor with a cargo hold loaded with food bound for England when, quite spontaneously it seemed, a devastating fire started belowdecks. The SS *Samland*, also out of New York and on its way to Liverpool, was the next ship to burst into flames in the middle of the Atlantic. When the SS *Devon City* caught fire off the coast of Nova Scotia, the mystery only deepened.

A labor dispute? Disgruntled crew members? A single longshore-man pursuing his own highly personal vendetta? Insurance scams? There were all sorts of theories. At Martha Held's, though, there were finally victories to toast.

CHAPTER 14

———

The shriek of the telephone woke Tom Tunney from a deep sleep, but he picked up the receiver on the first ring, instantly alert and expecting to hear Barnitz or, just as likely, an excited precinct sergeant reporting a new explosion. He was wrong. The caller was the police commissioner. And if that weren't surprising enough, Woods's instructions certainly were.

Tom hung up the phone and lay in bed, trying to imagine what could be so important that Arthur Woods, not an aide, would call at nearly midnight to summon him to a meeting in the morning. And why had the commissioner wanted to make sure Tom wouldn't be seen coming to his office?

Suddenly sleepless, Tom lay there wondering. Yet he couldn't repress a nagging fear that he knew what was to be revealed, and that his troubled instincts had been correct all along.

In the morning, Tom followed the PC's directions. The usual path to Woods's office at 240 Centre Street, the grandly domed Beaux Arts palace that was the new police headquarters, was straight up the broad limestone stairs to the second floor; left across acres of marble; a slow march through a gauntlet of uniformed aides and civilian deskmen; and finally to a pair of huge mahogany doors that, only on a lieutenant's command, opened up into the commissioner's private lair.

Today Tom traveled a decidedly more covert route.

The ornate headquarters had been squeezed onto a triangle of land, and a curving driveway, just wide enough for a single car, led to the rear of the building, near the triangle's peak. As ordered, Tom followed this drive on foot to a heavy wooden door that looked as if it might lead to a dungeon. A stone terrace jutting out from the floor above served as a canopy and, not unintentionally, also obscured the entrance.

The door was locked, as Tom was told it would be, and he knocked. He waited, and as he did he could hear the rumble of gunfire rising up from the shooting range in the building's basement. Before Tom could knock again, a uniformed officer he recognized as the commissioner's chauffeur opened the door.

The officer saluted and then led Tom to a wood-paneled elevator not much roomier than a coffin. The officer took a key chain from his pocket, inserted the key into the control panel, gave it a twist, and the elevator was engaged. He pulled a lever, and it started to rise.

The door of the elevator opened up directly into the commissioner's office, and Tom immediately inhaled the strong, comforting aroma of tobacco. It was a large, very formal room, a space designed to convey the position and power of its occupant. The walls were paneled in a forest of somber mahogany. An Oriental rug of a predominantly deep blue hue lay across the floor. The heavy curtains were drawn, the fireplace was unlit, and the golden wall sconces provided only faint illumination.

The commissioner sat like a king on his throne behind the mile-long wooden desk that Tom knew had been Teddy Roosevelt's when, seventeen eventful years earlier, the soon-to-be president had served as PC. Across from Woods in high-backed leather chairs were two men in civilian clothes.

Tom recognized one of them, and he was, as always, glad to see him. Guy Scull, like the commissioner who'd recruited him to serve as his deputy, was another Groton and Harvard man, and, also like Woods's, his pedigree seemed apparent at first glance.

He was old Boston and old money, a slender, wiry slice of a man who, with his chiseled features and punctilious demeanor, struck many in the department as aloof, if not entirely unapproachable. "My God," exclaimed one dumbfounded sergeant when told that Scull would be the deputy commissioner of detectives, "he looks like a portrait hanging in a museum. Not a cop."

But Tom had worked with Scull and had come to appreciate the soft-spoken deputy commissioner as, he would say, "a born detective" and, no less praise in Tom's striver's universe, "a workhorse." During the course of a still unsolved murder investigation that started back when Tom had worked out of a precinct in Brooklyn, he had spent a few evenings drinking with Scull. In those long nights, he'd learned a good deal about the man that he'd never have expected, and still had difficulty accepting.

The seemingly demure Protestant aristocrat was in his secret heart a raging adventurer: Scull had galloped up San Juan Hill with Roosevelt's Rough Riders; gone off to the Boer War as a newspaper correspondent; moved on to cover the Boxer outbreaks in China; fought marauding Mexicans along the border with the Texas Rangers; and also sailed to the Caribbean in search of the fabulous treasure that had sunk over a century ago along with the Spanish galleon *Good Faith*.

Tom had read somewhere that Scull had gotten married last summer, and he could not help wondering if married life had reined him in. It was one reason, Tom told himself, that he had never married. That, and never having found a woman who seemed more important than his work.

Tom did not know the other man seated across from the commissioner. He had a soft brown mustache that curled up toward his cheeks like the wings of a bird in flight, and he sat straight in his chair with a soldier's rigid formality.

Woods directed Tom to the remaining leather chair positioned in front of his desk, but even before Tom sat, the commissioner offered an apology.

You were right, he told Tom.

AT THE POLICE TRAINING ACADEMY, detectives were taught not to guess, but rather to be patient, to roll up their sleeves and chase after clues until they led to the solution. Induction, the instructors lectured, was the time-tested method for solving crimes: ascertain the facts, and then follow them like signposts to the only possible destination. Hunches, extrapolations, inferences—those were the lazy sleuth's dubious short-cuts. Even worse, they'd never stand up in court.

It was a cautious, methodical approach that, for his nearly two decades on the job, had served Tom well. But recently he'd strayed from this careful philosophy. There was, he felt with a shiver of concern, no time to lose.

"Every person was seeing events of unheard violence and magnitude pass him pell-mell, giving no warning," he would say in partial explanation for his impetuosity. Merchant ships were bursting into flames not long after they left New York Harbor. Chemical and munitions factories from New Jersey to California were rocked by fatal explosions. It was a time of swirling confusion and building mysteries.

After each new act of violence, theories took shape and suspicions flourished. Were unions the culprits? Anarchists? Antiwar activists? Yet there was no evidence to connect any group, any individual, to this campaign of destruction.

In fact, there was no proof that the events were deliberate. Perhaps the fires and explosions were accidents, a string of coincidences precipitated by a slippery disregard for safety as greedy American shippers and factory owners hurried to make a profit from the war in Europe.

Yet all along, Tom, the bomb squad veteran, knew. "There was a maddening certainty about it all," he had decided. In his policeman's mind, "it took no superhuman amount of reasoning to combine the abnormal destruction of property in New York with the strong suspicion of German activity."

But he had no proof. Not even a single clue. "The sum total of these reports was," he conceded with a gloomy resignation, "nothing."

Nevertheless, Tom, after weighing his options, had gone to see the commissioner. On that occasion, about four months before, he had walked in the front door and with no less directness shared his suspicions. Tom began by acknowledging that he had no facts to bolster his theory, only instincts forged by two decades on the job. But he was convinced that just as the Brescia Circle bombings were politically motivated, so were the shipboard fires and munitions plant explosions. He suspected that German agents, either American sympathizers or possibly even members of the kaiser's secret service, were responsible. He asked Woods's permission to begin an investigation.

Woods refused. For one thing, he didn't trust Tunney's motives. Perhaps the captain's unspoken intention was to unearth a scandal that would help push America into the war on the side of the Allies. It wasn't the role of the New York Police Department to manipulate foreign policy, especially when the department's activities might very well be contrary to the official government position of strict neutrality.

And even if Tunney's allegations had some merit, Woods viewed this sort of investigation as a federal matter, something the War Department should pursue. His men chased criminals, not spies.

But he didn't share all these thoughts with Tunney. He simply ordered Tom to put the matter aside. Tom and his men were expressly prohibited from making any inquiries.

Tom obeyed. The mysterious attacks continued. More property was destroyed. More lives were lost. By the spring of 1915 the tally of devastation was unsettling: over seventy fires and explosions, thirty-eight deaths, and an estimated $22 million in damages. Yet the tacit police department policy was one of studied indifference. "Keep our heads cool and our eyes open" was the rule, Tom moaned. And it left Tom stewing.

He perceived the dangers and knew there would be more destruction. He had theories, but he wasn't quite there. He couldn't prove who was responsible. Still, in his policeman's soul, Tom, the hunter, knew. Yet he was forbidden to act.

All that was about to end, though. And that morning next to Commissioner Scull sat the man in large measure responsible for the change: the head of Section V, the British secret service's New York station.

CHAPTER 15

———

In the first hours of the war a British trawler slipped into the rough waters off the North Sea Dutch islands, and in the dawn mist its crew methodically went to work. Sturdy grappling irons splashed into the sea and hauled up their heavy bounty—a German transatlantic cable. Once it was on deck, industrial-strength saber-toothed saws cut the thick, slimy cable; then, like a catch not worth keeping, the jagged pieces were thrown back into the sea.

By day's end, all five of Germany's transatlantic cables had been severed. The nation was effectively sealed off from direct cable communication with its embassies outside continental Europe and its ships at sea.

The Germans still operated, however, a powerful wireless station at Nauen, just miles from Berlin. Its strong signal continued to transmit messages to all parts of the world.

Germany realized the enemy could intercept the radio communications it sent to its outposts. But the wireless station at Nauen chattered on incessantly without a pang of concern: the messages were encoded, translated into a text—letters, arbitrary words, or numbers—that was incomprehensible without the codebook upon which the sender had based his message. Additionally, the cautious Germans often enciphered the code, wrapping the coded text in another layer of disguise where letters or groups of letters or numbers represented something entirely different according to an intricate prearranged pattern.

The Germans had absolute confidence in their carefully constructed inventions. After all, the Teutonic mathematicians who had devised the ciphers were, by training if not merely birth, the world's best.

Nevertheless, the fledgling British Cryptographic Service, a hastily recruited group of amateur cryptologists, mathematicians, and linguists, was determined to decipher the stream of messages its forests of antennae were intercepting. Working out of "40 O.B."—the secret designation of Room 40, a small warren in the Old Admiralty Building—the team went to work.

Room 40 quickly grew crowded with treatises on ancient codes requisitioned from the stacks of university libraries and the storerooms of the British Museum. Desks were piled high with recondite texts that delved into the esoteric domains of Playfair and Vigenère squares, alphabet frequencies, and word wheels. But most helpful was the mounting inventory of German intercepts. With typical Prussian thoroughness, these often included several readily comparable versions of the same message in different codes.

It was a painstaking, meticulous chase, long, futile days and nights, relieved by small eureka moments. They made remarkable progress. In a short time they succeeded in reconstructing several of the German ciphers.

In addition, British agents in Belgium and the Middle East had managed to get their hands on German diplomatic codebooks—including one for Code 13040, one of the two codes used to send important messages from the Foreign Office in Berlin to the embassy in Washington, and from there to German missions throughout the western hemisphere. The men in Room 40 now had the key to open stacks of previously locked top-secret diplomatic intercepts.

THE TROUBLE WITH SECRETS, THOUGH, is that they lose a good deal of their value once they are revealed. They are like capital that is to be hoarded, appreciated, but not spent. If the enemy knows you're reading his mail, he'll stop posting letters. The door to even greater revelations will be nailed shut.

But the information Room 40 was gathering was too consequential to ignore. Lives were at stake. The course of the war, it could be argued with convincing reason, could be affected. Something had to be done.

This was the dilemma that weighed heavily on the man known throughout Whitehall simply as C. This single letter with its magisterial, intentionally dramatic brevity was the code name of Mansfield Smith-Cumming, the head of London's Secret Intelligence Service (SIS, or, to those with higher clearance, MI6), then operating under the War Office as M11c. The cables Room 40 had deciphered revealed Abteilung IIIB's activities in America.

It was intelligence that, if shared with President Wilson, could help nudge an enraged America into war on the Allies' side. Or its disclosure could alert Wilhelmstrasse, and put an abrupt end to Britain's ability to read Germany's secrets.

C weighed the alternatives. In the end he wrote out a carefully crafted message by hand; signed it, as was his custom, in green ink with the letter *C*; and then ordered that it be flash-wired to "Head, Section V."

CHAPTER 16

———

Captain Guy Gaunt, CMG, RN, the British naval attaché to
Washington who also served as the head of Section V.

Guy Gaunt was the head of Section V, and he was also the unidenti-
fied man with the military bearing and the raffish mustache sitting
that morning in the commissioner's office.

Gaunt had been born in Australia. His family was comfortable
and distinguished—a brother an admiral, a sister a novelist of some

reputation. And Gaunt had lived his own adventures, leading a ragtag native fighting force in the jungles of Samoa that became celebrated as "Gaunt's Brigade," and then going on to command battleships and cruisers in the Royal Navy. As war clouds darkened European skies, Captain Gaunt had been sent to America. His official title was British naval attaché, and he was given an impressive suite of rooms in the embassy in Washington. But the title and office were bits of cover stretched to disguise his real job. Working out of the consulate office in downtown Manhattan at 44 Whitehall Street, he ran Britain's spy network in America.

It was Gaunt who had received C's memo. While careful not to reveal or even hint that the German codes had been broken, the secret service head had established in alarming detail that the German secret service was directing a campaign of sabotage against America.

As ordered, Gaunt promptly shared this intelligence with his liaison in the Wilson administration, Franklin Polk.

A DESCENDANT OF THE ELEVENTH president, another Groton old boy (although unlike the two policemen he had gone on to Yale), Polk was a former Wall Street lawyer who now worked as a counselor at the State Department. The president had also—in a deliberately informal way, since the whole notion of spies struck Congress as more appropriate for decadent European states with their histories of intrigues—selected him to coordinate the nation's nascent security operations.

It was Polk who had to make the decision about what, if anything, to do with Gaunt's extraordinary intelligence. The information, he recognized with a cautious, lawyerly prudence, remained unconfirmed. No names were provided, no operational specifics offered. Yet the implications of a secret war being fought by Germany against the nation, and on American soil no less, were staggering. It was an attack on the homeland that could not be ignored.

Yet whom could he—no, the nation—trust to conduct such an important, yet politically delicate, investigation? Who could effectively hunt down the culprits, and also be relied on not to create a storm of indignant, warmongering headlines as they reeled in the enemy spies?

There was the Secret Service, but a wary Congress had curtailed the agency's activities. In 1908, after a disreputable clique of public officials was implicated in a land fraud investigation, Congress quickly passed a law relegating the service's agents strictly to Treasury Department duties. Agents could pursue counterfeiters and had official authorization to guard the president, but the worried, self-protective federal lawmakers made sure that this was about all they could legally do.

The Bureau of Investigation (nearly three decades later its name would officially be changed to the Federal Bureau of Investigation) was President Theodore Roosevelt's retaliatory gambit. After the Secret Service had been stripped of its investigative powers, he slyly proposed the creation of a bureau of investigation, which would be part of the Department of Justice.

Congress grasped the president's shrewd game, and it was not about to establish another agency that might soon be scrutinizing its creators. It refused to authorize the bureau. Fuming, Roosevelt bided his time until Congress adjourned, and then had the last laugh: he established the Bureau of Investigation with an executive order.

But the agency that emerged from such manipulations was, perhaps inevitably, a hollow force. Bruce Bielaski, a plodding career civil servant with a night-school law degree, served as its passive, low-key head. Its men were not authorized to carry firearms, and, as an additional handicap, they had no official power to make arrests. The agents flashed shiny badges, but the humiliating reality was that they had not much more law enforcement authority than any citizen.

Bruce Bielaski, head of the Bureau of Investigation, which was
a precursor to the Federal Bureau of Investigation.

Then there were the military intelligence agencies. The Office of
Naval Intelligence (ONI), established in 1882, kept track primarily
of the daunting advances the European powers were making in their
warships. A studious team of a dozen junior officers pored over foreign
technical journals, while intelligence officers serving on U.S. ships in
overseas ports slunk about harbors and shipyards with discerning eyes.
An inventory of informative reports grew rapidly. But the ONI agents
were sailors, and they had neither interest in nor the detective abilities
to investigate nonmaritime matters.

The Military Intelligence Division (MID), set up by the army
three years after its sister service was created, was less reliable. It
functioned, when it functioned at all, as a tangled, ineffective bu-
reaucracy. Even the colonel who ran the division felt he had a duty

to alert the army chief of staff not long after Germany had marched into Belgium that "information on hand is now so old as to be practically worthless."

Ripening the prospect of future failures, the intelligence budgets of both the army and the navy had been repeatedly slashed over the past two years. Their activities had been deemed unnecessary now that peace-loving President Wilson was in office.

The president was committed to neutrality. It was a stance that grew in large part out of a deep-rooted, almost spiritual pacifism. "We will not ask our young men to spend the best years of their lives making soldiers of themselves," Wilson had pledged.

Yet at the same time, Polk knew, the president's neutrality was a farseeing practical political strategy. Wilson believed that an America that stayed out of self-destructive fighting, that energetically worked instead to broker peace, would emerge at the end of the war as a powerful player on the world stage, possibly *the* world power.

And, not least, Wilsonian neutrality made good economic sense. Business was booming. The European war had revitalized a stagnant America. Full employment had returned. Allied governments were placing colossal, unprecedented orders for raw materials and manufactured goods. The steel industry thrived. Farmers had markets that would voraciously buy all the crops they could harvest. Cotton prices shot up. The United States was no longer a borrower of international capital; in fact the National City Bank and the Morgan firms were lending huge amounts of money to the Allies, sums that would soon total in the hundreds of millions of dollars. The scales weighing the balance of international trade had tipped disproportionately in the United States' favor, too. Before the start of the war, American exports to Europe exceeded imports by $500 million. Over the next two years the advantage would grow to $3.5 billion. Neutrality was making America rich.

An investigation that might uncover convincing reasons for the country to go to war, that could put an end to these boom times, needed, Polk realized, to be pursued with a quiet caution.

Still, at the core of Wilson's neutrality there was a shaky, though less publicly articulated, ambivalence of which Polk, the Washington insider, was also well aware. The president, a proud and moralistic man, was prepared to lead the nation into war if he felt he had no justifiable alternative.

At the same time, Wilson engaged in all manner of philosophical contortions and rationalizations to avoid coming to that fateful realization. The president was quite happy to remain in denial.

When, for example, the outlines of the passport scheme had become known, the president quickly went to work to bury an inconvenient problem. The trail, it had become swiftly apparent, could conceivably be traced back to the German embassy, but Wilson didn't want to be forced to deal with the consequences of such a provocative discovery.

"I hope that you will have the matter looked into thoroughly," he wrote to his attorney general without any steel of conviction, "but that, at the same time, you will have all possible precautions taken that no hint of it may become public until it materializes into something upon which we have no choice but to act."

Or, as the president dexterously reasoned in a letter to an old friend: "The opinion of the country seems to demand two inconsistent things, firmness and the avoidance of war, but I am hoping that perhaps they are not in necessary contradictions and that firmness may bring peace."

Polk dutifully weighed all these considerations. He appraised the abilities of the various investigative agencies and, with no less rigor, thought long and hard about a president who wanted both peace and secrecy until "we have no choice but to act." In the end, a proud product of his class, he decided to approach people he knew he could trust.

Polk had served as New York corporation counsel, the municipal government's top lawyer, and therefore he had some professional history with Woods and Scull. Better still, they'd all come of age on the playing fields of Groton. They belonged to the same clubs, sat across the table from each other at dinner parties. They were heirs to the same traditions, to the same public-spirited concepts of duty and service. They were men of the same mind.

Polk arranged for Gaunt to meet with his old friend Guy Scull. After the deputy commissioner understood the importance of what was being discussed, he asked Woods to join them.

The British agent's revelations cracked like gunshots in the night. The commissioner listened, and an odd mix of anger and trepidation swept over him as he envisioned what lay ahead. Finally, he made a late-night call. He summoned Tom Tunney to a clandestine meeting the next day.

AFTER THE INTRODUCTIONS HAD BEEN made, Woods turned his attention to Tom. Just as C had not told Gaunt all he knew, and the SIS agent had not revealed everything to the policemen, Woods did not disclose to Tom all that had already been uncovered or discussed. That information still remained classified; and Woods also wanted his trusted man to move forward unencumbered by the preconceived notions of a British intelligence agent who no doubt had his own agenda.

This was a job, Woods strongly believed, that only a New York cop would know how to do. "Although city police forces did not usually take upon themselves to do such distinctly federal work," Woods later explained, "we felt it was necessary because of the commanding position of New York as the greatest city and the greatest harbor in the country containing thousands of people of different nationalities." The threat to New York had been confirmed, and Woods saw it as a personal attack. He would not rely on any other service to protect *his* city.

And he had an officer already in place who had experience in running undercover operations, who had successfully infiltrated terrorist groups. He had a man whose judgment and dedication he knew could be trusted.

He instructed Tom to pick a team of men and begin his hunt. The name of his command would henceforth be officially amended: the Bomb and Neutrality Squad. At the same time, Tom and his men were to tread quietly. It was crucial that their inquiries be kept secret. A public rush to judgment would not be in the national interest.

In the end, Woods candidly warned, wiser and more powerful men than those in this room would be making the decisions. Some secrets might remain hidden forever, he conceded with a gloomy prescience. But for now, Tom was to select the men he needed and begin his pursuit. He was to go wherever the clues would take him.

When Woods finished, Tom saluted. The others remained, but he left at once. The private elevator took him down to the first floor, and his solitary footsteps echoed against the marble as he made his way through the shadowy narrow corridor to the huge wooden door. Stepping out of the darkness into a city already transformed in his mind into a war zone, he set out to follow a new, devious trail.

CHAPTER 17

———

"We teach him how to fight," Commissioner Woods boasted with proud good spirit. "How to take on whatever trouble may come to the city."

The occasion was the police training academy graduation ceremony, and the commissioner, standing on a platform erected at one end of the long gymnasium on the top floor of the headquarters building, was making the commencement address. He was a forceful speaker, and his words this morning were meant to reassure New York mayor John Purroy Mitchel and the other officials in the audience. He wanted them to know that the new officers would be up to the task of protecting New York.

Tom, though, wasn't so sure. Sitting in the crowd, he had half a mind to jump to his feet and challenge Woods. But neither insubordination nor drama was Tom's style.

Still, he was in a shaky mood. It was not long after Woods and Scull had sent him off to fight a secret war, and in the frustrating opening battles his confidence had been the first casualty. How can you claim to teach officers to take on whatever trouble may come when you have no notion what that trouble will be? he wanted to scream. What good is teaching men to fight if they don't know whom to fight?

It was a time when, Tom would recall with a shudder, "I was being kept grimly busy." Only he had nothing to show for all his activity.

Not a single clue. Growing tired and dispirited, Tom lived day and night with a great secret: he was beginning to doubt whether this was a war he could win.

But he was not ready to surrender. Years of walking a beat had reinforced an important truth: a copper never knows what's waiting around the next corner. There was always the chance, however faint, that if he kept at it, he'd stumble onto something that would help him track down the men responsible for the bombings.

In the first harried weeks, Tom had started handpicking a new team for this new mission. It already included many of the bomb squad veterans, detectives like George Barnitz, Amedeo Polignani, and Patrick Walsh who had proved themselves in the Brescia Circle case. But the unexpected twists and turns of that investigation, all the "cloak-and-dagger stuff," as he described it with a deadly seriousness, had also driven home a few operational realities.

He would need officers who could work undercover, side by side with the unsuspecting targets, and for this mission that meant detectives who spoke German. No less essential—and this Tom had learned from Polignani's masterly performance—he required men who could find their own way through sinister worlds, who could work alone for weeks or months with little more than their wits, ingenuity, and steely courage for protection.

Tom was looking for something else, too. The commissioner had said the training academy taught recruits to fight, but that was not enough. Tom needed men who *wanted* to fight. Men who wouldn't back down, who wouldn't hesitate to throw the first punch or fire the first shot. He wanted officers who had the grit to stand up to the kaiser's well-trained spies.

It was the search for men with these qualities that had brought Tom to the academy graduation. The precincts, he was aware, had hundreds, perhaps even thousands, of German-speaking cops on their rolls. But most long-serving officers were, he suspected, immigrants, men who had been born in Germany.

Tom didn't want to go into battle with doubts about his own troops. He wanted to know where, if his officers were pressed to make difficult choices, their allegiances lay. Tom's cautious instincts told him it'd be better to recruit from a younger generation, men who'd been raised in German-speaking homes but born in America.

His brief stint as an agent runner had also provided another piece of hard-learned knowledge, and even now just the memory brought back a familiar sinking feeling. The responsibility of sending men off on dangerous missions had left him very uneasy.

His own life, by disciplined choice, had so far been lived without a wife. Why should he complicate it with sickening worries about other men's wives and children? He didn't want to have to endure the concerns that had tormented him when he'd sent Polignani, a young husband and father, into the enemy camp. This time he was determined to select unmarried operatives, and it stood to reason that he'd be more likely to find single men among the fresh, still-young recruits.

A week earlier, Tom had spoken with the training academy instructors. He outlined his requirements, but was vague about the actual mission; and the instructors, all longtime cops, had known better than to ask for details. In the end, he had a list of seventeen potential members for his squad.

Each of the candidates had been notified to report immediately following the swearing-in ceremony to an office on the second floor, adjacent to Deputy Commissioner Scull's. Tom wanted to move quickly, before the men had a chance to settle into the precincts and there'd be loose talk about the German-speaking team Captain Tunney was assembling. The last thing Tom wanted was for some inquisitive reporter on the police beat to get a hint that something was up and rush into print with his scoop. Headlines would only force his prey to burrow down deeper.

Tom made swift work of the interviews. He didn't try to test the candidates' ability to speak German; in truth, he didn't know enough, as he would joke, to order a beer in a Yorkville bar. Instead, he asked a few perfunctory questions and then let the men talk. They spoke about their childhood, their ambitions, why they'd joined the force. He listened, and observed.

Just as when he had selected an officer to infiltrate the Brescia Circle, he was convinced that it was best to work solely on instinct. There's no test, he'd say, that'll tell you whether you can count on your partner when you're outnumbered and an angry mob is circling. But Tom, who had been in that very situation, believed he could take the measure of a man and know whether he'd want him by his side in a fight.

Before the day was over, he'd picked three men. Valentine Corell and Henry Senff were easy choices. Corell, who had grown up in the Bronx, had a street kid's swagger and a Romeo's toothy smile. Tom imagined he'd charm his way even into a nest of spies. Senff was a bruiser, over six feet tall and built, it seemed, by the same firm that had put up the Woolworth Building. Another plus: he'd scored high marks on the academy's shooting range.

Detective Henry Barth.

The third recruit, Henry Barth, was more unlikely. He was moon-faced and doughy, but listening to him speak, Tom detected a keen mind and an easy, lighthearted humor. The way things were shaping up, Tom decided, it wouldn't hurt to have someone around who could make the men laugh.

His handpicked squad was ready.

CHAPTER 18

———

Tom had a dozen conflicting theories in his mind, and at a dozen different moments he found himself championing each one. But he quickly came to realize that any investigation into mysterious shipboard explosions would need to center, initially at least, on New York Harbor. He ordered his men to comb the waterfront. Be on the alert, he told them. But if pressed, even Tom would've conceded that he had no specific idea what they should be looking for.

There was, though, plenty to observe. The war in Europe had transformed the harbor. It hustled and bustled with a newfound energy. Trainloads of goods poured in from farms and factories all across the country, and Allied purchasing agents, their pockets bulging with money, arrived to make deals for the American supplies. "Any man who owned anything that bore a speaking likeness to a cargo-boat," Tom noted with a small pang of envy, "suddenly found himself potentially wealthy." The merchant steamship lines had never been so busy.

The harbor was also crowded, Tom sneered, with "thousands of ardent Boches," and every one of them, he felt, might be a potential suspect. England's tight blockade of the seaward channels had left a flotilla of imprisoned ships flying the red, white, and black flag. Their sailors prowled the harbor district, bored and restless.

LOWER MANHATTAN FROM BROOKLYN BRIDGE TOWER,
BY NIGHT, NEW YORK CITY.

A postcard depicting Lower Manhattan at night, as
viewed from the Brooklyn Bridge, circa 1910.

With nightfall the waterfront, the same as before the war, turned more sinister. The daytime commerce gave way to enterprises that flourished in the shadows. Whores and gamblers, thieves and thugs slunk through the lonely alleys and dark footpaths. Intrigues were the order of business.

Tom's men had entered a closed, secretive world. It was new territory for them, and their explorations were cautious, even tentative. Yet all the while the pressures to make a discovery kept mounting: the bombings continued.

Tom's files bulged with new reports. "On January 3," he complained, "there was an explosion on the steamship *Orton* in the Erie Basin for which there was no apparent explanation. A month later a bomb was discovered in the cargo of the *Hennington Court*, but no one could say how it came there. Toward the end of February the steamship *Carlton* caught fire at sea—mysteriously. Two months passed, and then two bombs were found in the *Lord Erne*. We might have had a look at them . . . if those who had found the bombs had not dumped them overboard rather hastily. A week later a bomb was found in the hold of the *Devon City*. Again no explanation. Nor any reasonable cause why the *Cressington Court* caught fire at sea on April 29."

Tom had files full of incidents, but little else. "Every ship that left port must have nothing in her hold except hungry rats, parlor matches, oil waste and free kerosene," he said with stiff exasperation. It was a mystery, and he didn't know how to pierce its shell.

THEN HE HAD IT.

Not a clue, nothing as substantive as that. But it was the beginning of an approach, a possible entry point that could lead to larger, more valuable discoveries. With no other strategy presenting itself, and spurred on at the same time by a detective's intuition, he decided it would have to do.

As for the credit, if there would be any—and at this preliminary point that was far from a certainty—it should rightly belong, Tom conceded, to Henry Barth. It was the new, bookish recruit who, in the course of a meandering discussion about the stymied investigation, had glibly quoted Shakespeare: "'There are land rats and water rats.'" A cop, he was suggesting, must deal with all manner of villains.

At the time, Tom had simply nodded in agreement. But that night as he lay in his bed in Brooklyn, the memory of Shakespeare's small wisdom popped up again in his mind. Unable to sleep, he tossed the line around in his mind until he finally established what had caught his attention.

In the morning he gave his order: the team would concentrate its investigation on a water rat.

He had just the man in mind.

CHAPTER 19

————

It wasn't anything Paul Koenig had done that prompted Tom's curiosity. Or, at least not anything specific. When Tom gave the order to focus on the Hamburg-American Line's chief security officer, he was unaware of Koenig's role in any crimes. But he was beginning to have suspicions.

The British blockade had effectively shut down his steamship line; nevertheless, PK—the initials instantly recognized all over the waterfront—was still very busy. His name kept popping up in the surveillance and background reports the team filed. Tom wanted to know why. He wanted to know what this nasty piece of work, a water rat if there ever was one, was up to.

He assigned a team of watchers, a dozen detectives working around the clock in three four-man shifts, to follow PK. I want to know everything about him, Tom ordered. Where he goes and whom he meets.

Tom had little reason to believe that PK was the head of the group planting the bombs. He was, Tom felt even at that preliminary point in his investigation, not the sort of man the haughty German high command Junkers would select to run their American espionage network. More likely PK occupied some middle rung on the operational ladder, his role that of a rough, intimidating presence, the tough guy who could be counted on to keep order among the underlings.

Tom—and here, too, pure instinct was at work—suspected that while PK was only a minor player in the scheme, he could point them in the right direction. Stick with him, and he'll lead us to the pot of gold, Tom told his men, unconsciously giving the leprechaun fables of his childhood an operational cast.

Then, even before the investigation had gotten fully under way, it nearly came to an abrupt end. After giving his men their assignment, Tom went across the street to the headquarters building and shared his broad strategy with the commissioner. Woods listened, and then, with his customary politeness, thanked Tom for keeping him informed.

The next day, however, Tom was summoned to Scull's office. The deputy commissioner revealed that Woods had spoken to him, and after their conversation he had begun to make some inquiries. The Bureau of Investigation, he said, had already given Koenig the once-over. He handed Tom a thin file as he explained that the BI had come up with nothing. Their conclusion: Koenig was not worth following.

Without the slightest trace of rancor, he suggested that Tom might want to reconsider his surveillance, or at least scale it back a bit. Perhaps, he said, it would be better if Tom allocated the majority of his resources elsewhere.

Tom didn't even pretend to give Scull's suggestion any consideration. The way Tom's competitive mind worked, he now had further incentive to focus on Koenig. It had become a matter of professional vanity: he'd show the feds how New York cops build a case.

Trust me on this, he told Scull.

The deputy commissioner nodded in mute surrender. Finally, he asked that Tom keep both him and the commissioner informed on his progress. But by then Tom was already walking out the door, eager to get back to work.

SURVEILLANCE WAS AN ART, AND a good shadow, like any artist, was born, not made. Twenty years on the job had made this insight one of Tom's articles of faith, and the weeks spent trailing Paul Koenig only reinforced it.

PK toyed with Tom's men. Day after frustrating day, he led them on a merry chase to nowhere. Whether his suspicions had already been raised by the feds' tail, or he was simply blessed with keen animal senses, Tom could only guess. But PK had been on to them from the start. He had proved to be, Tom said with a nod of respect for his adversary, "a slippery fish."

The watchers would be on the job, two men falling in discreetly behind PK and, as they had been taught at the training academy, another two farther in the rear, backups ready to take over in case the target made the primary team. But PK would lead them into a bustling crowd and then vanish, or so it seemed, into thin air.

Other times he'd head down into the subway, wait until the very last second before the train was ready to depart, and then rush on board. He'd be behind the closed door, the train screeching away, while the irate watchers were left standing outside on the platform.

Or, using a clever variation on that ploy, PK would enter the busy Belmont or Manhattan Hotel. He'd hurry through the lobby and take the rear stairs down to the basement. From there, a winding underground corridor led to a subway station. He'd hop onto the first train and disappear.

But PK's favorite game was to lull Tom's pavement artists into thinking that this time they had him fooled. They'd spend hours following him around town, all the time confident that their target suspected nothing. Then PK would hustle around a corner, the men would quicken their pace, sweeping around the same corner in pursuit—and he'd pop out of a doorway as they hurried by, greeting them with a taunting laugh.

Tom realized that he'd need to change his handwriting, to use the operational jargon, if he was to keep an eye on Koenig. He had thrown an obtrusive army into the field when, he now realized, a subtler strategy would have been more effective.

So, with a silent nod to Scull, he scaled back. He assigned one man to shadow and, in a bit of inspiration, another to walk ahead of PK. The new plan was for the two watchers to alternate positions. When the shadow charged ahead, the point man would fall back and take his place; and they'd go on switching back and forth throughout their shift.

As further insurance, he employed a fleet of unmarked cars. The vehicles, alternating positions frequently, would drive unnoticed through the heavy traffic, yet all the time their routes paralleled PK's travel on foot.

But arguably the most effective change, the one that vastly improved the entire quality of the operation, was Tom's careful selection of the men he now assigned to the chase. Swallowing a bit of pride, Tom acknowledged that not all the officers on his handpicked team had the watcher's gift. A man could be an excellent detective yet a poor shadow. It was the ability to look convincing while doing nothing—"a rare combination of artlessness and skill," as Tom put it—that characterized the successful watcher. Tom made sure that all the men he now put in the field could affect an entirely natural nonchalance that was, of course, pure artifice.

Now when Koenig rushed about the city, Tom's men followed.

They were taken on a tour of German New York—Pabst's in Columbus Circle, the German Club on Central Park South, and Luchow's on Fourteenth Street. Then at the end of each busy day, the winding trail would invariably lead back to the same destination: his office at 45 Broadway.

Yet although the team was now dogging PK's footsteps, it still had little to show for it. Koenig's extraordinary caution certainly suggested that he had something to hide—but Tom had no clear idea what that was.

Koenig's many meetings about town also revealed nothing out of the ordinary. "These were no more than the natural points toward which any German might gravitate," said Tom, with a professional's admiration for an agent who keeps to his cover. More frustratingly, Tom moaned, the watchers didn't dare get close enough to "pick up a scrap of conversation." Even if intrigues were being plotted across the table, Tom had no knowledge.

He realized he was caught up in a long battle, and there was no end in sight. His mood was low when at the end of another fruitless day one of his team called in to report that PK had returned to his office. Following the usual routine, he'd be holed up for hours, presumably working away at his desk.

Too bad we can't put a man inside 45 Broadway, the watcher said. It was an idle remark—and a pure impossibility.

"We might as well try to penetrate Berlin with a brass band," Tom agreed.

But even as he spoke, a strategy jumped up in his mind. It was a simple solution, one that he'd been circling for a while.

"We could listen in on his telephone wire," he decided.

EVER SINCE THE 1880S, WHEN Kansas City undertaker Almon Strowger invented what became known as the Strowger switch, it had become easy to listen in on a telephone call. Strowger's circuit-switched system, an ingenious electromagnetic contraption that clicked and clacked noisily like a telegraph key, did the operator's work. The Strowger switch automatically connected the relays and slides at the central telephone offices, completing the circuit that allowed people to talk to each other. Twist another wire around the right switch at the central office, and a party line was created: you could hear someone's conversation and he'd never know it.

Almon Strowger's switch.

Larceny, though, is the stepmother of invention. It didn't take long for Wall Street speculators to realize fortunes could be made with the sort of inside information collected by eavesdropping on telephone conversations. If you knew what a financier or mogul was plotting, you could invest along with him. The Metropolitan Telephone and Telegraph Company's central office at Cortlandt Street in lower Manhattan was crowded with sly men offering hefty fees to the technicians for connecting third-party telephone wires to tycoons' phone lines.

In 1892, pressured by the indignant financiers who had gotten wind of this scheme, the New York State legislature made telephone tapping a felony. The statute offered no exceptions to this prohibition.

The fact that it was illegal did not concern Tom. Laws, he believed, were made to keep criminals, not cops, in line. Besides, declared or not, this was war. Extraordinary measures were permissible. And, not least, PK's goading stung. It had become personal.

THE TAP ON KOENIG'S LINE was up in just one day. Whenever he picked up his phone, a detective in Tom's office now listened in and transcribed the conversation.

The typewritten pages of daily transcripts soon rose up in a small mountain on Tom's desk. He pored over them, reading and then rereading, looking for a lead. It was a nightly ritual, and one that grew more and more hapless. At the end of each exhausting day he found himself coming to the same disappointing conclusion: he had found nothing. Not an incriminating word, or even a hint of something worth investigating. Either Koenig was as cautious on the telephone as he was in his travels about the city, the consummate careful professional, or the feds had been right all along. He was that rarest of creatures: a man with nothing to hide.

It was now several months into the case, and Tom's mind was heavy with the dead weight of failure as he sat at his crowded desk and resumed his reading. He made his methodical way through pages and pages of Koenig's guarded conversations.

Then something he read caught his attention. It was an incoming call, and only a brief one. Yet it was clear that the caller was very angry. He hurled a furious volley of expletives at Koenig, and then accused him of treating him unfairly. "You're a bullheaded Westphalian Dutchman!" the caller ranted. That was when PK, whose instincts had led him to suspect his phone was tapped, hung up before something more incriminating could be said.

Nevertheless, Tom was intrigued. He read the frustratingly meager transcript again, only this time more slowly.

There were not many men who'd dare to attack Koenig. He wondered what had caused such animosity.

Two days later the same angry man called again. Once more he lashed away at Koenig, charging that he didn't deserve what had happened, that Koenig had taken advantage of him. Again the cautious PK, always on guard against eavesdroppers, promptly hung up.

But now Tom made up his mind to find the caller. He wanted to know what Koenig had done to provoke him. The explanation suddenly seemed very important.

CHAPTER 20

———

Unknown to Tom, the mystery caller was not alone in his outrage. Even as Tom pressed his hunt, in Berlin other critics of Koenig—of the entire von Bernstorff network—were openly venting their displeasure. Despite the initial success of the bombing campaign, they had grown impatient. The generals had come to realize that the sabotage campaign against American industry must be accelerated and expanded, or Germany would lose the war.

"We are at our wits' end to defend ourselves against American ammunition," the Supreme Army Command, its troops under heavy fire in France, had wired in desperation from its field headquarters in Charleville to the government in Berlin.

It was early in 1915, a dismal time after the unexpected reversals in the great battles of the previous year, a grim period when the humiliated generals were slowly growing resigned to the prospect of years of fighting on both the western and the eastern fronts. To make things worse, the army was running out of shells and bullets.

Soldiers were forced to huddle in the trenches, missions canceled, because ammunition needed to be conserved. Field artillery units couldn't shoot off test barrages to get the range of enemy positions. Batteries needed to receive permission from corps headquarters before opening fire, and even then there were strict orders limiting the duration of the shelling.

The ammunition supplies of the English, French, and Russians had also been depleted. Their antiquated factories too were incapable of replenishing the flow of deadly munitions required by this endless, fierce war. Yet their guns kept firing. Their supply depots were constantly refilled.

The Allies could purchase all they needed from the United States.

Send us your orders, too, and they'll be filled, America insisted with a cool equanimity whenever Germany complained. The State Department went so far as to release a formal statement, *Neutrality and Trade in Contraband*, to clarify—and justify—the government's position. American citizens, the State Department explained with what it hoped was great reasonableness, had a constitutional right to sell whatever they wanted to whomever they chose, and Congress or even the president had no legal right to intervene.

This self-righteous posturing, the German general staff sneered, was the same as America's vaunted evenhanded neutrality—pure hypocrisy. The United States knew full well that the diligent Allied navies had made it impossible for a single munitions ship to sail from New York to Germany. Woodrow Wilson talked loftily about peace, but a besieged Germany understood that American bullets were mightier than all the president's hollow words. The United States, like the United Kingdom, France, and Russia, had taken aim against the Fatherland's soldiers.

Worse, the American shells were cruel inventions. Ribbed and grooved, fabricated from hard steel, not cast iron like the less dependable European shells, they would hiss and whine like screeching furies as they flew toward the German lines. When they exploded, they burst into hundreds of shards, razor-sharp spears raining down in a menacing torrent. The embittered high command could never forget that each diabolical projectile was made in the neutral U.S. of A.

And the arms shipments kept coming and coming. Allied purchasing agents had signed contracts guaranteeing that they would buy all the munitions the bustling American factories could manufacture. Money was no longer a problem.

AT THE START OF THE war, it had seemed England would soon go broke. It was spending £5.5 million a day, and the nation's cash and credit reserves were dwindling perilously. France was no less shaky, and in the early days of the fighting it had requested a $100 million loan from New York's J. P. Morgan & Company, the world's largest bank. Without an infusion of capital, the defeat of the Allies seemed merely a question of months.

A financial rescue, though, was impossible. Secretary of state William Jennings Bryan would not allow any loans. They were, he declared, inconsistent with "the true spirit of neutrality." "Money," he piously told the president, "is the worst of contrabands—it commands everything else. . . . I know of nothing that would do more to prevent war than an international agreement that neutral nations would not loan to belligerents."

American banker and philanthropist
John Pierpont "Jack" Morgan Jr., May 10, 1915.

Only J. P. Morgan Jr.—"Jack" to kings, prime ministers, pres-
idents, and Wall Street barons—saw things differently. He didn't
want to prevent war. He wanted the Allies to win. He was determined to find a way to get them money, and he was damn sure no
one, neither the secretary of state nor the president, was going to
stop him.

Morgan had not inherited only his father's immense wealth and
prestige when in April 1913 he became the senior partner of J. P. Morgan & Company. He was also heir to a haughty, patrician fondness for
aristocratic England and its leisurely old-world ways.

In London he had a town house off Park Lane. In Hertfordshire
he owned Wall Hall, a grand manor house with a three-hundred-
acre working farm and its own cricket team, which he cheered on
with uncharacteristic passion. And in Scotland he had Gannocy,
where he went to shoot, ride, walk about the moors, and rhap-
sodically contemplate "the heather just turning brown and cloud
shadows chasing each other across them." In his self-confident
heart, Morgan was as English as he was American; that is, it was as
natural to him to live the comfortable, rarefied life of an entitled
Englishman as it was to live the comfortable, rarefied life of an entitled American titan. It would be, Morgan felt with an unshakable
Episcopal conviction, a betrayal of his proud heritage, of the values
and beliefs that shored up his privileged world, if he did not do all
that was in his considerable power to help England, and the Allies,
win the war.

Inventively, he initiated a bold scheme that sidestepped the government's objections to loans, signing the British Commercial Agency
Agreement after a meeting with British prime minister Herbert As-
quith and munitions minister David Lloyd George. J. P. Morgan &
Company had become Great Britain's purchasing agent for all the nation's war supplies in the United States. A similar arrangement would
soon be made with France.

These huge expenditures would be backed by Allied gold reserves and the sale of American securities owned by overseas investors. This was a vague, if not largely hypothetical, credit line, but Morgan for once was not too punctilious about the security he required. As for the American factories, once their gleeful owners learned they'd be doing business with Jack Morgan, they stopped worrying about getting paid. His guarantee was as good as gold—perhaps, in these unsettled times, even better.

Yet Morgan, with a dunning banker's tenacity, had not given up on the possibility of American banks making loans to the Allies. Even as the newly created export department of J. P. Morgan started to orchestrate the purchase of American supplies for Britain and France, Morgan continued to work to change the U.S. government's position. He preferred bullying to charm, and in his blunt, assertive way he focused his energies on Robert Lansing, then a counselor in the State Department (and within six months Bryan's successor).

Lansing, who already saw the war as a battle between righteous democracy and evil absolutism, was sympathetic to Morgan's arguments. Fellow conspirators, they smoked cigars in Lansing's office and plotted. Then Lansing hurried over to the White House, where he told the president that if the prohibition on loans wasn't lifted, Canada, Australia, Mexico, and Argentina would profit from war orders that would have gone to American factories. Wilson listened, and agreed to give the matter more thought.

Days later, Morgan, in Washington to preside at a meeting of the Advisory Board of the Federal Reserve, found time for a fifteen-minute conversation with President Wilson. Before Morgan had left the Oval Office, the president had agreed that J. P. Morgan & Company could extend $12 million in commercial credit to Russia.

President Woodrow Wilson, photographed at his desk in the Oval Office, circa 1913.

A commercial credit, Wilson knew full well, was for all practical financial purposes a loan. But in another of his convenient rationalizations, the president had convinced himself that it was a different sort of transaction entirely. American neutrality, he proclaimed, had not been broken; or if it had been, he simply refused to acknowledge the cracks.

Nevertheless, a precedent had been established, and now a flurry of multimillion-dollar credits from a consortium of banks led by J. P. Morgan & Company went to the Allies. Soon after these arm's-length agreements were in place, without much discussion or even a hint of a governmental reprimand, a direct $30 million loan was made to France. This was quickly followed by a $50 million loan to Great Britain. "This should be orally conveyed, so far as we are concerned, and not put in writing," the president, trying once again to straddle the fence, insisted.

But these loans were insufficient. The great killing machine ran on money; capital was squandered as promiscuously as lives. All the previous credits and loans had merely been preliminaries. A desperate Anglo-French financial mission came to New York in search of a $1 billion loan.

The commission was unwilling to pledge collateral. The general credit of two great nations, it argued with a still-proud majesty, should be sufficient.

American bankers had a more cynical assessment: both countries were already tottering on the brink of financial collapse, and if the Allies lost the war, things would go from terrible to hopeless. One billion dollars was a lot to lend on nothing more substantial than friendship and good wishes.

Once again Morgan, relentless and supremely powerful, rallied his Wall Street troops. He led a nationwide banking syndicate that underwrote an unsecured Anglo-French loan of $500 million. Bonds would mature in five years and bear a steep 5 percent interest. The interest payments made it an attractive investment—if the Allies won.

With half a billion dollars at stake, plus interest, neutrality was becoming a thin and increasingly abstract philosophy for America. Yet this sum, too, was not enough. The need was constant; wartime spending was a very repetitive habit. Within three years the loans to the Allies would total $3 billion, $2.1 billion coming from J. P. Morgan & Company.

In England and France, Morgan was cheered as the nations' savior.

In Germany, he was cast as the devil. "Something must be done about that man," Nicolai brooded.

AS FORTUNES OF DOLLARS FLOWED to the Allies, von Papen, the German military attaché, received orders to assess the activity in the American munitions industry. After consulting with Heinrich Albert, the well-connected commercial attaché, he sent his report.

Koenig's sabotage campaign lacked the organization and discipline of a Prussian military operation. It was amateurish. The bombs were too crude. The recruits were unreliable. As a result, the factories, he cabled back, were working at full capacity. Allied transports, he wrote, crowded the harbors, waiting to be loaded with arsenals of American-made shells and bullets.

"Something must be done to stop it," he pleaded.

General Erich von Falkenhayn, the chief of the general staff, read the cable, and then wrote plaintively across the page: "Not only must something be done, as the Attaché says; something must *really* be done."

CHAPTER 21

———

General Franz Gustav von Wandel made the initial approach. As the war minister, the staff officer responsible for the Prussian army's running with its vaunted efficiency, he certainly had both sufficient authority and position. But Nicolai, who prided himself on his ability to judge men, had not chosen von Wandel simply because of his place in the military hierarchy.

In a command top-heavy with imperious Junker aristocrats, von Wandel, a general who had risen up through the infantry ranks, was the exception. He was an unfailingly gracious, instinctively friendly, almost avuncular commander. His men loved him, and perhaps that was because he loved them too.

It would've been easy enough to order a junior officer to accept the mission. Nicolai had no doubts he'd march dutifully off to America like a prisoner to the hangman. But Nicolai's own tense experiences behind the lines had taught him that obedience was an insufficient guarantee of success. And the string of fiascoes orchestrated by von Bernstorff and his crew of incompetents had only reinforced his old lessons.

As Nicolai had predicted, von Wandel won the candidate over from the start. He began with a disarming ardency, insisting that he was speaking not as a general but as one patriot to another. The flattered officer already riveted, von Wandel proceeded to announce that the kaiser himself had ordered the mission he was about to share. The words carried a genuine gravity; it was impossible to doubt that they were true.

You have been chosen, von Wandel revealed, to bring discipline and ingenuity to the covert war against America. The captain would work in conjunction with the von Bernstorff network, but at the same time he had the authority to be an independent operative. He would have the funds and the power to launch any plot he deemed feasible, to recruit any agents he needed. He would be, the general said, "a spider spinning his own secret webs."

"You cannot give us a 'No,'" von Wandel concluded, nearly begging.

"Your Excellency, my train will leave on Monday morning," Franz von Rintelen replied without a moment's hesitation.

Captain Franz Dagobert Johannes von Rintelen, the naval intelligence officer who masterminded much of the German sabotage effort in the United States, circa 1919.

ON PAPER, CAPTAIN VON RINTELEN was the perfect operative for this mission in America. He had been born in Frankfurt in 1878 to a good family, although not nearly as grand as he liked to imply, with interests in banking. After graduating from gymnasium, he did some early service in the navy and then followed his father into finance.

His first stint was as representative of the Deutsche Bank in London, where he perfected his English, learned how to dress, and, with the liberating freedom that came from being far from home, added the "von" to his name as coolly as if he'd been born to it.

In 1905 he came to America as a representative of the Disconto-Gesellschaft, Germany's second biggest bank. He lived at the New York Yacht Club—the only other German members on its exclusive rolls were the kaiser and his brother Prince Heinrich—and had his office at the white-shoe banking firm of Ladenburg, Thalmann & Company. With his amended pedigree, continental manners, and well-cut clothes, he was considered a gentleman by those New York circles that cared about such things. Tall, rail thin, with his dark, thinning hair brushed back, a mischievous sparkle in his blue eyes, and an athlete's grace, he was a rakish bachelor invited to dinner parties from Newport to Southampton. During his three years spent as a young banker running out and about nearly every night, he made many well-connected friends in business and society.

In 1909 he left for Mexico, and then traveled on to South America for his bank. A year later he returned to Germany, where he married a woman of considerable wealth and fathered a daughter.

With the outbreak of the war, von Rintelen rejoined the navy, serving as a captain-lieutenant attached to the admiralty staff. His initial responsibilities were financial, perfunctory assignments involving payrolls and transfers of admiralty funds to ships in foreign ports. But soon his superiors, appreciating a keen and resourceful mind, directed him into intelligence operations.

Zeppelins had been used with great success in bombing Antwerp, and he was drafted to be part of the team planning similar raids on

London and Liverpool. Days and nights were spent hunched over large-scale maps specially printed on the admiralty's own presses. Guided by his experiences in the cities, he drew ominous red circles over targets he decided would be vulnerable to an aerial attack. Only one location was off-limits to the zeppelins: the kaiser insisted that in all circumstances Buckingham Palace, home to his royal relatives, must be spared.

His next assignment took him undercover. Three hundred new machine guns, the naval corps had learned with some excitement, were sitting in a shed in Copenhagen, awaiting shipment on the first boat to Russia. He was ordered to make sure the much-needed weapons wound up instead in Germany.

Using the alias William Johnston, a London businessman, he checked into the Hotel d'Angleterre in Copenhagen and, after several happy evenings buying rounds of drinks in the hotel bar, succeeded in making friends with the Russian purchasing agents.

I'm not actually a businessman, he confessed at one evening's end to his new drinking buddies. He revealed that he was a member of the British secret service, and that he'd been instructed to help them get machine guns to the Russian army. There were some unexpected twists and turns as his brash scheme proceeded to play itself out, but in the end the Russians, encouraged by the British agent, loaded the guns onto a steamer flying the French tricolor. The flag was one more lie, and the boat chugged across the Baltic to Hamburg.

These were the broad facts, the details all documented with military thoroughness in Captain von Rintelen's service records. However, Nicolai, who had been keeping his eye on von Rintelen for a while, was convinced they told only part of the story. Moreover, it was largely the unrecorded qualities, the intangibles, that had convinced the Abteilung IIIB commander to snare his new recruit.

Nicolai felt he'd discovered an agent with a fox's cunning and a seducer's charm—a man, the spymaster predicted, who'd be able to move effortlessly around America. He'd find his way into factories and boardrooms, into waterfront saloons and labor rallies, wherever he needed to go. He'd listen to the chatter and read the rising wind of opinion and know at once whether an operation would strike deep at the American will.

At the same time von Rintelen, Nicolai was certain, would be a guiding beacon to his men. He'd recruit agents and helpers, and they'd be devoted to him. He'd truly believe in his own invincibility, and his adoring agents would feed on his colossal self-confidence. Nothing would be too bold.

All of Nicolai's intuitive judgments were happily seconded when von Rintelen showed up for his briefing at the Königsplatz headquarters. There was much to go over, and von Rintelen took it all in undaunted.

His operational life would begin as soon as he got off the boat in New York Harbor. Malvin Rice, a German sympathizer who claimed to be a board member of DuPont, had sent word to a member of the Reichstag that he could arrange for Germany to purchase significant quantities of explosives. There was no hope of getting the matériel to Germany, but at least it would not be used to fill the Allies' shells. Von Rintelen was given half a million dollars to fund the initial orders.

Even as he accepted the money, Nicolai could tell, von Rintelen was as skeptical about the scheme as, in truth, he was himself. Yet confirming his expectations, his newest operative didn't argue, or even suggest the possibility of failure. Von Rintelen simply accepted the assignment, confident that if Rice had been truthful, he'd get the job done.

Nicolai's faith in his new recruit soared even higher when word was passed on about the brash promise an unintimidated von Rintelen had made the following day to the powers at Wilhelmstrasse. There he was, a naval reserve captain standing before Karl Helfferich, the vice chancellor, and Arthur Zimmermann, the deputy foreign minister, and von Rintelen vowed, "I'll buy what I can, and blow up what I can't." The stolid politicians could not help bursting into admiring smiles at the young officer's bold words, and neither could Nicolai when an account of the meeting reached him too.

At Wilhelmstrasse, von Rintelen received a *Kaiserpass*. Signed by the foreign minister, it was an exceptional passport, issued only to officials on the most important government missions. Written in the formal, antiquated German of Frederick the Great's imperial world, it informed all authorities, embassies, and legations, military and civil, to give the bearer every assistance he requested.

That night von Rintelen sewed it into the lining of his suit. In the morning, he left for the Stettiner Bahnhof, where he boarded a train that would take him to Norway, and to the ship that would sail for America.

THE CODES WERE IN TWO capsules in his mouth, pressed against his cheek, to be swallowed at the first approach of a British cruiser. It was April 3, 1915, and von Rintelen was on the deck of the *Kristianiafjord* as it steamed toward New York Harbor.

He was traveling under a Swiss passport, printed by one of Nicolai's artists, that looked as good as the real thing. It was issued to Emile V. Gaché, a name that was von Rintelen's contribution; a fellow naval officer in Berlin had married a Swiss woman, and von Rintelen had borrowed her brother's identity. She had also filled him in about all the relations he had just acquired, a Swiss family Gaché crowded with nieces, nephews, aunts, and uncles; given him a photograph to keep in his wallet of the little mountain cottage that was his new home; and tutored him on the intricacies of the Swiss civil code—because the last thing a good Swiss would want to do was break a law.

Von Rintelen, scrupulous in his tradecraft from the start, had made sure that his new initials were sewn onto his linen. Then, taking another shrewd precaution, he'd had the items laundered so the monograms would not look new.

He had been told that the British cruiser *Essex* was stationed just beyond the three-mile point delineating American waters. As the *Kristianiafjord* neared, he placed the two tiny capsules in his mouth. They contained the diplomatic codes he'd been instructed to deliver to the ambassador and his attachés. If enemy seamen boarded, the "most secret" codes would vanish with a quick gulp.

But the steamer made its way without incident into New York Harbor. Looking out toward the city in the distance, von Rintelen felt as if whole new vistas of intrigue were opening up in front of him. He had all he needed: a righteous cause, an evil enemy, and a burning desire to succeed.

He had come to establish what he proudly called the Manhattan Front. He would take charge of the entire misused and undisciplined network, and redirect the attack. He saw himself as "the Dark Invader," making his way behind the lines, sneaking into enemy territory. A cold confidence swelled up inside him. He would make the city a battleground.

CHAPTER 22

———

In Mexico, Frank Holt decided that his past was finally past, that the crimes of a Harvard professor had been forgotten. The time had come to reclaim a bit of the life he had lived as Erich Muenter.

During the long days and the even longer solitary nights, he had worked out a plan. As Frank Holt, he'd enroll in a small backwater college where there'd be no chance of encountering any of his former Harvard colleagues, and he'd start a fresh climb up the academic ladder. He had a new name and a new look, but, he assured himself, he still possessed a first-rate mind. With perseverance, he'd clear a path through the dismal thickets of academe and make his way back to its sunnier groves.

He moved to Dallas and in 1908 enrolled in the Agricultural and Mechanical College at College Station, Texas. It was a rancher's world away from the Ivy League, and Frank Holt disappeared into the crowd of new students. He studied for a degree in German language and became the department's star pupil. His impressed professors marveled at his knowledge and the deftness of his mind. Upon graduation, they assured him, he'd head off to a promising academic career.

In the bottom of his suitcase, Holt still kept a three-year-old clipping from a Chicago newspaper: "Lunatic Professor on the Loose."

But that sort of ignorant name-calling, he was convinced, belonged to another lifetime and, for all practical purposes, another person. Frank Holt was his own man.

Then he met a new Leona.

LEONA SENSABAUGH HAD THE SAME Christian name as the wife Muenter had poisoned, but that was all they had in common. This Leona was a bouncy blond coed at the college, a fun-loving young woman who spoke with a Texas twang and had a cowgirl's playfulness.

Her father was a prominent Methodist minister in Dallas, but the preacher's daughter had her own rebellious soul. She dreamed of a sophisticated life in exotic, faraway places. She'd had her fill of cowboys and tumbleweeds. In Frank Holt, with his meticulous manners, his cosmopolitan airs, and his erudite talk, she saw a man who would take her to big cities and perhaps even one day to foreign lands.

"Mon cher," she called him; it was their lovers' game to talk to each other in French, one more shared allegiance to a life beyond Texas. Meanwhile Holt, eager to win this new, impressionable Leona, wrote her poems. Yet even in love, he dwelt on death:

> When I am dead
> Will those with whom I have long toiled
> Thro' burdened years and restless days,
> Stand round an upturned mound of earth
> And speak their hearts in tones of praise?

It was a whirlwind courtship spurred on by his confident talk of a vague but distinguished academic future, and they were soon married. When Holt graduated in 1909, Leona bought him a gold pin engraved with the year '09. Her intention was to commemorate her husband's accomplishment. He attached the pin to his jacket lapel and wore it daily, a tacit symbol of his successful escape to another life.

Holt became a college instructor. To any uninformed observer— say, his critical father-in-law the minister—Holt had joined the makeshift ranks of the itinerant academics, the untenured roving flock who moved from school to school whenever a suitable opening appeared. But Holt was following a more purposeful agenda. As he traveled about the country, he was shaping his new identity, constructing a new biography.

There was a stint as assistant professor of German at the University of Oklahoma; "he speaks Spanish and French fluently, and has studied at the University of Berlin, and studied in Rome and Paris and has traveled over Europe," the local paper reported, although with only a small smattering of truth, about the new faculty member. From there he moved on to teach French at Vanderbilt University in Tennessee. A year later he was at Emory and Henry College in Virginia, as the school's French and German instructor.

Then finally, in 1913, he obtained a place in Cornell University's PhD program; at the same time, the university hired him to teach undergraduate German and French. Holt had completed his long, diligent trip back to the Ivy League.

PART III:
THE MANHATTAN FRONT

CHAPTER 23

———

Who was the caller? And why was he so furious with Paul Koenig? Those were the questions Tom felt he needed to answer if his meandering investigation was ever going to move into a new, more productive phase.

He summoned his team, and the entire squad crowded like school-boys around the rows of scuffed wooden desks in the big room. There was an unusual formality to the moment. It was not Tom's style to make speeches; this, in fact, would be the first. His way was to lead by example, to throw himself into a case and expect his men to demon-strate an equal commitment. The sincerity of his diligence was their motivation.

But today Tom believed a crucial moment, perhaps *the* crucial mo-ment, in the investigation had arrived. For Tom, for every man in the room, the investigation had been a deeply disappointing quest. The files were jammed with incident reports, and still, as he had repeatedly complained, "the sum total of those reports was—nothing." Now at last he had a scent, and his blood was rising.

Tom stood facing his men, his broad back pressed against the glass door to his office, a large and impressive presence in his blue uniform with its shiny gold buttons. He did not raise his voice; his tone, by all accounts, was steady. But his usual flippancy deserted him, and his face was as grim as an undertaker's. It was this demeanor—rigid, stolid, and authoritative—that affected the men as deeply as his words.

It was a short speech by any standard. He began with a confession. For months Koenig had led them quite a chase. A disciplined quarry, he was so circumspect in his movements and speech that, Tom now divulged for the first time, he had despaired of ever latching on to a single incriminating clue. Finally, however, they had uncovered something of potential importance: Koenig had an enemy.

Anger, Tom went on, his knowledge acquired firsthand in years of precinct house interrogations, could be a very effective weapon. "It's a knife waiting to be driven deep," he said. He told his men he wanted to take the caller's anger and make it work for the investigation. He wanted to give the caller a chance at revenge. But before that could happen, Tom said, he needed to know the caller's identity.

"Find him!" Tom concluded, the two words as much a prayer as a command.

THE MEN WENT TO WORK. The first part of the investigation was, like so much of detective work, drudgery, but it soon produced results. An officer went to the telephone company central station on Cortlandt Street and, with no further official imprimatur than the authority of his uniform, received permission to sort through the records of the incoming calls to Koenig's office on lower Broadway. The logs were not in any logical order, but the detective already knew the precise times and dates of the two acrimonious conversations. In short order, they were found.

Fortuitously, both had been made from the same number. A quick search of phone company records revealed its location—a public booth in a saloon on the Lower West Side of Manhattan.

Tom heard the report, and at once his hopes collapsed. How many men must traipse into the saloon each day to grab a beer and use the phone? More than likely the caller, taking his lead from the security-conscious Koenig, had intentionally chosen a busy public phone. He must have known a well-trafficked location would make any attempt to identify him difficult, if not impossible. Tom decided that he was reading the handwriting of another well-trained professional. His only lead appeared to have taken him to another very dead end.

But, as Tom would later recall, "crucial events can almost always be traced to some trivial circumstances." The triviality that kept this crucial case alive was that his officer found New York's only, or so it seemed to an amazed Tom, "bartender with a good memory."

Perhaps business was slow, and that gave the bartender plenty of time to stare out across the room with rapt attention. Or possibly the bartender had been nursing a long-running grudge, since the man apparently entered the saloon only to use the phone, never reaching into his pocket to buy a beer. Then again, it was no less likely that the bartender was one of those rare sorts who truly never forget a face. But whatever the reason, when the detective went through the perfunctory motions of asking the bartender if by any chance he remembered a fellow who showed up in the late afternoon on a couple of occasions to use the phone, the bartender shot back that he did.

"Yes, he came in once in a while," the bartender went on breezily. "Don't know his name, but I'm pretty sure he lives in the neighborhood. Around the corner, I think."

The detail in the bartender's description was no less miraculous: about five feet ten inches; thin; sparse dark hair; and, he added snidely, "a bit mousy."

Within the hour, half a dozen detectives were combing the neighborhood, knocking on doors and asking discreet questions. It didn't take them long to find their man: George Fuchs, an unemployed German immigrant.

TOM SUGGESTED TO BARNITZ THAT they could bring Fuchs in for questioning.

Barnitz nodded. His years working with Tom had taught him that the boss was not asking for his advice. In time, Tom would work things out in his own mind. The sergeant's role was purely rhetorical, the mute audience whose silence spurred the thinking on.

After a while, Tom spoke up again. He explained that even if Fuchs was arrested and given the third degree, there was still no guarantee he'd talk.

Once again Barnitz agreed.

There was more silence. Then, just as Barnitz was growing uncomfortable, Tom shared an idea. He would put an operative close to Fuchs. Someone Fuchs would trust and confide in.

Sourly, Barnitz asked Tom how he intended to do that.

Once again Tom didn't respond. He sat across from Barnitz, but it was as if he'd left to go to some distant, private place. And when he finally spoke, Tom had it all pretty much figured out.

His plan was to give the unemployed Fuchs a job. That is, Tom went on, we get Fuchs to think we're giving him one. That way we become his new best friend. After all, he asked, what man wouldn't trust someone coming to his rescue with a paycheck? Tom predicted that if they played it right, Fuchs would talk.

THE OFFICIAL-LOOKING LETTERHEAD BORE THE name of a wireless telegraph company that existed only in Tom's imagination. The address was a building near police headquarters; the landlord was quite willing in the unsteady times to rent an empty suite of offices for a week.

As for the letter itself, Tom dictated it on the fly, and Barnitz took it down; another detective did the typing.

"Dear Sir," it began, according to Tom's imprecise memory of the text he had deliberately crafted to be both vague and at the same time full of promise. "There is a position immediately available in our company and it has come to our attention that you would be the proper man for this job. We would be pleased if you would call at the office of the company next Tuesday at 10 a.m. to discuss work and wages. Yours Sincerely," and here Tom, with what he hoped looked like an executive's self-important flourish, signed one of the many cover names he had used in the course of his long career. The envelope was stamped, and then, a sign of Tom's recognition of how much was riding on this ploy, hand-delivered to the post office so there'd be no reason to worry about its being picked up as scheduled from the local mailbox.

At ten on the designated Tuesday, Detective Corell, dressed in a double-breasted business suit and looking, he hoped, like a prosperous telegraph company executive, sat waiting behind a desk in the rented suite. Tom had cast Corell because even when not playing a carefully scripted role, the detective was a hail-fellow, personable sort, a man who wore an ingratiating smile perpetually frozen on his handsome face. Also, of no less operational value, Corell spoke German fluently. It was a tacit bond with Fuchs that Tom hoped would be useful in cementing a budding friendship.

Down the hall from Corell, hidden behind a closed door but still near enough to hear a summons for help, were Barnitz and a few other men. They'd burst through the door if Fuchs became suspicious and showed signs of running. But Tom deeply hoped it wouldn't come to that.

For a while, though, it looked as if it wouldn't come to anything. Ten o'clock came and went without any sign of Fuchs. And so did ten thirty. Tom had remained on Centre Street, and the reports being telephoned in from the watchers casually loitering in the building's lobby were a growing concern.

What if, it suddenly occurred to Tom for the first time, Fuchs had already found a job? For all Tom knew, he had ripped up the letter after just a glance. Or maybe Fuchs had come to the building at ten as specified, only to turn suspicious. Had Tom stationed too many men in the lobby? Had Fuchs felt he was walking into a trap? Whatever the reason, as it grew later and later, Tom began to lose any hope that Fuchs would appear.

Then, just minutes after eleven, his phone rang: Fuchs had taken the bait. He was on the elevator, heading up to the telegraph company office.

Tom's lurching world began to steady itself. Now it would be up to Corell.

The job interview began with an apology. Fuchs explained that he'd overslept, and his candor struck Corell as an encouraging sign. Either the man was naive, or he was simply stupid; and either trait, or both for that matter, would make him susceptible to being played.

With an equanimity that might have sounded the alarm in a more suspicious mind, Corell insisted it didn't matter. Could happen to anyone, he said affably. In fact, he confessed with a laugh, he was always late.

The interview continued along in this breezy, good-humored fashion. But it wasn't long before Corell, with a playful clap of his hands that signaled the end of the formalities, announced that there really was nothing further to discuss. The telegraph company was looking for someone who spoke German, and George Fuchs was certainly the right man for the job.

Why don't we get out of here and get lunch? Corell suggested. He made it clear that it would be the company's treat. They could eat, have a beer or two, and work out when Fuchs would start and what office he'd like.

An elated Fuchs agreed that that was a good plan.

CORELL WAS MASTERFUL. THE TEAMS of watchers at the adjacent tables were unanimous in their praise. He did not hurry, and he kept the pitchers of beer arriving at the table.

The two men talked about their families, their shared German roots. And with a conspiratorial wink, Corell confided that Fuchs was getting a cushy job. A man could saunter in most days after having slept late and the dumb bosses would be none the wiser.

Fuchs raised his glass in happy anticipation of working in such an undemanding environment, took a healthy swallow, and then chimed in with obvious delight, "Be a nice change from my last job."

"Who did you say you were working for?" Corell asked. His tone did not betray anything. It was as if it were the most casual of questions between two drinking buddies. But Tom would later say the entire case was riding on Fuchs's answer.

"That bullheaded Westphalian Dutchman," Fuchs said, nearly spitting out the words. "He is some relative of my mother's. She was a Prussian, though, *Gott sei Dank*!"

Corell offered a sympathetic laugh, while at the same time he did his best to disguise any evidence of the excitement Fuchs's words had ignited. He felt that if he did not rush things, he'd soon learn why Fuchs was so angry.

"This bullheaded Westphalian Dutchman," Corell asked absently, "he have a name?"

"Paul Koenig."

As the pitcher was drained dry, Corell, with deliberate caution, steered the conversation away from Koenig. But the meal ended with an appointment for lunch again the next day. They had dinner together the evening after that, too. Fuchs began to think of his generous new employer as a friend. And as the beer flowed, in time the rest of the story followed.

ONCE UPON A TIME, HE was living in Niagara Falls, New York, Fuchs began as if telling a fairy tale. He was sharing an apartment with his mother when Koenig and his wife came to visit.

Fuchs played the gracious host to his relatives from the big city, giving them the full tour of the falls. But afterward, when the two men were alone, Koenig shared a secret: he hadn't come up from New York City to see the falls. His real interest was the Welland Canal.

That was when Fuchs knew. He had suspected something from the start; Koenig hadn't seemed like a tourist on a holiday. Now he was certain. There was only one reason Koenig would want to inspect the busy shipping channel. His cousin was a saboteur.

Fuchs could see where this was heading, and in his mind he was already counting the money he could make. Yet he realized that the harder Koenig had to work to make the deal, the more Koenig would value his services—and the more he'd pay. He let his cousin go on talking, hinting.

Finally, Koenig asked if Fuchs would go over to Canada and take some snapshots of the locks for him. His tone was offhanded, as if he were suggesting Fuchs take pictures for his scrapbook.

"Why don't you go yourself?" Fuchs asked.

"They would probably pick me up if I did," he answered. There was no need to complete the thought: once Koenig's ties to the Hamburg-American Line were discovered, he'd never be able to talk his way out of a jail sentence.

"Well, that's why I won't take any camera over there with me," Fuchs said with some vehemence. "But I'll go if you want a report."

And so George Fuchs became a spy. He was following in the footsteps of another Abteilung IIIB agent, Horst von der Goltz, who a little more than a year earlier had been recruited by von Papen to destroy the canal.

Using the cover name George Fox—Fuchs decided an American-sounding name would arouse less suspicion—he registered at the Welland House in Welland, Canada, a short walk from the waterway. The next morning he hiked to Port Colborne, the Lake Erie mouth of the canal, and followed the towpath north. As he walked, he made notes on the ship traffic, the construction of the locks, and where the guards were placed. The next day he made his way an additional twenty-seven miles to Lake Ontario, all the time gathering intelligence.

As soon as he was back safely in Niagara Falls, he hurried to Koenig's hotel room and shared what he had seen. Koenig was full of praise for his new operative, but he also wanted a written report. "Mail it to me at Post Office Box 840 in New York. Sign it just 'George'— nobody would know who that was even if they did find it," he instructed.

Fuchs mailed off his report, and then waited. As the days passed without any word from Koenig, Fuchs realized that he very much wanted to hear from him. He had enjoyed the excitement of being a player in a secret high-stakes game, and the fact that he was being paid for having so much fun only made it even better. When Koenig finally wrote to offer him a job, Fuchs left the next day for New York.

At the starting salary of $18 a week, he joined Koenig's Bureau of Investigation, the name chosen by PK in an ironic tribute to the government's organization. Together they went to work planning the attack on the canal. It was quickly decided that Fuchs would hire the men, locals from Buffalo, who'd row a boatload of dynamite across the upper Niagara River into Canada. Koenig had already signed on his assistant, Richard Leyendecker, and his secretary, Fred Metzler, to light the fuses that would blow a vital stretch of the canal to pieces. All that remained was for Koenig to set the date.

While this was being worked out, Fuchs, the novice field man, was given a variety of assignments. He prowled the waterfront, observing which ships were being loaded with munitions, and then relayed the information to the office on lower Broadway. He did special guard duty at Albert's office, never realizing that the safe across the room contained a fortune in cash. He was sent to Hoboken to confront a would-be German agent who, after being hired to do an errand for von Papen, was trying to blackmail the attaché for more money. Modeling his tough-guy manner on Koenig's, Fuchs convinced the blackmailer he'd be making a dangerous mistake if he didn't back off. The man was never heard from again.

There were other assignments, too, all part of a rapid tutelage.

Fuchs proudly felt he was becoming quite good at his new trade. But then he made the mistake of getting a cold.

One Sunday Fuchs woke up with a fever. His body ached; his coughs left him shaking; and he couldn't get out of bed. He missed a day's work. And at the end of the week, his paycheck was a day short.

He complained to Koenig. But Koenig could not be swayed. Always suspicious, he doubted that Fuchs had been too ill to work. But even if Fuchs had been sick, PK went on to argue with a tyrant's logic, illness should never be allowed to interfere with service to the Fatherland. Koenig refused to pay for work that was not done.

The relationship between the two relatives quickly degenerated. Fuchs held a grudge, and his gnawing resentment made him testy. Koenig, for his part, was not willing to tolerate anything less than total, subservient respect.

He fired Fuchs, charging him with "constant quarrelling with another operative, drinking, and disorderly habits." Never missing an opportunity to be vindictive, Koenig also announced that he was docking the ex-operative another day's pay: $2.57.

It was the indignity of the loss of $2.57 that had fueled Fuchs's unrestrained anger. It had goaded him into making the angry calls. It had driven him to share the story that incriminated Paul Koenig. It had cost Abteilung IIIB a key operative in its American network. And it had given Tom the evidence he needed for an arrest.

BUT TOM STILL DIDN'T HAVE any information on the explosions. That was why he'd originally launched the investigation into Koenig, why he'd followed PK and tapped his phones. Yet for all his work, for all his progress, Tom wasn't any closer to an answer. He still didn't know who was planting the bombs.

If he arrested Koenig, the one potential lead he had would disappear. Koenig, he expected, was not a man who would talk; he'd happily go to his grave rather than reveal a secret to the enemy. Fuchs, however, didn't know anything more than what he'd already shared. And there was no likelihood of his getting new information; he'd already been summarily shoved out of the network.

So Tom made a tactical decision, and then ran it by Woods and Scull for approval.

He explained his plan: We make a deal with Fuchs to buy his silence, while at the same time we let PK run free. We follow him. Here, there, everywhere. See where he takes us. We can scoop him up whenever we get nervous. We have him cold.

Tom insisted that the most important mission was to stop the bombings. Arresting Koenig, he said, would be as futile as cutting the tail off a snake. The snake would still live. It'd wriggle off to strike again. They needed to "kill the snake," Tom said.

He believed that if his men continued their surveillance of Koenig, there was a good likelihood that in time they'd be led to the bombers.

Woods agreed. "Kill the snake, Captain," he ordered.

CHAPTER 24

———

No one was there. It was a bad enough start, but things soon got worse.

Von Rintelen, like Tom but for quite different reasons, had the bombings on his mind as he stood with his valises on the New York pier where the *Kristianiafjord* had docked. He had been told that Malvin Rice, the DuPont board member, would be waiting to greet him. Straight off they were to go—"arm in arm," Nicolai had teased—to the depot where Rice had stored the explosive powder von Rintelen would purchase.

When he'd first heard the plan, von Rintelen had practical reservations. He doubted that significant quantities of valuable explosives would be kept from Allied purchasing agents waving bundles of cash simply on the promise that Rice had a mystery client who'd be around in a month or so to make a deal. He had considered sharing this concern with Nicolai, but he'd decided not to; for all he knew, the great spymaster's faith had been predicated on machinations from which he was excluded. But now von Rintelen's fears had been confirmed. There was no sign of Malvin Rice.

He stood on the pier feeling entirely alone. His mission weighed on him. The rash pledge he'd made at the Foreign Office bound him to a perilous strategy: since he could not buy the munitions, he'd need to blow them up.

Alone in enemy territory, the full impact of what he was setting out to do struck him with a nearly unnerving force. "Single-handedly," he'd write, "I now ventured an attack against the forty-eight United States!"

Von Rintelen considered his next move. One of the golden rules of tradecraft, he told himself in an attempt to calm the waves of apprehension crashing over him, was that nothing goes as planned. A field agent must take setbacks in stride. With that maxim in mind, he decided that Rice's nonappearance was not worth worrying about. He'd move on to the other instructions he'd received in Berlin: the delivery of the new "most secret" codes hidden in the two capsules.

From the dock, he took a taxi to the German Club on Central Park South. He had been a member before the war, and, for the time being at least, he'd take a room. Most evenings, he'd been told in Berlin, he'd be able to find Captain Boy-Ed, the naval attaché, and Captain von Papen, the military attaché, holding court in the bar. His plan was to introduce himself and, when the moment was right, hand over the codes.

The two diplomats were not pleased to see him. Days earlier they had received a cable from Berlin announcing von Rintelen's imminent arrival, and they had been sulking ever since.

As soon as von Rintelen sat down, they made it clear that they did not need his help. The network, they insisted haughtily, was running fine without von Rintelen's interference. Boy-Ed was particularly disdainful. He wore more gold stripes on his sleeve than the junior naval officer, he pointed out, and therefore he had no intention of taking orders from him.

Von Rintelen tried to deflate the hostile mood by sharing news he had brought from Berlin. In recognition of their service, Boy-Ed had been awarded the Order of the House of Hohenzollern and von Papen the Iron Cross. He might as well have informed them they'd received lumps of coal, so total was their indifference to anything he had to say.

Von Rintelen realized he had no choice but to accept their ill humor. "I had anyhow not expected them to break out into whoops of joy when I made my appearance," he recalled years later with a philosophical detachment made easier by the passage of time. After handing them the new codes, he quickly left the bar.

He checked out of the German Club, too, and instead found a modest hotel on Fifty-Seventh Street. He didn't want to be near the attachés; he was done with them. Anyway, it would be better tradecraft, he decided, to "disappear into obscurity."

His first day in New York had been measured out in failures. Still, he told himself as he settled into his new hotel room, he would persevere. He didn't need Rice, or the two military attachés. He'd find his own assets, formulate his own plots. The Fatherland was counting on him, and he would get the job done. "It was," he reminded himself with a steely resolve, "high time that something *really* was done."

CHAPTER 25

———

Living in a familiar city gave von Rintelen a great sense of freedom. He openly inhabited two worlds, yet both were in their different ways aspects of the same operational cover.

By day, using a variety of aliases and wearing rough clothes, he prowled the waterfront, a spy conducting reconnaissance. He saw the English, French, and Russian transports waiting to be loaded with munitions, and each ship became a tangible target that brought a pressing clarity and focus to his mission. He noticed the roving cliques of bored German seamen hanging about the harbor, and he recognized at once that they were invaluable assets waiting to be recruited. He observed that many of the stevedores were Irish, and when he heard them openly snarling about having to load a ship flying the Union Jack, the talent spotter in him rejoiced. This was a visceral hatred he would exploit. And he met with a brooding, suspicious Koenig who nevertheless arranged sit-downs with many of the security chief's assets.

Discovering that the men in the field had grown wary of von Papen and his incompetence, he jumped at the chance to be their savior. He announced that the days of "the Kindergarten," as he had sneeringly dubbed the old network, were over. Berlin had sent a professional, not another diplomat dabbling in espionage. He would protect his agents, von Rintelen promised. He pledged to help them win many victories for the Fatherland. From now on, he stated with a persuasive finality, they worked for him.

And at night he'd shed his shabby clothes and aliases and play Franz von Rintelen, the fun-seeking aristocrat. He went merrily around town in white tie, society's newest handsome leading man.

He had taken up residence in the gilded sanctuary of the New York Yacht Club, and invitations arrived for dances, dinners, and country weekends. He tried to accept them all, a man seemingly committed to nothing more than a good time. Hiding in plain sight, he believed, was often the best disguise.

All the time, day and night, as he made his way about the city gathering intelligence and forging contacts, his confidence kept building. He had taken hold of the mission, and an operational plan was taking shape. America, he had discovered, was too soft, too trusting, too unprepared. He felt invincible.

This was his resilient, self-assured mood when he received a letter summoning him to a meeting with von Bernstorff. He went to the suite at the Ritz-Carlton on Madison Avenue suspecting that the ambassador would reiterate the attachés' offhand dismissal of his services. He was not disappointed. There was not even a pretense of polite conversation.

Von Bernstorff immediately demanded to know why he had come to America. His abrupt tone made it clear that he felt von Rintelen was not needed.

Von Rintelen, however, was no longer the man the military attachés had confronted, the novice operative who had literally just gotten off the boat. Unyielding, he stated that he was a soldier sent by the highest authorities in Berlin. His mission, he announced emphatically, was clear: "America is the unseen enemy," he said, and he would do whatever was necessary to save German soldiers from its shells.

The count bristled. The kaiser's ambassadors were not accustomed to receiving presumptuous lectures from junior officers. Indignant, he started to reprimand von Rintelen.

Unintimidated, von Rintelen reached into his pocket and, with deliberate drama, placed the *Kaiserpass* on the table.

"'Alle meine Behörden und Beamten sind nunmehro gehalten . . . ,'" he quoted: all the kaiser's subjects were to offer the holder whatever assistance he requested.

"Even an ambassador," von Rintelen said stiffly. Then with great formality he excused himself, walking out of the room like a soldier on parade.

CHAPTER 26

———

The Manhattan Front's headquarters was a newly rented two-room office suite on Cedar Street in the throbbing heart of New York's financial district. Emblazoned on the door was "E. V. Gibbons, Inc."—the two initials appropriated from von Rintelen's Swiss pseudonym—and below it, the words "Importers and Exporters."

In one room was the cover staff—Max Weiser and his secretary. A longtime legitimate exporter, Weiser not only knew his way around the waterfront but also came recommended by the German consul. At any one time he had several legitimate business deals going, but even when things were slow, his secretary was under orders to keep typing busily throughout the day. In the humble back office, von Rintelen set up shop.

Now that the whispered word was out around the German neighborhoods and meeting places, someone was always hoping for an audience with Mr. Gibbons. A procession of imperial navy sailors, assets who had previously performed tasks for Koenig's network, as well as a variety of shady characters eager to get backing for improbable schemes traipsed through the offices. Von Rintelen met with them all, showing most of them the door after only the briefest of interviews.

One afternoon Dr. Walter Scheele appeared without an appointment.

He had been Abteilung IIIB's lone agent in America before the war, and he arrived with a letter of strong recommendation from von Papen in his outstretched hand and a new invention hidden in his pocket.

Von Rintelen read the letter and then offered the wizened, elderly man a seat. Clearly nervous, Scheele began by explaining that he was a chemist by profession, president of the New Jersey Agricultural Chemical Company, but decades ago he had served as a lieutenant in the German field artillery and still remained a loyal son of the Fatherland. He had come, he said hesitantly, because he had created an invention that Mr. Gibbons might be interested in acquiring.

"You can trust me," von Rintelen assured him, moving his chair conspiratorially closer to his guest. "I am the most discreet man in New York."

Scheele waited, gathering his courage. At last he pulled his invention from his pocket and placed it on the desk.

It was the size and shape of a cigar, and it appeared to be made of solid lead. Von Rintelen stared at it with bewilderment.

If Scheele noticed a derisive glance, he chose to ignore it. Instead, with a confident professionalism, he explained how his "lead cigar" worked.

The interior of the lead tube was divided in two by a copper disc he had soldered into place, Scheele began. In one compartment was picric acid; the other held sulfuric acid. Wax plugs placed at both ends made the cigar airtight.

Von Rintelen was confused. He still didn't understand the device's purpose.

His puzzled look seemed to amuse the chemist. As if it were entirely obvious, Scheele explained that the two acids would eat their way through the copper disc—and when they did, their mingling would result in an intense flame.

The disc, he went on, was merely a timing device. It could be thick or thin, and depending on its size, the inevitable combustion caused by the merging of the two acids would occur in either days or weeks. But best of all, Scheele revealed—a performer saving his best routine for last—as the fire burned, the lead casing would melt away. *No clue would be left behind.*

Concluding, he said that what he'd invented was nothing less than the perfect sabotage device—inexpensive, dependable, easily concealed, and untraceable.

Trying to disguise his excitement, von Rintelen said he'd need to see if the device was as good as Scheele claimed. He wanted a demonstration. But a scheme was already taking shape in his mind.

The next day the experiment took place in a New Jersey woods. Under von Rintelen's watchful eye, Scheele placed a wafer-thin copper disc in the tube. Then he placed the device on the ground. Step back, he warned.

Whoosh! A bright stream of flame suddenly shot up from the cigar. It was so intense that for a moment von Rintelen feared that he might be blinded. Swiftly, he jumped back; and then, from the safety of his new vantage point, he watched with fascination as the device melted down into a tiny slug of lead.

When the demonstration was over, he turned to see Scheele leaning nonchalantly against a tree, a beaming smile on his weathered face. "That was pretty good, wasn't it?" Scheele asked with self-satisfied pride.

"I'll say it was!" von Rintelen rejoiced.

CHAPTER 27

———

As quickly as the invention had burst into flames, the operational significance of the lead cigar became clear to von Rintelen. He'd arm Scheele's devices with copper discs thick enough to delay their combustion for about two weeks, and then plant them on ships carrying cargo to the Allies. The ships would be in international waters when the destructive fires erupted, and in the smoldering aftermath there'd be no clues as to what had caused the blaze. Visions of raging shipboard fires, the racing flames exploding American shells meant to target German troops, filled him with gleeful anticipation.

He promptly wrote Scheele a large check and sent him back to his laboratory in Hoboken to begin manufacturing the sinister cigars. In the meantime, he started recruiting men to plant the devices.

Using one alias, he went to several of the captains of the interned German ships and signed them on as supervisors of the sabotage operation. Next, using another alias, he met with groups of Irish stevedores.

He never revealed that he was working for Germany; he simply made it clear that he was out to harm England. Shared animosity, plus some cash, was sufficient to get their attention.

With the efficient authority of a chemistry teacher, he explained how the cigars were constructed. Then, deciding that candor was now necessary, he boldly stated that the devices needed to be smuggled aboard ships transporting explosives to Europe. To a man, they all agreed that it could easily be done. They were ready to start at once.

Now that the men were in place, however, von Rintelen faced an unanticipated problem. Scheele's laboratory in Hoboken was tiny and makeshift. It was not suitable, the chemist explained, for the sort of nationwide sabotage operation von Rintelen was planning. They'd need, he insisted, a much larger space, preferably a metalworking plant where the lead cigars could be manufactured in quantity.

Von Rintelen listened, and immediately realized the contradictory obstacles he now faced. He needed a large-scale manufacturing plant. At the same time it had to be a covert operation; the bombs must be manufactured in secret. Yet the bigger the factory, the more likely that it would attract the attention of the American authorities. Unable to find a solution, in his frustration he began to make discreet inquiries, asking his expanding circle of American acquaintances for advice.

It was Bonford Boniface, a waterfront lawyer with a penchant for outrageous schemes and cheap whiskey, who came up with the answer. A friend of Weiser's, he had no allegiance to Germany. Weeks ago he'd drifted into the network simply because it offered him the opportunity to make some extra money. Now he bounded into the back room of the E. V. Gibbons offices and bellowed that he'd thought of the perfect place to manufacture the devices.

Von Rintelen noticed that Boniface's pince-nez was askew. Wearily, he suspected that today the lawyer's drinking had begun just after breakfast. He told Boniface that he was busy; perhaps he could come back tomorrow. It took all von Rintelen's discipline not to add, *When you've sobered up.*

But Boniface plowed on as if he hadn't heard. "Why not manufacture your bombs on one of the interned ships?" he suggested without preamble.

Rintelen thought about it for a moment and then decided that if Boniface wanted a drink, he was ready to buy it. It was a magnificent plan. "We are to transplant ourselves, with all our schemes, devices, and enterprises, on board one of the German ships and thus place ourselves in a most admirable situation," he would later write, still excited by the lawyer's strategy. "Germany within American territorial waters! What possibilities!"

And what choices! There were more than eighty interned vessels, from large passenger liners like the *Vaterland* to smaller fighting ships like the *Emden*. Before the scheme could move forward, he'd need to pick one for his workshop.

CHARLES VON KLEIST WAS AN old salt. He'd been born into an ancient aristocratic family, but he had wanted nothing to do with his gilded heritage. After shipping off to sea on a windjammer when he was a boy, von Kleist had spent the next forty years behind the mast, rising to the rank of captain and sailing around the globe too many times to count. Now a feisty seventy, bald, his carefully groomed goatee as white as snow, he had settled in Hoboken and spent most nights drinking with crowds of admiring German sailors from the interned ships. His wild stories were famous, and a few of them might also possibly be true.

The old sailor was a favorite of von Rintelen's. The spy enjoyed the shamelessly embroidered sea yarns, and he also had a bounder's fascination with aristocrats—especially those who didn't flaunt their distinguished families.

Not long after his conversation with Boniface, von Rintelen met up with von Kleist for a drink and shared his plan. He let it sink in, and then confided, "Well, Kleist, this is going to be something out of the ordinary. We must find a ship where the captain will play the game; where the crew will abide by the orders given; and where, above all, the whole crowd will keep their mouths shut."

Von Kleist pulled on his goatee thoughtfully. "Well," he said finally, "you are asking a good deal. Qualities like those are a rare combination to find on board one vessel."

Still, the old sailor began to throw out several possibilities. But no sooner had he mentioned a ship than he'd find a reason to dismiss it. As the list of failed candidates grew, von Rintelen began to despair.

Suddenly von Kleist banged his fist on the table in triumph. "I think I've got it! It is the steamship *Friedrich der Grosse* you want!"

Over the next week the ship was transformed into a factory. The firm of E. V. Gibbons ordered large quantities of lead and copper tubing, as well as machinery to cut the metal to precisely calibrated lengths and thicknesses. Under the cover of darkness, the purchases were carried up the gangplank and smuggled on board the steamer.

At night, the hold of the ship became a hive of activity. Teams of sailors went to work, the blades of a half dozen machines whirling in a purposeful, high-pitched buzz as they cut through the lead pipes. Once the cigars had been cut to size, copper discs were inserted. This was careful, meticulous work. Each disc first had to be cut to precisely the thickness that Scheele's experiments had determined would take fifteen days to dissolve. Finally, they had to be soldered into place—a genuine challenge, since the pieces of tubing were small and very narrow. It took an entire week to fabricate approximately one hundred lead cigars.

When the shells were ready, sailors delivered them to Scheele in Hoboken. His lab was hidden away in a crawl space above his firm's offices; it could be accessed only by climbing a ladder to an artfully camouflaged trapdoor.

The chemist locked himself into this secret room and, in solitude, filled each device with the copper-eating chemicals. A careless slip of his hand or a too-sudden gesture, and the incendiary acids might run into each other and explode. He'd be burned alive. Scheele worked with a nerve-wrenching slowness, always aware that his life depended on his precision. By the time he fixed the last wax caps on the last cigar, he was completely undone. His hands continued shaking for hours.

The finished devices were packed into a small wooden box and taken back across the Hudson River to the office on Cedar Street. The box was stored in a drawer of von Rintelen's desk. The cigars would not explode for fifteen days, but the thought of working in such close proximity to enough explosives to set the entire building aflame was sufficient motivation for the spy to move quickly. He told Weiser to gather all the Irish stevedores for a war council that evening.

No sooner had the stevedores filed into the back room than they told von Rintelen they had news to report. The *Phoebus,* a British transport, had started loading munitions. It was a large order, and the work would not be finished for several days.

Von Rintelen opened his desk drawer and removed the box. He gave each of the men several of the devices. He was as jovial as if he were handing out real cigars.

The next morning the dockers carried barrels, cases, and sacks filled with American-made shells and bullets onto the *Phoebus*. And in their pockets were the combustible devices. When they were certain no one was looking, from time to time they bent down and, all stealth, wedged a cigar unobtrusively into a dark corner.

As they went about their surreptitious work, von Rintelen strolled along the dock where the steamer was berthed. He glanced at the British sailors on deck, carbines slung over their shoulders, ready to prevent saboteurs from interfering with their valuable cargo. Didn't the fools realize it was too late? he gloated. Didn't they know they couldn't stop Franz von Rintelen? That he was invincible? But of course he said nothing. He simply continued on along the waterfront, his mind near to bursting with its secret, joyful pride.

The *Phoebus* sailed the next day, and von Rintelen waited impatiently for news. Each morning he eagerly read the *Shipping News,* but no report about the *Phoebus* appeared. He had calculated the date when the copper disc would dissolve and the acids would combust, but this day passed, and there was still nothing in the paper.

He began to grow anxious; doubts filled his thoughts. Perhaps Scheele had miscalculated the necessary amounts of acid, and the devices wouldn't work. Or maybe they had been discovered and tossed overboard. Or maybe, he suddenly feared, the Irish stevedores had played him, and the plot had been reported to the authorities. The next knock on his door might very well be the police.

But two tense days past the deadline, he picked up the *Shipping News*: "*Accidents*. S.S. *Phoebus* from New York—destination Archangel—caught fire at sea. Brought into Liverpool by H.M.S. *Ajax*."

He ordered the men on board the *Friedrich der Grosse* to get back to work that night making more lead shells. He sent word to Scheele to purchase additional quantities of acid. The first battle had ended in a glorious victory: the *Phoebus*'s cargo had gone up in flames, and the ship had foundered. Now the main attack would begin.

CHAPTER 28

———

Tom prayed for another miracle. After he reported last month to Commissioners Woods and Scull that his team had identified Fuchs and was making progress in building a case against Koenig, Tom had brushed off their praise. Modestly, he admitted that it was more luck than anything else that had finally moved the investigation forward.

Now once again stymied, the Koenig surveillance bringing no new leads and ship explosions suddenly escalating, Tom regretted his previous cavalier disdain. He'd happily settle for another gift thrown his way.

He soon got it. Only this time the clue came not over a tapped phone, but from the French ambassador.

Four bombs had been discovered packed among bags of sugar in the hold of the steamship *Kirkoswald,* en route from New York, when it docked in Marseille. The French police removed the explosive charges and, after some heated debate, finally agreed to send the bombs back across the Atlantic to Ambassador Jean-Jules Jusserand in Washington. Protocol required that they be delivered to the State Department, the ambassador determined. From there, the now harmless devices made their laborious way to Mayor Mitchel's office at City Hall in New York, then on to Commissioner Woods, who promptly handed them over to Tom.

The bombs were like nothing Tom had ever seen before. They were metal tubes, about ten inches long, divided into two compartments. The potassium chlorate (the French report made no mention of picric acid) and sulfuric acid that had each filled one of the two sections had been drained, but it was clear how the bomb was meant to work. The acids would eat through the thin copper disc separating the two compartments, and when the fluids merged, an explosion would take place. For some unknown reason, though, this time the internal copper discs had not dissolved. The bombs aboard the *Kirkoswald* had been found intact.

The devices were a mystery, and—frustratingly—at the same time they were Tom's only clues. If he was ever going to get anywhere with his investigation, the bombs, he decided, would need to be the starting point. They were the evidence that could lead to the men behind the sabotage—if only he was smart enough to make sense of what he had in front of him. These were puzzles, Tom sternly told himself, that he must solve.

He picked up a device in his hand, feeling its weight and then running his index finger along the cold metal. It seemed harmless; in fact, it occurred to him that the bomb was about the size and shape of a cigar.

Looking at it with greater scrutiny, he saw that the device was, in its diabolical way, a work of art—an ingenious design, built from good-quality metals and fabricated with careful workmanship. It was nothing like the crude, makeshift weapons thrown together by the Brescia Circle bombers or any of the other anarchist groups he had encountered. This was the work of a skilled, rather artful professional.

That told him something, he decided. There had to be someone involved with a sophisticated knowledge of chemistry and design. Perhaps the mastermind was an engineer, a chemist, or a science professor. Another thought: the saboteurs were well funded; metals of this quality were expensive.

It suddenly occurred to Tom that they must be working out of a factory or a manufacturing plant. The lead tubes and copper discs were cut with precision, the edges smooth to the touch. Only industrial electric saws, he imagined, could do this meticulous work. Of course the factory could be anywhere in the country, but it was, he wanted to believe, an insight that could prove valuable as the case progressed.

He put the device down and closed his eyes. Deep in thought, he tried to focus on what else the bombs could tell him. To his great annoyance, only stray, irrelevant notions ran through his mind.

Then he remembered that the *Kirkoswald* had carried supplies to France. The other fires—and over the past two months a long list had grown even longer—had also occurred on ships making deliveries to the Allies. No bombs had been found on those vessels, bolstering arguments that the blazes had been accidents. Yet now this tangible evidence confirmed his working theory: the bombs had been placed on the vessels by either German spies or their henchmen. He had been right all along.

However gratifying, this realization did not bring him any closer to identifying the saboteurs. And it certainly wouldn't stop future bombings. Tom needed to dig deeper.

He opened his eyes and, with nothing else to consider, picked up the report written by the Marseille police. It had been forwarded along with the devices, and some anonymous diplomat, in either the French embassy in Washington or the State Department, had thoughtfully gone to the trouble of translating the three pages into a very efficient English. Tom had already read it several times, but now, as he went over the pages again, a single sentence drew him like a magnet: the bombs had been found hidden among bags of sugar.

What if—

But before he could even complete the thought in his mind, he was shouting for Barnitz.

Tom told his aide that he wanted him to check the cargo records of all the ships that had reported fires. He needed to know if they had also been carrying sugar shipments.

Barnitz moaned. He'd need to go over the manifests of at least nearly thirty ships. Danger didn't bother him, but the monotony of following a paper trail loomed as certain torture.

Tom ignored the sergeant. He wanted the results by noon tomorrow, he ordered.

Barnitz's report was a revelation. Not only had every one of the ships plagued by recent fires carried a cargo of sugar, but the detective had also discovered an ominous corollary: sugar was highly flammable. The experienced shipboard fire crews reported that next to munitions, sugar was their biggest fear. A blaze fed by bags of sugar, they knew only too well, took just moments to swell into a raging inferno.

Sugar! It was a whole new avenue to explore, opening up the investigation with a suddenly promising clarity. Encouraged, Tom decided he now understood how the saboteurs had planted the devices without being noticed: the bombs had been loaded along with sugar shipments.

But how had they done it? Tom wondered. And when? At the refinery? On the piers? On board the ships? He made up his mind to get the answers.

SUGAR FOR EXPORT WAS PACKED in two kinds of bags.

Tom learned this firsthand as he toured the refinery in Long Island City. He had decided that since he was not sure what he was looking for, he'd better visit the plant himself. Perhaps, he hoped, he'd see something that would start him thinking.

He spent a long day learning all about the sugar-manufacturing business. He followed the entire process, from the arrival of raw sugar at the refinery to the bagging and shipping of the finished orders. It was a noisy, hectic education, his eyes and ears assaulted by pounding assembly-line machines and busy, shouting human chains of workers.

The incessant clatter made it difficult for Tom to think. But as he watched the refined sugar being bagged, he was struck by an idea: *If I were a saboteur, that's how I'd do it. I'd put the devices right into the bags.*

He made his way over to a long table where a half dozen workers were sewing closed the bags that had just been filled. He watched them work. It was all done by hand with fast, sure stitches, using thick red thread and a big needle.

Without a word, he grabbed one of the sewn bags and ripped it open. It came apart easily.

Startled workers jumped to their feet in anger. Tom showed them his badge and backed it up with a menacing look. They sat down immediately.

He ordered one man to stitch the bag closed again.

The worker was confused, but he didn't dare disobey. It was done in moments, and when Tom examined the handiwork, he saw that it was impossible to tell that it had previously been opened.

Tom moved on to the adjacent table. Here the tops of the heavy muslin bags were stitched closed by machines. He grabbed a bag and tried to repeat his previous experiment.

It took several attempts, and a bit of muscle, before the machine stitches came undone. And when the bag was resewn, the new stitches were obvious.

Lesson one, Tom told himself: The saboteurs most likely plant the devices in the hand-sewn bags. That should narrow the search considerably.

But no sooner had Tom come to grasp this knowledge than he realized he was getting ahead of himself. He had skipped a crucial part of the process. The saboteurs wouldn't plant the devices in just *any* hand-sewn bags of sugar. They'd target only orders bound for Allied boats.

He quickly made his way to the shipping department and spoke to the clerk. He needed to learn how many people knew the final destination of a shipment when it left the refinery.

The clerk said there were only two. He was one. The shipping clerk, he explained, knew the destination of every order. The other was the lighter captain. He would pick up the shipments from the clerk and pilot the barge carrying the sugar out to a specific ship.

It was a short drive back to Centre Street, and all the while Tom's thoughts were racing. Lesson two, he decided, with a mounting sense that he was getting closer to unraveling the mystery: the lighter captain inserts the bombs into the hand-sewn bags of sugar before he delivers the shipment to the boat.

A strategy had settled in his mind before he even walked into the squad room. He'd order his men to begin surveillance of the waterfront lighter captains. He'd follow the seamen as they loaded their barges at the piers and then steered them out into the harbor to the Allied boats. And in the process, he'd find his saboteurs.

CHAPTER 29

————

With nightfall, curtains of gray mist and heavy shadows fell over the Hudson River. The silence grew thick and deep, too. Yet the lightering—the process by which barges brought cargo to vessels too large to be anchored at the port facilities—was done only at night on the empty, dark river. For month after taut month, it had been a particularly challenging surveillance for policemen more accustomed to the sidewalks of New York.

There had been the night, for example, when something suspicious caught Detective Senff's eye, and he gave chase to a sailor by the West Forty-Fourth Street pier. Senff ran through a maze of shadows; and then suddenly he had fallen into the water, and the tide was carrying him away. Three beefy detectives dived in after him, and only after a frightening struggle were they able to pull him to shore.

On other evenings, they'd chase after a barge in their police motorboats, only to realize that stealth was impossible: the sound of their barking engines might just as well have been a cannon barrage echoing through the silent night. They'd cut their engines and try to drift, but then the lighter barges would pull swiftly away. Or they'd stay back, trailing a distant blinking light as it headed out to sea, only to discover when at last they caught up that they'd been following the wrong boat all along.

Yet after all the fruitless months, the team decided that they had finally found something. On several nights they'd watched as a motorboat stole up to a lighter. The detectives were a half mile or so off, and at night their binoculars were nearly useless, but each time the furtive shadows scurrying about the long barge suggested that some sort of covert transaction was taking place. Engines roaring, they'd charge toward the lighter, but by the time they arrived, the mysterious motorboat along with its crew would always have vanished.

Tom was unable to get his proof, but still he was convinced: the devices were delivered to the lighter captains at sea. They'd arrive by motorboat, and then the bombs would be concealed in bags of sugar.

It was the only time, he reasoned, that made sense. Once the barge pulled up to the vessel's side, there'd be no opportunity. The stevedores would quickly hurl the cargo into the hold, and then the hatches would be sealed. Why else, he told himself with the brimming confidence of a man who felt he had solved a difficult problem, would the motorboats rendezvous at sea with the barges? They had to be dropping off a consignment of bombs.

Tom set a trap, and this time, to ensure that it would succeed, he stationed his men on land. He realized that the mysterious motorboats not only went out to sea but also returned to shore. He'd catch them when they docked.

Even as Tom shared his strategy with Barnitz, he knew it was a flimsy plan, its success at best improbable. For one thing, his men couldn't cover the entire length of the New York waterfront; there were the entire East River and Hudson River shorelines to patrol, as well as the New Jersey side of the Hudson. And even if they did get lucky and spotted the motorboat coming in to tie up, there was always a strong chance that the crew would bolt, disappearing without a trace into the dark, twisting city streets that fanned out from the waterfront.

But for once everything went as planned. Shortly after 2:00 a.m., a motorboat docked at a pier on the Lower West Side. A single man climbed out, and Tom's detectives were able to follow him unnoticed. He walked slowly, seemingly without a care, and stopped in front of a brownstone building on Twenty-Third Street.

Before he put his key into the front door, Barnitz had grabbed his arm, and Detective Corell snapped handcuffs on his wrists. Moments later, Barnitz gleefully radioed his boss that they were bringing the suspect in.

Tom waited in his office at Centre Street to meet the saboteur. There were dozens of questions he wanted to ask. He looked forward to rounding up the rest of the network. Before the day was over, Tom was sure, he'd have the information that would put an end to the months of bombings.

Tom soon got to ask his questions, but he didn't get the answers he'd been expecting.

The man was a crook, not an enemy agent. For the past four months he and his crew of river pirates had been motoring out to the barges under the cover of darkness to buy bags of stolen sugar from the lighter captains. He was making 400 percent profit on each bag he resold.

He didn't know anything about bombs.

Tom's men arrested five lighter captains that day. Very quickly, they all confessed—to selling sugar illegally. As for the shipboard explosions, they were as puzzled as Tom was. Mike Matzet, a burly seaman who was used to doing things his own way, even barked at Tom, "That's why we thought there was no harm in selling the sugar. Take all you want, we told him. The damn ship will never get over anyway!"

Tom had to agree that Captain Matzet was probably right. After four futile months following a seemingly promising trail, he was no closer to a solution than when he had started. And the morning paper, he saw, had reported another fire at sea.

CHAPTER 30

——

It was Tom who initiated the meeting, and he entered the commissioner's office with the same grim resolve he'd summoned up as a boy reluctantly going off to confession. Only this admission of guilt, he knew, would be worse, much worse; so much more had been at stake than merely the fate of his own insignificant soul.

It was the day after the arrests of the river pirates and the lighter captains, and in those twenty-four hours Tom was as low as he had ever been. He had barely eaten, and sleep had been impossible. His restless thoughts were filled with recurring visions of the many wasted nights he'd ordered his men to spend huddled in motorboats on the dark river. He had been so confident, and in the end so wrong. The nuns in county Cork had taught that arrogance was a deadly sin, but they had never hinted that his transgressions could harm innocent victims too. Yet a sorrowful Tom felt that his wrongheaded certainty—so much valuable time squandered!—left him personally culpable for any new damage the explosions caused. Atonement seemed impossible. And punishment—demotion? reassignment?—seemed probable.

He marched into Woods's office as gravely as a man going to his own funeral. The commissioner sat behind the Teddy Roosevelt desk, and Scull was in a leather side chair, puffing on a pipe.

Tom saluted, and still at attention, he addressed the commissioner. I was wrong, he confessed stiffly. Without omitting any of the painful details or, for that matter, offering any excuses, he went on to explain how his theory linking the bombs and the sugar shipments had proved to be a mistake.

When he was done, Tom girded himself for what would happen next. He was a proud man, but even more painful was the prospect of leaving his job when there was so much more to do.

Woods's face did not betray any emotion. He simply ordered Tom to take a seat.

The commissioner waited until Tom had settled into the chair. Then he asked, "Where do we go from here, Captain?"

Tom would always remember that Woods's tone was not malicious. There was no lash of criticism. And Tom would always be grateful, especially since it was a kindness he felt he did not deserve.

"I'm not sure," Tom admitted truthfully.

So Woods, still at heart the Groton master, offered a parable. "When you are bound on a long trip," he began, as Tom would later relate the conversation, "and you mislaid your ticket, it is second nature to go through your pockets one by one knowing full well that it is not in any of them, for you 'just looked there.' Then you find it in one of the pockets where you knew it could not be."

Tom understood. He left the commissioner's office determined to go back through his pockets.

THE INVESTIGATION RETURNED TO THE piers, and this time Tom ordered his men to focus on the Chenangoes, as the stevedores who loaded the shipments of sugar onto the lighters were called. Perhaps, he now wanted to believe, they were the accomplices who concealed the devices in the bags.

Stevedores on a New York dock loading barrels of corn syrup
onto a barge on the Hudson River, circa 1912.

A dingy second-floor room that looked straight out on the pier was rented in a nearby flophouse, and this became the team's observation post. Watchers with binoculars monitored whether any of the Chenangoes lingered among the bags of sugar or carried any suspicious packages to the job. After three weeks of surveillance, a despondent Tom admitted, "The wickedest thing we ever found was an occasional pint flask on the hip."

So, digging still deeper into his pockets, Tom went back to the bombs themselves. He decided to investigate sales of chlorate of potash and sulfuric acid—the two ingredients listed in the French report. His men examined reams of sales receipts from explosives and chemical manufacturers and tracked down dozens of people who had bought the chemicals in commercial drugstores. In the end, Tom was forced to concede, the team "found nothing of consequence." None of the purchases had even provoked a lingering suspicion.

Tom had reached the point where he had to accept that his pockets were indeed empty. He had racked his mind, but no clue, as far as he could tell, had been overlooked. He couldn't think of anywhere else to search. Worse, the investigation had dragged on futilely for so long that he feared for his men's morale. His squad had grown callous; they now accepted that more bombings were inevitable. And Tom, too, was suffering through his own cruel internal struggle. Resigning himself to live with defeat did not come easily to him.

Then one morning Tom's phone rang, and a revitalizing energy was brought to the case. The caller was Robert Martyn, the French military attaché, and as Scull would later be quick to point out, this was the second time France had come to the investigation's rescue.

With a deferential politeness, Captain Martyn wanted to know if Captain Tunney would perhaps be interested in information that had come his way. It involved, he said obliquely, someone seeking to purchase a quantity of explosives.

"What kind?" Tom barked. He'd received too many reports of people buying nothing worse than firecrackers to show any immediate concern. And, he'd later admit, the prospect of dealing once again with the French chafed him.

The attaché explained that it was trinitrotoluene.

The more common name, Tom knew, was TNT.

"Yes," Tom said. "We would be interested."

CHAPTER 31

———

The attaché's information set Tom and his men off on a confusing, circuitous, and dangerous trail. It started with a war exporter named Carl Wettig, an acquaintance of the French diplomat. Wettig had been approached by a friend of a friend who wanted to buy a small quantity of TNT for, he explained to Wettig, "test purposes."

The prospective purchaser lived at the Hotel Breslin in downtown Manhattan and, Tom quickly discovered, was known to the hotel management as Paul Siebs, yet he often used the name Karl Oppegaarde. A man with an alias trying to buy TNT gave Tom some concerns, and the instructions to Wettig that he should deliver the dynamite to an address in New Jersey where the exporter would finally receive payment only added to them.

Tom could have ordered Wettig to walk away from the deal; if Siebs (aka Oppegaarde) didn't get his TNT, then Tom would no longer need to worry about what he'd planned to do with it. But all his instincts told Tom that diligence would be rewarded. He decided to let Wettig get the dynamite, and then they'd, as he put it to his squad, "play follow the explosive."

With Detective Barnitz glued to his side as a burly chaperone, Wettig went to a munitions store in Perth Amboy, New Jersey. Twenty-five pounds of TNT were bought and then carried back across the Hudson and handed to Mr. Siebs, as he was calling himself that day.

The Hotel Breslin, at the southeast corner of West Twenty-Ninth Street and Broadway, still stands today. This photo is circa 1910–1915.

Tom had been waiting at the Hotel Breslin, too, and as soon as the dynamite was delivered, he pounced. He immediately asked what Siebs intended to do with twenty-five pounds of TNT.

"I don't have the slightest idea," Siebs shot back.

Tom raised a beefy hand. He could have slapped Siebs for such impertinence and never given it a second thought. But before he could land a blow, Siebs, now shaking with fear, began to talk.

Dr. Herbert Kienzle, a German clock maker whom he knew only in passing, he explained hurriedly as if speed would make it all seem more logical, had first approached him with the proposition that led him, through another friend, to Wettig. The clock maker had instructed that the TNT be delivered to a garage on

Main Street in Weehawken, New Jersey. A Robert Fay would be waiting at the garage, and he would pay Siebs for both the dynamite and his services.

Tom asked him about Fay. He wanted to know why Fay needed the dynamite.

If Siebs was tempted to answer, "I don't have the slightest idea," he wisely stopped himself. Instead, he plaintively insisted that he really, truthfully, didn't know.

Tom believed him. The whole complex tale of, as he put it, "passing the TNT" was so improbable that Tom felt it had to be true. His head was swimming with all the names and connections, but at the same bewildering time he felt he was on to something promising. Employing a small army of cutouts—from Fay to Kienzle to Siebs aka Oppegaarde to Wettig—was the behavior of a professional concerned with operational security. But what was this operative truly trying to hide?

With his renewed sense of the chase, his spirits lifted, too, and Tom set out to find Fay. He wanted to discover who this mystery man was, and why he had asked a German clock maker to get him twenty-five pounds of TNT.

THE FOLLOWING DAY TOM MADE two operational decisions, and each was a gamble that, he knew full well, could end badly. But Tom felt he didn't have much choice. He had reached that desperate juncture in a case when gambles and hunches were all he had left in his arsenal.

The first occurred when detectives George Barnitz and James Coy, playing the roles of sturdy deliverymen hired by Wettig, brought the twenty-five pounds of TNT to the Weehawken garage. There was no sign of Fay, but Barnitz appealed to one of the workers. He told the man that they wouldn't be paid unless the package was delivered directly to Fay. Could he help them out?

The worker gave them the address of Fay's boardinghouse on Fifth Street. Fay wasn't there, either, but the landlady was chatty. She invited the two men in.

"Mr. Fay," she told them, was "a real gentleman." Paid his bills, even subscribed to a magazine. Sociable, too. He had a roommate, a Mr. Scholz. Then, her voice dropping to nearly a whisper because she knew she really shouldn't be saying so much, she revealed that Fay was an inventor. She admitted that she didn't know that for a fact. But he had a table in his room where he was always drawing some kind of plans, and so she had figured out that was his profession. Finally, she told them they could leave the package; she'd make sure that Fay would get it.

Covert operative Robert Fay, inventor of the rudder bomb.

That's when Barnitz went off to telephone Tom. He asked if he should give the landlady the package.

Tom knew Fay had been expecting the dynamite, and Wettig had promised it would be delivered. And Fay's intricate precautions suggested he was a suspicious sort. Any deviation from the arrangements, Tom suspected, could make him bolt.

But the alternative would be to leave twenty-five pounds of TNT in a boardinghouse in the middle of the town of Weehawken. With a professional objectivity, Tom reminded himself that TNT was harmless without a proper detonator—most of the time. He also knew that accidents were possible. In certain circumstances—too much heat, a tight, airless space—it could combust.

Tom weighed the possibilities in his mind: Fay's going on the lam; or half of Weehawken going up in smoke.

Losing Fay, Tom decided at last, was a risk he couldn't take. He told Barnitz to leave the package.

Yet no sooner had Tom made that difficult decision than once again his instincts were put to another hard test. Detectives Coy and Walsh, joined by James Sterett, had been staking out the Hotel Breslin, covering all the exits to make sure that Siebs did not suddenly disappear. After several uneventful hours of surveillance, they saw a man stop by the front desk, ask if Mr. Siebs was in, and then take the elevator to his floor.

He was in his youthful thirties, with a bushy black mustache above an easy smile, and dressed in a sharply cut double-breasted brown suit. He was a handsome man, and the swagger in his walk suggested he was well aware of it.

Walsh asked the hotel clerk who had rung Siebs if he had caught the visitor's name.

"A Mr. Fay," said the clerk.

Moments later Coy was on the phone with Tom. He needed to know if they should bring Fay in.

Tom considered. If Fay was in custody, Tom could go one-on-one with him in the interrogation room. Most men would crack after a few slaps with a nightstick. But the signs pointed to Fay's being a professional. There was a chance he'd take a beating, and all Tom would have to show for his efforts would be a bruised fist and a broken nightstick. Besides, Tom reminded himself, there was no guarantee Fay had anything to confess. Maybe he really was an inventor. Maybe he did need the TNT, as Wettig had been told, for "test purposes."

Yet if his men tailed Fay, the prospects were tantalizing. There was no telling where he'd take them, or what they'd find out. Fay might be the man who would lead them to the group behind the shipboard explosions.

As long as, Tom realized with a sudden twist in his stomach, his men didn't lose Fay. There was always the possibility that Fay would walk out of the Breslin and then disappear into the city, never to be seen again. Koenig, after all, had shown them how easily a professional could shake a tail in New York.

"Follow him," Tom ordered. "And if you lose him, don't come back."

CHAPTER 32

Lower Manhattan, New York City, with ferry in the foreground, circa 1912. Identified buildings include *(from left)* the Woolworth Building (with tower nearing completion) and the Singer Building.

The open deck of the Forty-Second Street ferry didn't offer many places to hide, so all the detectives could do was bury their heads in their newspapers. They hoped they looked like typical commuters, and that Fay, standing by the rail and looking straight across the Hudson to the New Jersey shoreline, didn't notice them.

When Fay left the Breslin a little more than a half hour ago, Coy, Walsh, and Sterett had been in pursuit. The three detectives followed him onto the ferry to Weehawken.

After the ferry docked, they stayed with him as he walked up the steep hill into town and headed into the garage on Main Street. Fay remained in the garage long enough for the detectives to make new operational plans. Borrowing a car from the local police, they sat in it and waited.

Hours passed, and they began to wonder what Fay was doing. Or if there was a back door to the garage they hadn't spotted.

But patience, they told themselves, was at the heart of every successful surveillance. Besides, all they could do was wait—unless they dared to telephone Captain Tunney and suggest there was a possibility that somehow Fay had escaped.

Suddenly a dark sedan pulled out of the garage. Fay was at the wheel, and there was a husky, well-dressed passenger next to him in the front seat. Was this Scholz, the roommate the landlady had mentioned?

The car drove through Weehawken and then headed north, taking a twisting route that ran along the cliffs of the Palisades. The police car kept its distance but never lost sight of the dark sedan.

The road took them past large homes, brick villas newly built by Wall Street financiers to take advantage of the glorious sunsets shimmering across the Hudson, then a movie studio where D. W. Griffith had shot the outdoor scenes for his earliest dramas. Soon the countryside became wilder, a thick forest of scrub oak trees.

Fay stopped the car, and both he and his passenger got out. They walked into the deep, dark woods.

The detectives couldn't decide what to do. They could follow the two men, but the likelihood of their traipsing through a pitch-dark forest undetected seemed slim. Besides, Fay had left his car at the side of the road. He must be coming back, they told themselves.

They waited in the darkness, and it was as if they could hear the ominous ticking of each passing moment in their heads. What could he be doing in the woods for so long? They tried a variety of possibilities out on each other, but nothing in the end seemed reasonable.

The longer they waited, the greater was their dread. How could the detectives explain to Captain Tunney that they had watched passively as Fay had walked off?

Fay and his passenger returned, though. They drove directly to the boardinghouse. When the two men entered, the watchers breathed a sigh of genuine relief.

The next day was Saturday, and at noon when Fay and his friend— they were now sure the big, dapper guy was Scholz—emerged from the boardinghouse, six detectives were in position up and down the block. Barnitz, on orders from Tom, had arrived before dawn to take charge.

There were also, parked in a nearby car, two Secret Service agents. Tom had asked that the agents be there; New York cops had no power of arrest in another state, and Tom had decided that it was time to bring Fay in. The many cautious steps that set up the covert delivery of the TNT; the meeting with Siebs; the strange disappearance into the Jersey woods in the middle of the night—Tom wanted explanations for a growing list of questions.

Still, Tom was willing to let Fay roam for a while longer. He wanted to see where he'd go, what he'd do. With the Secret Service agents, there were eight men on his tail. It was what watchers call a bandbox operation, cozy to the point of being airtight. There was no conceivable way Fay could suddenly vanish.

They followed Fay as he and his companion got on board a Grant-wood streetcar. One detective hopped on board, too, while the others followed in two unmarked cars.

Fay and his friend rode the streetcar out of Weehawken and then continued on foot to the woods outside town. They walked at a leisurely pace, never looking back over their shoulders, never glancing about suspiciously. They seemed to be two friends out for a stroll. When they reached the spot where they had entered the woods on the previous night, they once again disappeared into the forest.

Barnitz sent Sterett and Coy in after them. Careful, he warned. But stealth was impossible. Leaves crackled under their feet. Twigs snapped. They were only two men, but it sounded as if a cavalry brigade were riding through the woods.

Fay turned around sharply and peered back. The two detectives froze.

After a moment, Fay continued. The officers followed. But it wasn't long before Fay came to a halt. He looked about nervously, suddenly suspicious. Fay finally moved on, and when he did, the detectives decided it would be prudent to return to the cars.

The eight men waited. Hours passed. When it started to get dark and there was still no sign of Fay, Barnitz understood he had nothing left to lose. Let's bring him in, he ordered, and the detectives and Secret Service agents went charging into the woods.

It was nearly midnight when Tom picked up the ringing phone in his office. His mood was subdued. He had been waiting all evening for Barnitz's call, and he knew that every passing minute was a cause for alarm. He'd had hours to prepare himself for the worst. Yet he had kept hoping.

"We lost him," Barnitz announced, his voice as pained as if he'd been shot in the gut. "Fay has vanished. No sign of him anywhere."

CHAPTER 33

———

The police were coming for him. He could hear their muffled footsteps in the hallway as they got into position. He waited, panicked, not knowing what to do. *Bang!* They were pounding on the door, shouting, "Open up! This is the New York Police Bomb Squad! Open up!" He was completely frozen, unable to move, unable to think. The door crashed open. A team of detectives, big, fierce men, came charging in. And Thomas Tunney, full of menace, was staring him in the face.

It was at this point in his dream that Franz von Rintelen would wake. He'd be shaking, and his body would be dripping with a cold sweat. Getting back to sleep was never easy; and anyway, he feared the nightmare would simply return.

He had been having this dream for weeks. It had started not long after he'd observed plainclothes detectives poking about the waterfront, watching the Allied ships being loaded and asking questions. A conversation with Koenig, who paid an officer at headquarters, detective Otto Mottola of the warrant squad, $25 a week to keep him informed, had provided more specifics. The detectives, Koenig had learned, were members of Captain Tunney's bomb squad. They had been assigned to investigate the ship fires.

As for Tunney, the mole Koenig was running reported the captain had a reputation as "a bulldog," a fierce and relentless cop. And once von Rintelen had a name, Tunney became the personification of all his mounting fears. In his agitated mind, Tunney loomed as a constant, stalking adversary.

Von Rintelen grew so troubled, he would later confess, that it wasn't only his dreams that were a source of torment. He suffered "hallucinations that every knock at the door, during the day or during the night, was an invasion of the Bomb Squad of the New York Police." Or he'd be having a drink at the Yacht Club bar and he'd become convinced that he "was being watched." To lose the surveillance team, he'd take a taxi "to a remote quarter of the town"—but they'd be there, too. "I was still being shadowed," he'd recall. He felt skewered by every stranger's glance.

Yet the ubiquitous watchers were not Tom's men. Tom had still not connected any names directly to the network mounting the bombings. They weren't British agents either. While Room 40's wranglers had decoded Wilhelmstrasse's cables announcing the imminent arrival of von Rintelen in Manhattan, Section V, the SIS's New York station, was not yet sufficiently concerned to be watching his every move.

In truth, there was no basis for von Rintelen's fears. His skittish mood was that of any field agent behind the lines. A galloping internal terror was part of the mission.

At the same time, his fears, real or imagined, sharpened his edge. They drove him forward. He consoled himself by proving his bravery each new day. He would not allow himself to be deterred. He threw himself with an almost manic energy into a variety of outlandish schemes. Nothing seemed too ambitious, too far-fetched. He was a proud patriot answering his country's call to battle.

A driven man, he launched many plots.

ONE BRASH AND HIGHLY EFFECTIVE operation had its roots in a Russian count's love of claret. It was the long, sobering spring of 1915, when the

Russian army was on the march. They had pushed back the Austro-German forces, charged through Galicia and Austria, and were now advancing through the Carpathian Mountains. As the German general staff made preparations for a retaliatory counterstrike, von Rintelen soberly calculated that although he was far from the front lines, he could do his bit too. With an impressive ingenuity, as well as some shrewdly manipulative psychology, he went on the attack.

His opening gambit focused on Count Nicolai Ignatieff, the Russian military attaché in Paris. Ignatieff was an aristocrat and a soldier, a distinguished gentleman who by virtue of both his noble birth and his martial accomplishments wielded great power in the ruling czarist circles. The count was also a man who paid great attention to the cut of his clothes, the paintings that hung in his houses, and the horses in his stables. But his greatest passion, and most famous indulgence, was the care with which he stocked his cellars. He was renowned as a connoisseur of wines, a man whose "nose" was respected even by sophisticated Parisian oenophiles.

With cunning dexterity, von Rintelen went straight for the count's vanity. For assistance, he recruited a wellborn German American woman whose sympathies remained bound to the Fatherland. Now living on Fifth Avenue, she had frequented Parisian society before the war and knew the count well. Von Rintelen dictated the letter she was instructed to send, and she took down every word in an ornate, flowing cursive:

> My dear Count, a good friend, a Mr. E. V. Gibbons, hopes to import the finest claret into America. It would be an invaluable assistance if Monsieur le Count, with his extraordinary knowledge, could help select the choicest vintages and recommend the most esteemed vineyards.

The count's reply was quick: I would be delighted to help Mr. Gibbons; please have him contact me directly. And now that the introduction had been made, the wellborn lady vanished and Max Weiser, the sly importer-exporter whose presence in the front room gave von Rintelen's operation a veneer of legitimacy, took over.

In a flurry of letters and telegrams, Weiser, acting on behalf of E. V. Gibbons, Inc., wrote first to the count and then to the vineyards that the Russian, after much consideration, had selected. With the count's imprimatur helping the deal to move swiftly along, a large consignment of the finest bottles of claret was soon shipped to the E. V. Gibbons company in New York.

The Abteilung IIIB paymasters were furious. Von Rintelen had insubordinately used funds originally intended to buy munitions to purchase cases of wine. Didn't he realize there was a war on? This sort of indulgence was close to treason.

But von Rintelen was unapologetic. He explained that the transaction had helped to establish two important principles. First, E. V. Gibbons was a reputable firm that promptly paid its bills. And second, it forged a relationship with the influential Count Ignatieff.

Once tempers had been calmed, he also brought another beneficial consequence to the spymasters' attention: Germany had made money on the deal. The cases of wine had all been sold in just two days for a heady profit.

With the powers in Königsplatz appeased, von Rintelen made his next move. A letter from E. V. Gibbons, Inc., to the count suggested that the Russian army employ the long-established and well-capitalized firm to act as its purchasing agent in America. It would be a mutually advantageous alliance: the Gibbons company was in a position to obtain whatever the troops needed, and the Russian army would be dealing with a firm they could count on. Gibbons would like, the letter concluded, to negotiate a significant contract for the purchase of military equipment.

Once again, the well-mannered count responded with alacrity. Based on his experience, he would be only too glad to recommend Mr. Gibbons and Gibbons's distinguished firm to the Russian purchasing agents already in New York. To expedite the process, the count listed their names and addresses.

Playing the role of Mr. Gibbons, a successful American-born exporter, von Rintelen met with one of the Russian agents in the lobby of the man's hotel. The Russian, an infantry captain, was not impressed. He barely had time for Mr. Gibbons, summarily announcing that all the necessary army purchases had already been consigned to other firms. Abruptly, he rose from his chair, prepared to escort Mr. Gibbons to the door.

Von Rintelen did not move. He remained seated, relaxed, even slouching a bit as if to emphasize that he was not intimidated. The Russian glowered. Von Rintelen returned his stare with an easy smile, and offhandedly noted that this decision would "sadden a very good friend."

The Russian ignored this news. Instead, he said he was in a hurry. With an imperious wave of his hand, he summoned a bellboy to fetch his hat and coat.

Von Rintelen still did not budge. But now with a great casualness, as if it were the most uncalculated of remarks, he asked the captain if by any chance he happened to know his good friend Count Ignatieff, the military attaché. He said he would be most grateful if the next time the captain was in Paris, he could convey his warmest regards.

Now the captain hesitated, and von Rintelen pounced. He withdrew the count's laudatory letter from his pocket with a proud flourish, and passed it on to the Russian.

It was as effective in its way as a *Kaiserpass*. The Russian had only to start reading the letter before he began apologizing profusely. Full of embarrassment, he said that it was quite possible that he'd been too hasty. Perhaps Mr. Gibbons would like to accompany him to his room, where they could discuss the possibility of a purchasing contract in depth.

"Amazing" was how von Rintelen, with customary modesty, described the twelve contracts that were subsequently negotiated and then signed by the imperial Russian embassy in Washington. The Gibbons firm was to provide saddles, tinned meat, bridles, mules, horses, field kitchens, boots, shoes, underwear, gloves, and small-arms ammunition.

It was a large and varied order that vastly exceeded Weiser's legitimate manufacturing connections. The old man worried that the Gibbons company would be unable to obtain the items that had been ordered. But von Rintelen was not concerned. He never had any intention of delivering the supplies to the Russians.

Nevertheless, von Rintelen did not hesitate to take the contracts to his New York bank. With the agreements as collateral, he received a $3 million loan from the impressed bankers. He thanked them, and then deposited the funds in an account he'd opened under another alias at a different bank.

All in all, von Rintelen felt it had been a fairly successful scheme. He had diverted orders of Russian army supplies using a dysfunctional company, and at the same time he'd made $3 million. The goods weren't to be delivered for another forty-five days, so he figured he had plenty of time before he would need to invent an excuse for the "unanticipated further delay." His sincere regrets, he hoped, would buy another month or so.

This contrivance, however, threatened to fall apart when an officer from the Russian embassy telephoned to request an immediate conference. There was a new concern, he announced mysteriously. Mr. Gibbons apologized, but he was afraid a meeting would not be possible; he was very busy. The Russian insisted. Back and forth they went until von Rintelen, more out of curiosity than any desire to accommodate, wearily agreed that he would be available tomorrow morning.

Two huge Russians he had never met before arrived at his office precisely at the appointed time. It was imperative, they explained, that the contracts be fulfilled at once. They had been authorized to offer a substantial bonus for early delivery. To demonstrate the severity of the situation, they shared telegrams from the War Ministry. The supply shortages, the beseeching telegrams revealed, were dire. The Russian army was running out of bullets.

This was heartening news for von Rintelen. But he was also canny enough to understand that if the Russians couldn't get what they needed from him, they would go to another purchasing agent. After all, money was not a problem; J. P. Morgan and his munificent loans had seen to that. And another agent might actually make sure that the goods arrived in Russia.

"What are the most important items?" he asked. His improvised plan was to suggest a compromise; or, more accurately, to let them think he was offering one.

The Russians held a hasty, whispered discussion, and then one spoke up. Tinned provisions and ammunition were essential, he stated. They were needed at once.

Gibbons promised to give them a definitive answer by that evening. And as soon as the Russians left, assisted by the resourceful Weiser, he went to work.

They telephoned brokers and, to both Weiser's and von Rintelen's astonishment, they were quickly able to obtain all the required tinned provisions and ammunition. Another miracle: the goods could be delivered to the docks the next day.

The Russians were ecstatic. They chartered a steamer that would leave without delay once the crucial goods were loaded.

But von Rintelen, of course, was not going to allow much-needed war matériel to reach the enemy. That night in the shadowy hold of the *Friedrich der Grosse* he gathered his sailors and dockhands and gave strict orders: he wanted no fewer than thirty of the cigar bombs carried on board along with the Russian supplies. Lay them in the wood shavings, he instructed. They'll be more effective.

The fully loaded steamer headed out of New York Harbor, and, he recounted, "I waited for four days in a state of fever." If the bombs didn't ignite, if the crew managed to put out the fires, if any of a dozen too easily imaginable events occurred and the goods arrived in the port of Archangel, von Rintelen would not have been able to forgive himself. He'd have procured bullets for the Russian army that would be aimed at German troops. He worried that for once he had been too smart, his scheme too convoluted, its success contingent on too many factors beyond his control.

But on the fifth day he read in the *Shipping News* that the steamer had caught fire on the high seas. The blaze was so intense that the crew had to escape in lifeboats. They were rescued by a passing American merchant vessel, and from its deck they watched as their steamer disappeared beneath the waves.

The two Russians, pale and wringing their hands, soon appeared in Gibbons's offices. Mr. Gibbons commiserated; he too was deeply upset. A tragic accident, he offered. But fear not, he went on. E. V. Gibbons, the count's great friend, would not let them down. He would outfit another ship, no, *two* ships, with ammunition and tinned goods, services for which, naturally, he'd want an additional check and an additional bonus. And this time he would engage private detectives to ensure that there was no possibility of saboteurs sneaking on board.

Yet once again fires broke out at sea, and on both ships to boot. And once again the Russians were distraught. But it never occurred to them to suspect that their contractor had engineered the fires; after all, fires were occurring mysteriously on other ships, too.

The Russian embassy signed twenty-one contracts with E. V. Gibbons, Inc., and not a single shipment was delivered. When the Russian agents finally became belligerent, and possibly suspicious too, Mr. Gibbons responded to their harangue with stoic calm. When they grew abusive, he took his hat, offered a polite "Good day," and left. By the time the enraged Russian embassy prepared legal papers, von Rintelen, using another alias, had set up new offices on William Street for the "Mexico North-Western Railway Company." The firm of E. V. Gibbons no longer existed.

The principal of the defunct company, nevertheless, was cheered by an article he read on the front page of the *New York Times*. Russian minister Prince Miliukov had reported to the Duma that the consequences of the delay in the transport of munitions from America were becoming more and more serious. It was likely, the prince said, that the new offensive would need to be postponed.

CHAPTER 34

————

But there were just too many ships. Lavishly spending the fortune J. P. Morgan had conveniently provided, the Allies continued to buy supplies, and their boats continued to leave New York Harbor. It had become impossible, von Rintelen realized, to sabotage all of them. He needed to come up with an additional strategy.

He found his inspiration on the front page of the *New York Times*. The dockers had gone out on strike. But since the union had not sanctioned the action, the newspaper reported, port officials did not anticipate a lengthy disruption.

As he read the article, von Rintelen's churning mind filled in the gaping holes in the *Times'* brief account. The reason the work stoppage would be short-lived, he knew, was that the protesters had no chance of receiving strike pay to compensate for their lost wages. He also knew why that was: Samuel Gompers, president of the American Federation of Labor (AFL), wanted England to win the war. He'd never sanction strike benefits for men whose actions were impeding the Allied cause. And this, von Rintelen decided in his mounting fury, was further evidence that America's neutrality was a sham.

Yet von Rintelen's anger was also the impetus for what he admittedly described as a "fantastic" scheme: he'd form his own union. The more he played with the idea, the more persuasive and feasible it grew:

"A union which was properly registered could proclaim a legal strike, and the law could not interfere. If, in addition, we could pay strike benefits, it might be possible to achieve something, and I certainly had the money to do so."

So he set to work. In the course of a previous, abandoned adventure, Frederico Stallforth, a German citizen now working as a financier on Wall Street, had introduced him to David Lamar, notorious as "the Wolf of Wall Street."

David Lamar, the "Wolf of Wall Street," a con man and
financier who worked with Germans, circa 1913.

Everything about the charming, wealthy Georgia native was false—including his charm, his wealth, and his southern accent. Lamar had cut his teeth on phony stock deals, been convicted of impersonating a Pennsylvania congressman, gone on to real estate scams where he'd promised to put up skyscrapers on land he never owned, and escaped one seemingly certain conviction after he hired the savage Eastman gang to beat the daylights out of a witness. Von Rintelen, who knew a bit about fabricating stories and coming up with inventive plots, was impressed.

But more than any of these bold crimes, what established Lamar's credentials with the German spy was the fact that he'd worked for J. P. Morgan and succeeded in fleecing the company for well over $1 million. When the two men subsequently encountered each other on the street, an enraged Morgan slapped Lamar across the face and then stormed off. Any man who had pulled a fast one on Morgan— and in von Rintelen's world the Anglophile financier was the devil incarnate—was his friend. And being slapped by the tycoon was as distinguished an honor as receiving the Iron Cross. Von Rintelen quickly decided Lamar would be the perfect front man for his union.

It was called Labor's National Peace Council, and in addition to Lamar it attracted a collection of theologians, university professors, members of Congress, and even a former attorney general, all united in their sincere opposition to the export of American munitions. Halls were rented, rallies were held, speakers were paid, petitions were sent to President Wilson. But none of the activists had any notion that they were, as von Rintelen merrily bragged, "in the service of a German officer."

At the same time, Lamar was sent off to use his persuasive powers to enroll New York dockworkers in the new union. To help this recruitment drive along, von Rintelen, as generous as J. P. Morgan, gave Lamar nearly $400,000 for bribes and expenses.

But the Wolf of Wall Street became the Wolf of the Waterfront. Lamar pocketed Abteilung IIIB's money as cavalierly as he'd pocketed J. P. Morgan's funds. The $400,000 was spent on a lavish estate he was building in the Berkshires.

All along Lamar had given convincing assurances to von Rintelen that he'd made great inroads with the dockers. Hundreds of men, he guaranteed, would enroll in the union. When the long-planned recruitment rally was held, von Rintelen, brimming with confident expectations, waited eagerly in the back of the hall. Not a single recruit turned up. It didn't take the spy long to discover that both his money and Lamar had vanished. But who was E. V. Gibbons to complain?

Instead, he hired a new front man, Frank Buchanan. A former president of the International Union of Structural Workers who'd recently been elected to Congress from a Chicago district, Buchanan was a gruff, fiery speaker, and an effective one, on the infrequent occasions when he wasn't drinking.

Buchanan led the fight in Washington for embargo legislation, and von Rintelen sent the personable Captain von Kleist and the canny Weiser to the docks. Once von Kleist started handing out bulging packets of "strike pay," dockers were lining up to join the new union. For some, it was a matter of conviction: they didn't want to load munitions on Allied ships. For others, it was simply a practical decision: they'd be paid for not working.

When von Rintelen, still hidden away behind the scenes but always the decision maker, sent word that the time had come for a strike, nearly 1,500 dockers walked off the job. This success established the union's credentials.

He dispatched his well-paid union executives to ports around the country, wiring fantastic sums to each new city; halls were hired, literature was printed, and longshoremen were recruited. As a result, a series of strikes broke out in ports throughout the United States. Dockers all across the country refused to load Allied transports. The National Peace union had quickly become an effective force.

The fortunes the armaments manufacturers had planned to make from the war in Europe were in jeopardy. And with their livelihoods at stake, they fought back with a clawing ferocity. Millions of dollars were poured into the treasuries of the older unions. Gompers was enlisted to travel around the country to persuade the dockers to come back into the AFL's fold. Reporters were fed stories about the shady hidden powers behind the new union; "See Lamar's Hand in 'Labor' Peace Move," one headline in the *New York Times* revealed. A clique of friendly senators initiated an indignant federal investigation into "the operation of alleged lobbies to influence Congressional legislation" to prohibit arms shipments.

Yet as his union's power lessened and members returned to the AFL, von Rintelen remained philosophical. "So the fight went on, and ground was lost and won again. Ultimate success would be a matter of money and nerves."

CHAPTER 35

———

Von Rintelen's mood was also steadied because, as he proudly put it, "I had a finger in so many 'shady' deals." He even grandly plotted to provoke a war between the United States and Mexico. "If Mexico attacked her [America]," he reasoned with a statesman's pragmatic logic, "she would need all the munitions she could manufacture, and would be unable to export any to Europe."

For months this inchoate political strategy had been taking shape in his always active mind, but when he read that General Victoriano Huerta was in New York, von Rintelen decided to put it into action. The general was the deposed ruler of Mexico, and he'd been moping in Barcelona as he plotted the military coup that would return him to control. Now, like Lenin at Finland Station, Huerta was passing through New York on the way back, he hoped, to his homeland and to power. Von Rintelen was determined to help the general realize their mutual ambitions. But he needed to find a way to get to him.

In the end, he ambushed the general. As Huerta, surrounded by a retinue of Mexicans in velvet-collared overcoats, made his way out of a black limousine and bounded into the lobby of the Manhattan Hotel, von Rintelen pounced. Jumping up from the seat where he'd passed tedious hours poking at the potted palms with his cane as he waited, he confronted the general.

Mexican military officer Victoriano Huerta (1854–1916),
who was president of Mexico from 1913 to 1914, with
members of his cabinet. Huerta is seated on the right.

Huerta was wary, and his men moved threateningly toward the stranger. But von Rintelen was bold. He looked Huerta in the eyes and, with all his self-possessed authority, announced that he was a German officer. "I would like to do all I can to help you reclaim what is rightfully yours," he declared.

The meeting that took place that afternoon in Huerta's suite was a long and careful negotiation. The agreed-upon terms left each man feeling as if he'd won a great victory: German U-boats would deliver covert shipments of weapons along the Mexican coast; Germany would provide significant sums to outfit a Mexican rebel army; and once Huerta was restored to power, his troops would attack the United States and be assured of Germany's complete support.

When the meeting concluded, von Rintelen hurried off to send a cable to Berlin. And in the adjacent hotel room, Section V's listeners waited impatiently until they could retrieve the Dictaphone that had recorded the entire discussion and send a cable to London. Their target had been Huerta, but to their surprise and excitement, they had also snared a German agent.

When Huerta checked into the Manhattan Hotel earlier in the week, Guy Gaunt, the British station chief in New York, had dispatched a team with orders to put a recording device in the general's suite. They surveyed the rooms and decided formal conferences would most likely be held around a large round table in the middle of the sitting room. So they moved the table closer to a window framed by flowing curtains, concealed a Dictaphone in the folds of the heavy fabric, and trailed a connecting wire out the window and over the ledge to the room next door.

Headphones on, a British agent was able to listen to every incriminating word between the man they now knew was a German spy and the would-be ruler of Mexico. When the Mexicans left for dinner, the SIS agents would retrieve the recordings from the target room and deliver them downtown to the Section V field office for transcription.

IN THE WEEKS THAT FOLLOWED, Huerta continued on his tour of America, and von Rintelen waited anxiously for a response from Berlin. Yet all the while, the German agent also kept busy; "I had plenty to do in the meantime," he boasted.

Unknown to von Rintelen, though, his activities were at last being monitored. Section V was now on his tail.

Without disclosing his sources or precisely what activities had been discovered, Gaunt had also suggested to Tom that the New York police should keep an eye on von Rintelen too. However, even if the British agent had provided more details of von Rintelen's discussion with the Mexican general, Tom would still have needed stronger evidence to arrest the German spy.

There was no specific law against espionage. The closest statute was the Defense Secrets Act of 1911, which made it a crime to deliver national defense information to a person who was "not entitled to it." Previous state secrecy laws had even vaguer language, and these federal statutes were largely concerned with treason, unlawful entry into military facilities, and the theft of government property. Not until America declared war would Congress, after much contentious debate, pass the Espionage Act of 1917. This law made it a specific crime to spy on or to interfere with American military operations. But in the days of this covert war, as the network of German spies established itself in New York, Tom's power to make an arrest was severely restrained. He needed to catch the spies in an act of sabotage, or at least firmly establish that they were planning one.

WHEN BERLIN'S RESPONSE TO VON Rintelen finally arrived, it was enthusiastic. Even better, the Foreign Office swiftly reinforced its words with action. Eight million rounds of ammunition were purchased in St. Louis, awaiting shipment to Huerta's men; another three million rounds were on order. An initial payment of $800,000 was deposited into Huerta's personal account in the Deutsche Bank in Havana; $95,000 went into a Mexican account that was also in his name. And von Papen, who had spent time in Mexico before the war, was sent down to the Texas-Mexico border to draft plans for the invading army's attacks on Brownsville, El Paso, and San Antonio.

An elated Huerta received these reports, cut short his stay in San Francisco, and sped south by train. His plan was to disembark at Newman, New Mexico, twenty miles from the border. General Pascual Orozco and his well-armed men would meet him, and this honor guard would drive him triumphantly into the country that would soon be his once more. But as Huerta descended from his Pullman, a U.S. Army colonel backed by twenty-five soldiers and two deputy marshals arrested the general. The charge was sedition.

He was incarcerated in El Paso, then released on bail. Ordered to remain in America until the charges were adjudicated, he was invited to a dinner at Fort Bliss. The general saw the invitation as a conciliatory gesture. Perhaps it was, but a day later he took sick.

Yellow jaundice was the official diagnosis. Poison was the widespread, and more persistent, rumor. Whatever the cause, the illness was fatal. General Huerta died on American soil. He could see the promised land through the window of his hospital bed, but he never returned.

VON RINTELEN HEARD THE NEWS in New York. It was night, and he'd just left a dinner party. As he was standing on the street in evening dress, looking to hail a taxi, a man hurried by behind him.

"You are being watched," the unseen presence whispered in the background as he passed close enough to touch him. "Look out! Don't wait for Huerta. He has been poisoned."

Von Rintelen summoned up all his discipline. He showed no emotion, focusing his attention on the taxi that had pulled up. But as he was getting in, his eyes darted up the block and he recognized the tall, lean figure of Boniface, the lawyer who had been his coconspirator in many schemes.

Seated in the cab, the spy struggled to remain calm. Perhaps, he tried telling himself, Boniface was mistaken. But when he glanced with a contrived casualness out the rear window of the taxi, he saw that an ominous dark sedan was right behind him. It followed him all the way to the Yacht Club.

The next day his fears received additional confirmation. Von Rintelen learned that Koenig had dispatched Boniface. Several of the security chief's well-placed sources alerted him that the Huerta affair had blown von Rintelen's cover, and he sent off the lawyer, a man unknown to the police, to warn the spy. A new caution, von Rintelen realized, was required.

CHAPTER 36

——————

For von Rintelen, though, the game was too entertaining. Prudence was difficult. And he was always thinking. Sinister schemes would without warning snake their way into his thoughts. In that unexpected way, a routine reconnaissance trip to the New Jersey piers in search of abandoned sheds where stolen rifles might be stored inspired a new plan.

Accompanied by Boniface and Weiser, he had marched up streets and lanes, crossed railroad tracks, sauntered through lots littered with debris, and continued on past dismal marshes until they found a derelict pier where a motorboat could be covertly tied. But no sooner had they made this discovery than von Rintelen's eyes fixed on a nearby spit of land. It was, he decided at first sight, a "most valuable" target.

It was long and oddly shaped, jutting out for more than a mile into the Jersey City harbor like, it had long ago been decided, a colossal sea creature's head and neck. In spooky tribute to this forbidding shape, it had picked up the name Black Tom. These days Black Tom bustled with a grim activity that lived up to its monster's name.

It was the largest munitions depot in the country. Cargo trains from manufacturers all over America delivered shipments of shells, bombs, and ammunition straight to the series of piers that were lined up in an orderly row on one side of the spit. All day, sunrise to sunset, an army of workers unloaded this deadly cargo from freight trains and then onto the boats that would carry the lethal supplies to Europe.

Von Rintelen stared at this nest of enemy activity, and one clear, powerful image took shape: a gigantic, ferocious explosion, billows of smoke and fire reaching far up into the sky. "Black Tom destroyed!"

It would all be, he reasoned, so easy. There would be "little risk." An impromptu plan materialized: "Some peaceful summer evening—all arrangements properly made—a powerful speedboat at hand for us to disappear into the vastness of the Hudson River—it was all so remote from observation, from possible harm that might be done to human life."

A more detailed operational strategy would need to be drawn up. Field agents would have to be recruited, then trained for the mission. But from his first sighting of the gigantic munitions depot, von Rintelen was determined to launch a mission that would reduce Black Tom to smoke and ashes.

AS VON RINTELEN'S AMBITIOUS PLOTS unfolded with varying degrees of success, there was always one constant. His major offensive against America—the shipboard fires—continued with a vicious, and gratifying, effectiveness. A rhythm of constant, puzzling destruction pounded the harbor. "We continued to place bomb after bomb," he boasted with a soldier's pride.

It had started as a makeshift attack, a ragtag group of German sailors and Irish longshoremen bringing the cigar bombs aboard any ship that caught their attention while it was being loaded in New York Harbor. But with the passing months, it had grown into a larger, well-organized national sabotage operation.

Decisions were now made by a group von Rintelen christened the Executive Committee. They met Saturday afternoons in the windowless back room of the Hofbrau House on Broadway and Twenty-

Seventh Street. Seated around a table covered with a red-checked cloth, they hoisted steins of beer as they carefully selected targets and planned attacks.

It was a small but dedicated group. There were Scheele, the chemist; Eno Bode, the wealthy superintendent of the Hamburg-American Line, who relished the opportunity to play the secret agent in his old age; and Otto Wolpert, the coarse, brutish pier superintendent of the Atlas Line, whose years on the waterfront had given him many invaluable contacts. The chief field officer was Erich von Steinmetz, a trained Abteilung IIIB operative.

Von Steinmetz was a mystery to von Rintelen. They had met by prearrangment at Martha Held's, and all von Steinmetz would reveal was that Nicolai had sent him months earlier to America on a most important mission. Von Rintelen pressed, but the Abteilung IIIB agent would not disclose the operation. It was top secret, he repeated. The most he would offer was that it had failed, but he had been exonerated. His new orders were to report to von Rintelen and assist the Manhattan Front.

Under the Executive Committee's guiding hand, the sabotage attacks spread around the country. Von Rintelen went to Baltimore, where with the help of Paul Hilken, the worldly, well-connected son of the local German consul, he recruited a network of field operatives from the local piers. Von Steinmetz was dispatched to New Orleans. A third team of agents went to San Francisco. Soon the *Shipping News* carried reports of ships sailing from ports throughout the country being engulfed by mysterious fires.

There was a new recruit, too, who brought with him an invention that had the potential to be as effective as the cigar bombs. It was an ingenious device: a container holding TNT that attached to a ship's rudder. With each turn of the rudder blade, a metal rod in the container would wind up a firing mechanism until the TNT detonated.

Von Rintelen ordered a test. The young man took a motorboat out into the harbor one evening and drew up alongside the rudder of a large munitions transport. He jumped into the water with only a small splash and quickly fixed his device to the ship's rudder. It took about a minute. Then he moved on to another munitions ship and repeated the stealthy procedure.

Days later the *Shipping News* reported two disturbingly similar accidents. Two transports had their rudders torn away at sea. The damage to their sterns was so severe that its crew had to abandon one boat, while the other was towed back to harbor.

Von Rintelen was ecstatic. "What the incendiary bombs could not achieve was reserved for . . . [the new] machines," he rejoiced.

The young inventor's name was Robert Fay.

IT WAS ALL GOING SO well. Yet with hard-nosed objectivity, von Rintelen found himself forced to concede that his operation was under attack. He now had definitive proof that the New York police were on his trail. The report from Koenig's mole had sounded the alarm. And any hopeful doubts about this intelligence had been erased by his own observations: teams of watchers now often followed him openly around New York. His premature vision of Tunney bursting through the door could very well turn out to be prophetic.

But, he also realized, there was no preemptive move he could make. He wasn't going to abandon his mission and run back to Germany. There was nothing he could do other than proceed.

Now that his nightmare had become a reality, his courage put to a genuine test, it was almost a relief. His dread had been a thousand deaths. The fact that his long-smoldering fears had proved true brought an unexpected calm. He'd come at last to the place where he'd never wanted to be, and yet he was able to convince himself that he would prevail.

So what if the New York police knew his name? His tradecraft had been meticulous. He was certain they had no "direct and clear proof." He had left no tangible clues. The best they'd come up with, he assured himself, was "that Rintelen was often seen in society in evening dress and lived at the New York Yacht Club." He was smarter, craftier, than any New York cop. Tunney would never catch Franz von Rintelen.

CHAPTER 37

F rank Holt's arrival at Cornell was the end of a remarkable journey. It had, Holt told himself with delighted pride, proceeded precisely as he had planned it six years ago in the Mexican hill country.

Leona was elated, too. The man she had met in a small-time Texas college that churned out farmers and cattlemen was now at an Ivy League university, writing a dissertation entitled "The Effect of the Work of Shakespeare on German and French Literature."

She was troubled that her husband was working too hard, often all through the night. And there were days on end when he wouldn't speak a word to her. But Leona attributed all this to Frank's diligence and the intensity of his focus. Who was she, she reprimanded herself, to question that sort of commitment?

The other faculty members grew to appreciate the industrious Holt, too. Clark Northrup, a member of the English department who became a close friend, was one of many Cornell professors impressed with Holt's "well-founded scholarship," his "abilities as a teacher," and his intelligence.

The fiction had become the reality. In Holt's mind it was as if he'd never had a previous, more complicated life with another Leona.

Then in April 1914, a notice appeared in the German department office. All members of the department were expected to attend the annual Jacob H. Schiff Lecture "to promote the study of German cul-ture." This year's distinguished speaker was Professor Kuno Francke. Of Harvard. And the man who eight years earlier had been Erich Muenter's thesis adviser.

Holt considered his predicament; and then he ran. He told Leona he had sudden business in New York and left that very afternoon. It was odd, but then her husband was often unpredictable, even impul-sive. But weren't all great thinkers that way? she consoled herself.

Two days after the lecture, Holt returned to the Cornell campus. He had narrowly avoided a potentially damaging, perhaps even fatal, encounter, and his well-timed escape was only further proof of his shrewdness. Hadn't he always been one step ahead of them all? The coroner? The police? His in-laws? He had outsmarted everyone.

Then in one unexpected instant his luck seemed to have run out. On a bright fall day in 1914, a day when the leafy campus was painted in a bold blaze of autumnal colors, Holt was walking to the library when he saw Nathan Gould, a colleague during his days in the Har-vard German department. Gould was coming toward him.

It was too late to run, or even to attempt to conceal his face. Gould stared straight at him with an unmistakable look of shocked recogni-tion.

The two men stood opposite one another, only feet apart.

Holt did not speak. He couldn't find the will, and he didn't know what to say. It was as if fissures were suddenly spreading through his carefully constructed world, breaking apart the invented life he had built.

Gould continued to stare at him, his mind running wildly. "I did not know the man was guilty," he'd later say, sharing the progres-sion of thoughts cycling rapidly through his head at that icy moment. "Had never felt convinced of his guilt. Muenter, as I had known him, always was a good man. He seemed to be living right at Cornell, and was doing good work."

After a long moment, Gould walked on without a word.

Holt rejoiced. His invincibility had once more been tested, and again he had triumphed. It was confirmation, he realized with excitement, that the time was swiftly approaching to move on to his next important secret mission.

PART IV:
SPINNING THE THREADS

CHAPTER 38

———

Tom did not like Guy Gaunt. He was too glib, too much a dandy, and most annoyingly of all, the British agent kept too many secrets. But Tom was a professional, and he appreciated that Gaunt had resources and information that the police did not possess. When Gaunt, in his usual cryptic way, told him weeks ago about von Rintelen, Tom had listened.

Tom was now simultaneously following two trails and two quarries—Robert Fay and Franz von Rintelen. He was uncertain if their activities were related. Or, for that matter, if either man would prove to be of any value to the main thrust of the case—solving the ship bombings. But, Tom reminded himself, in detective work there are blind alleys and main streets, and there's no sure way of knowing which one you're exploring until you get to the end. Determined, he pressed on.

Still, even the memory of the meeting with Gaunt when he had first heard von Rintelen's name left him simmering with irritation. At Gaunt's urgent request, he had shown up at Station V's downtown headquarters at four one afternoon, only to find the British agent in evening clothes. Either he was getting ready to go off for a night on the town, or, no less possible, Tom speculated, he had just returned from a long night that had stretched into the next day.

Gaunt never bothered to explain, and Tom, whose entire life had passed without any occasion to suit up in white tie and tails, was not about to give him the satisfaction of asking. And the guarded conversation that followed, he complained to Barnitz, played out more like a coy dance of veils than an intelligence briefing.

Gaunt had begun portentously, announcing that a man named Franz von Rintelen was a German agent.

Tom grudgingly conceded that he had never heard the name, so Gaunt provided a few details. Von Rintelen was a former naval officer, a banker, and a man-about-town who lived at the New York Yacht Club.

Tom listened, then asked Gaunt to explain how he'd reached the conclusion that this high-society banker was a spy.

Stiffly, Gaunt refused. The transcript of von Rintelen's meeting with Huerta was in the safe across from his desk, but he was under orders not even to suggest it existed, let alone share it.

Tom tried another approach. He asked if there was evidence of von Rintelen's involvement in any crimes.

Gaunt answered that he could not respond to the question.

Tom persisted. He asked if Gaunt would at least identify the man's associates. Could he share any names?

The intelligence officer conceded that he had no knowledge of any associates. At last speaking with complete truthfulness, he explained that this was the reason he was asking for Tom's help.

Asking, but not giving. That's what the Brits call cooperation, Tom thought, the Irish in him stirring dangerously.

But no sooner had he returned to his office on Centre Street than he assigned a team to watch von Rintelen. With the ship bombings still his priority, the best he could do was spare two men. And they covered von Rintelen only on random days; there were other, more pressing leads that still needed to be pursued. Nevertheless, their orders were clear. See where he goes, whom he speaks to, Tom instructed them.

In this haphazard way, on his tail for a day and then off for two or three and sometimes even four, they had been at it for weeks, and had nothing definitive to show for their efforts. Maddeningly, the watchers' reports could be used as evidence to bolster either of two conflicting hypotheses: von Rintelen was a frivolous socialite making his fun-loving way about New York, or he was an Abteilung IIIB professional living his cover with scrupulous discipline.

Depending upon the day and his moods, Tom's opinion vacillated. But he was not about to call off his men. There was something about von Rintelen's nonchalance, the way he didn't try to lose the surveillance team, that struck him as a bit too deliberate. Same for his partying; it too seemed almost diligent, part of a disguise.

The exterior of the New York Yacht Club on West Forty-Fourth Street, 1913.

Wanting to get his own feel for the prey, Tom had sat lookout one afternoon in a car across from the Yacht Club. As he watched von Rintelen walking up the block, Tom was certain he detected the parade-ground stiffness of a Prussian military officer in his stride. All Tom's policeman's instincts screamed to him that von Rintelen was more than he appeared to be. But try telling that to a judge, Tom thought. For now, all Tom could do was watch. And wait.

CHAPTER 39

———

A nd Robert Fay was still missing. When the mystery man with the stash of TNT had suddenly vanished from the New Jersey woods, Tom, pounding his desk like a drum in his fury, ordered all his available men into the field.

They were split into two teams. Under Barnitz's steady command, one group staked out the boardinghouse on Fifth Street in Weehawken, where Fay and his friend Scholz lived. The other spread out along Park Place in lower Manhattan, their eyes focused on the front door of the Kienzle Clock Company, the offices of Dr. Herbert Kienzle, the elderly German clock maker who had originally ordered the dynamite for Fay.

Tom, the resolute commander, waited impatiently at his desk. So much, he felt, depended on their finding Fay. If Fay had made the surveillance team and bolted from the woods—and there was no reason to think that wasn't the case—then Tom might never discover what the German intended to do with the explosives. Or whom he worked for. Of course, it was also possible that Fay was just one more cutout in the lengthy chain. He could already have passed on the TNT, and the next news would be the report of a ship on fire or a munitions factory going up in smoke.

Tom tried to persuade himself that his doubts had gotten the better of him. Wasn't it just as reasonable to believe that Fay had strolled into the woods along one path and, on little more than a whim, simply taken another way out? But it wasn't a very likely proposition, he had to concede. And the longer Tom stared at his silent phone, the smaller and smaller, he was forced to admit, the likelihood became.

When the phone finally rang, it was Barnitz, and his news was one more blow. An express wagon had pulled up to the boarding-house, and a trunk had been loaded into the rear. A couple of detectives had gone off in pursuit, and when the driver stopped to make another pickup, one of the officers vaulted into the back. "There's a plain calling-card on the trunk," Barnitz reported. "It reads 'Walter Scholz.'"

Immediately Tom's low spirits sank deeper. Scholz was Fay's room-mate, the companion they had seen accompany him on two occasions into the woods. If Scholz was packing his belongings and getting ready to move on, then it seemed probable that Fay would be heading off, too. If he hadn't already fled.

Tom asked where the trunk was delivered.

A storage warehouse in Weehawken, Barnitz said.

Tom had to make a decision. He could grab the trunk. It might, after all, contain a clue to where Fay had gone to ground. For that matter, the twenty-five pounds of TNT could be inside. That would be another reason to take possession; hesitate, and there was always the small chance that the warehouse could be reduced to a smoldering hole in the ground.

Tom told Barnitz that he wanted men outside the warehouse in case Scholz picked up his trunk. He also wanted the watch on the boardinghouse to continue. Round-the-clock, he ordered.

It was a cold, quiet afternoon in Weehawken, and Barnitz's men cursed the icy weather and the tedium.

IN NEW YORK, THE OTHER team was on the move.

When the clock maker left his office just before noon, he had headed out on a meandering route across lower Manhattan. Kienzle went into one downtown building after another, and two detectives, keeping a careful distance, went in after him each time. But it was all business; in one office, the clocks were running too fast, in another too slow. The old man made the necessary mechanical corrections and then continued on.

As Tom received this discouraging report, he began to wish that he could adjust time too. Instead, he continued to hear it ticking ominously away. How soon, he wondered, before the next fire broke out on a transport ship?

It was after five when the exhausted surveillance team trailed Kienzle into the lobby of the Equitable Building on lower Broadway. Bored after the long, uneventful day, they watched him head toward the elevators. No doubt he'd be going to another office to repair another clock, the team predicted as they waited by the front doors and made a big show of focusing their attention on the building directory.

Kienzle let one elevator pass without boarding. Then another. And in the next wonderful moment the watchers were all at once on full alert: Fay and Scholz, beaming smiles on their faces, had just bounded across the lobby to greet the clock maker.

There was a brief conversation that the detectives could only wish they could hear; and then Fay, after excusing himself, walked to the row of telephone booths on the other side of the lobby. When he closed the door to make a call, Detective Sterett hurried into the next booth.

The partition was thin, and the attentive detective could hear every word. Fay was talking to someone in the garage in Weehawken, asking if a package had been delivered. "It hasn't, eh?" he heard Fay say before hanging up the receiver.

The next moment Fay was back with his two friends, and the trio went off to a noisy restaurant on Fulton Street for dinner. The detectives took a table far across the room. They watched enviously as plates heaped with steaks and chops were consumed all around them, but they knew Captain Tunney would have their heads if they dared to bill the department for a full dinner. Instead, they spent well over an hour nursing a single mug of beer apiece, at the same time dodging the withering glances the waiter was shooting at them.

After dinner, the clock maker said his good-byes, and the two young men went off for a night on the town. They wound up at the Grand Central Palace, a block-long fortress of a building on Lexington Avenue between Forty-Sixth and Forty-Seventh Streets that had been erected over the New York Central tracks leading into Grand Central Terminal.

The cavernous ground floor of the Palace was jumping; a bar stretched across one wall, and up front on the stage a band was playing. The handsome Fay quickly found a slinky blonde to dance with, and she waved to a friend who seemed happy to be with Scholz.

The detectives crowded around the bar, sticking to nickel beers and keeping their eyes fixed on the dance floor. Fay kept buying the women drinks, and the couples were getting friendly. In a sudden moment of panic, Sterett wondered what they should do if the two Germans split up, each going off with a woman. While the others kept vigil from their seats at the bar, he hurried off to call the captain.

"Fay!" Tom shouted, his voice exploding through the receiver and startling the detective. "He's our man. You stick with him no matter what." If they lost Fay again, Tom made it clear, heads would roll.

But it wasn't long after midnight that both Fay and Scholz, looking a bit worse for wear and with no women in tow, were back at the Weehawken boardinghouse. Barnitz was parked down the block, and when he saw the two Germans going in the front door, he uttered a silent prayer of thanks. The case was finally back on track. Fay hadn't gone to ground, and everything was once again possible. "I could've kissed them both," he reported to Tom, who was feeling precisely the same way.

"POKING THE BEAR WITH A stick" was what detectives called it. It meant taking the initiative, supplying the stimulus that could push a stalled case forward. If it worked, the suspects would be goaded into action, and then you'd have them cold.

It also was a tactic, Tom had learned firsthand, that had its risks. The "bear" could panic and run. Or, once provoked, he could turn mean, and when that happened there was no telling whom he'd lash out at. But a case where the poking would be done with a stick of TNT gave Tom a whole new set of powerful reasons for reconsidering this strategy.

Still, Fay's abrupt disappearance had unnerved Tom, and the discovery of Scholz's packed trunk had only made things worse. He was certain the two men were preparing to leave town. He was not willing to gamble that when they did, his men would be able to find them again. Better to force the issue, he decided, while we still have them close at hand.

Carl Wettig, the war supplies exporter whose conversation with the French military attaché had originally set the entire investigation in motion, was once again recruited to help. Following Tom's earlier instructions, he had purchased the dynamite that was ultimately delivered to Fay's boardinghouse. Now for an encore Tom wanted him to play the persistent, hustling businessman.

Wettig telephoned Fay and suggested that they go off together and test the dynamite. Reading the script Tom had written, he promised that if Fay was satisfied, he'd get him all he needed. And at a good price, too, he ad-libbed to Tom's delight.

When Wettig arrived at the boardinghouse the next afternoon, Tom's watchers were down the block in a parked sedan, silently cheering him on.

"He's in," Barnitz reported to Tom.

Tom said he wanted to be told the moment Wettig left, and then abruptly hung up the phone. He tried to stay calm, but he could not help feeling that it had been a mistake to throw Wettig back into the middle of the operation. This wasn't a job for an amateur. He'd be skittish. They'd see through him. I should've used Barnitz, Tom chided himself.

As soon as he had the thought, Tom realized it was foolishness. One look, and they'd make Barnitz as a copper. Fay already knew Wettig. He trusted him. This will work, Tom decided, desperately trying to convince himself.

But now Wettig was inside the house, and anything could be happening. Tom waited, and waited. Then his phone rang: Fay and Scholz had walked out the front door, and Wettig was trailing right along. "One big happy family," Barnitz reported gaily.

Fay led the way to the streetcar line. A car passed, but he didn't signal for it to stop. Then another car, and still no signal.

He's wary, Barnitz thought as he watched from his sedan. He suspects something.

A third car approached, and Fay gave a small wave of his hand and it stopped. He gestured for Scholz and Wettig to board first, and at the very last moment, as the doors were closing, he jumped inside.

Barnitz cursed. He had promised the captain they'd have a man with Wettig at all times, only he hadn't counted on this.

Then he saw Detective Pat Walsh. He'd been in an alley behind the boardinghouse, covering a rear door, and he was sprinting up the block like a track star to the next streetcar stop. When the door opened, Walsh climbed aboard and took a seat right behind Wettig.

Barnitz's black sedan followed the streetcar. As it continued past the shops to the outskirts of town, Barnitz realized Fay was on his way to the now-familiar woods.

Barnitz hung back; there was no rush. He let three or four vehicles get between him and the streetcar.

He pulled up across from the woods just in time to see the three men walking through the underbrush and heading into the deep forest. This was how he'd lost Fay the last time, and Tom had given precise instructions so it wouldn't happen again.

Barnitz ordered the team to move in. There were six detectives and two Weehawken cops. Cautiously, each step a careful, stealthy undertaking, the officers slowly spread out across the woods in a wide circle. The three Germans were trapped in the middle. Using the trees for cover, the officers held their positions.

Fay emerged from a ramshackle wooden shed. He had a package in one hand, and a hammer in the other. He took a short brown stick of TNT out of the package and broke off a small fragment, about the size of a coin, with his fingers. He placed the piece of explosive on the surface of a broad, flat rock.

"Let's see what we got," he said to the two other men. They immediately started backing away.

In one quick move, Fay raised the hammer high above his head and brought it crashing down against the tiny chunk of TNT.

Bang! The noise echoed through the woods like a gunshot. The handle of the hammer snapped off in Fay's hand.

Barnitz had seen enough. He charged out of the trees, his revolver raised. The other officers followed. "You're under arrest!" Barnitz shouted.

"Who is in charge of you all?" Fay asked. He had recovered from the initial surprise with impressive speed.

"I am," Barnitz answered.

"Well, I will tell you I am not going to be put under arrest," Fay said defiantly.

Barnitz stared at him with stony indifference. He wanted to see where this would go.

"If I am, great people will suffer!" Fay insisted, his voice suddenly rising. "You will surely have war. It cannot be—it is impossible," he announced with genuine indignation.

"I will give you any amount of money if you will let me go," Fay continued. He spoke grudgingly, as if his offer were a great kindness.

"How much will you give me?" Barnitz asked. He was eager to play along. Up to now, they'd had a lot of suspicions but little hard evidence. And a shrewd lawyer could probably make the charge for illegal possession of explosives disappear.

"All you want—any amount!"

"Fifty thousand?"

"Yes, fifty thousand, if you want it."

"Got it with you?" Barnitz challenged.

"No, I haven't got it all, but I can get it. I'll pay you a hundred dollars now as a guarantee, and I'll give you the balance at noon tomorrow."

Barnitz called over two of his detectives. He wanted witnesses.

"All right, where's your money?" he demanded.

Fay took some bills from his pocket, counted out a hundred dollars, and handed the money to Barnitz.

Barnitz took the money, and made a big show of recounting it in front of the men. Then he put the bills in his suit pocket, and slapped handcuffs on Fay's wrists.

Twenty minutes later, Fay was being booked at the Weehawken police station. The charge—attempted bribery.

CHAPTER 40

—————

The interrogation room at headquarters had once been a subbasement supply closet, and the long walk downstairs felt like a descent into the dark depths of hell itself. Two officers led the handcuffed Fay down the flights of stairs and roughly seated him on a stool in the middle of the room. Then they left, slamming the steel door behind them.

Tom waited outside, purposely letting the minutes slowly pass. He wanted Fay to see the dried streaks of blood on the walls, and give them some thought. Threats weren't always necessary; imagination, he had learned, could often be a much more persuasive weapon.

There were other, more tangible arguments available to Tom, too. In the days following the arrest for bribery, his men had searched Fay's room at the boardinghouse and torn apart the garage.

In addition to Wettig's TNT, they found another 25 sticks of the explosive, 450 pounds of chlorate of potash, 400 percussion caps, and 200 bomb cylinders. Nailed above Fay's desk at the boardinghouse was a detailed chart of New York Harbor, and in the top drawer of his dresser were the ownership papers for a motorboat that they traced to a slip opposite West Forty-Second Street. Tom felt pretty sure he was finally on the right path. And the regulation German army pistol hidden beneath the bed had left Tom convinced he knew whom Fay was working for.

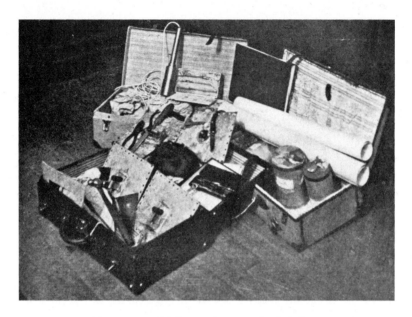

The contents of Robert Fay's suitcases included two
maps of the harbor, rudder bomb components, a wig,
two false mustaches, and an atlas.

But what tied all the evidence together into one tight, incriminating knot was the discovery of dozens of intricate mechanisms for
bombs. The devices were unlike any Tom had ever seen. They were sophisticated pieces of engineering, significantly more advanced in both
workmanship and design than the cigar bombs.

Were the new devices to be used by the same group that had planted the
bombs on the *Kirkoswald*? Or were they the weapons of a separate network
planning its own, independent attacks? And how did they plan to smuggle
them onto the targeted boats? No less a puzzle, how did the bombs even
work? Tom had studied the mechanisms for hours and still could not figure
out how the explosive charge would be detonated.

He had many questions, and after giving Fay some time alone with
his thoughts, he entered the interrogation room. Tom loomed above
Fay like a colossus; and the resigned look set firmly on his face an-

nounced that he was determined to get the answers he wanted, one way or another.

THE THIRD DEGREE WAS NOT necessary. Tom asked one question, and Fay's confession came pouring out. He spoke as easily as if he were sharing the story of his life with a stranger he'd just met in a bar.

A year ago, Fay began, he'd been a German army lieutenant fighting in the muddy trenches in France when he had an epiphany. What if, it occurred to him as shells rained down, the French seventy-fives and the British eighteen-pounders ran out of ammunition? What if the enemy artillery batteries couldn't obtain more shells from America? What if the flotilla of munitions boats heading out from New York never arrived in France?

Once these sudden, unexpected speculations had popped into his head, he found he couldn't let them go. Before the war, he had been an engineer. A rather accomplished one, he told Tom as if simply stating a fact. He'd always loved tinkering, coming up with new inventions. Now, he realized, he needed to invent a machine that could save his life. He was in the middle of a roaring battlefield, yet he knew his future, his very survival, depended upon his immersing himself in the task. He went to work.

Fay's commander was impressed enough with the drawings he made to summon the battalion intelligence officer. When this officer learned that Fay had lived in America before the war and spoke fluent English, he sent a cable to the headquarters on Königsplatz.

A week later, Fay was in Berlin. One team of Abteilung IIIB officers studied his drawings, while another, English-speaking contingent tried to trip him up with questions about finding certain addresses in New York and whether he could name the branches of the federal government.

When the spymasters were satisfied, Fay joked to Tom, "they told me to 'Go west, young man.'" A boat from Norway, a phony passport stamped by the U.S. immigration authorities, and Fay was walking the streets of New York, rejoicing that he'd outsmarted fate. His life would never be crushed out by an Allied shell. He'd escaped the front line and become a spy.

His first operational decision was to recruit his brother-in-law. Walter Scholz had been working as a gardener on a Connecticut estate, and after Fay flashed the thick roll of dollars they'd given him in Berlin, it didn't take much discussion to persuade Scholz that planting bombs was a lot more lucrative than planting flowers.

As for Dr. Kienzle, at the start of the war the clock maker had written to the Foreign Office to volunteer his services in America. Before Fay had left Berlin, his Abteilung IIIB handlers had provided the old man's name as a reliable contact.

When Fay informed Kienzle at their initial meeting that he needed explosives, the clock maker started making inquiries. He first approached his friend Max Breitung, and from there the request for dynamite was passed dutifully along among a shady entourage of German sympathizers until it finally reached Wettig.

"The next thing I knew," a crestfallen Fay concluded his tale, "I was standing in the woods and an army of detectives came charging from out of nowhere, waving their revolvers, and shouting that I was under arrest."

BUT IT WAS A DIFFERENT Fay who told Tom about his invention. He was proud of his work, and he spoke with the confident authority of a man who knew he'd created a unique and effective weapon.

The core of the bomb, he said, was a clockwork mechanism designed to fire two rifle cartridges into a chamber filled with ninety pounds of TNT.

As for getting it on board, that wasn't a problem: there was no need to smuggle the bomb into the cargo hold. The device would be attached underwater to the rudderpost of the ship as it lay in the harbor.

But its most ingenious aspect, Fay revealed with undisguised enthusiasm, was its detonation. The bomb's clockwork heart would be
connected to a wire attached to the rudder. As the helmsman steered
his boat, each turn of the rudder would wind up the mechanism
tighter and tighter until it fired the cartridges into the TNT.

A ninety-pound blast, Fay boasted, would tear the rudder off like
a toothpick, and leave a hole in the hull big enough to drive a car
through. And it'd be the helmsman, he declared with a mischievous
schoolboy's grin, who'd be responsible for setting off the explosion
that wrecked his own ship.

It was a foolproof plan, Fay said with pride. Along with Scholz, he
had spent hours in the motorboat, ostensibly fishing, but in reality
exploring the harbor. There was not a single obstacle, he'd learned,
to prevent a fisherman from guiding his little motorboat up close to a
munitions ship.

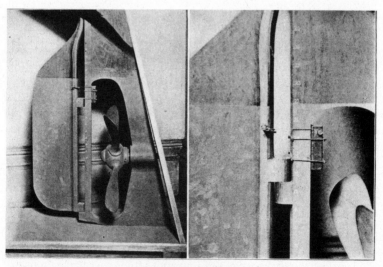

Robert Fay's rudder bomb.

During the course of one single dark night, he could sidle up to as many as ten ships getting ready to sail to England and France. Diving suit on, he'd slip noiselessly into the water and within minutes attach his device to the rudder.

"Ten ships, ten explosions," Fay said matter-of-factly. And ten shipments of shells and bullets that would never kill German soldiers.

TOM HAD HEARD ENOUGH. FAY had told him, he realized, a deliberately edited story. His pretense of candor was all artifice. The spy hadn't lied, but at the same careful time he had not revealed the larger, more consequential secrets that surrounded his mission. With a sense that his long investigative journey could soon be coming to an end, Tom took control of the interrogation.

"What ships have you blown up?" he asked.

"None." Fay insisted that he'd been finalizing his plans when the detectives pounced.

Tom felt Fay was not telling the truth, but he was willing to let the lie go unchallenged for the moment. This was their first talk, and already there was sufficient evidence to build a daunting case against the German agent. A few more sessions, and Fay's predicament would sink in. When the district attorney dangled a sentencing deal, Fay would cave. He'd give up all his secrets. Time, Tom was confident, was on his side.

"Were you responsible for the five fires in the hold of the *Craigside*?" he tried.

"No."

"Did you make the bombs that were found on the *Arabic*?"

"No."

Tom reeled off the names of four more ships that had caught fire since the agent's arrival in New York. And again Fay insisted that he knew nothing about any of the disasters.

Tom tried a different tack. He reached into his pocket and removed the cigar bomb casing that had been found on the *Kirkoswald*. He handed it to Fay. "Did you ever see that?" he asked.

"No."

"Didn't you make that?" Tom suggested.

Fay let out a small laugh. "I did not," he said, enjoying the moment. "That's a joke." He studied the device with more attention. "I see now why they sent me over to this country," he said as he returned the small steel cylinder to Tom. "They wanted someone to make bombs that would do some damage. That's crude work."

"You're right," Tom agreed truthfully. And at the same time he hoped a bit of flattery would encourage Fay to answer the one big question that had been at the center of his thoughts since the moment of the spy's arrest.

When Barnitz had jumped out of the Jersey woods, Fay had dogmatically insisted that he could not allow himself to be arrested. "If I am," he had pleaded, "great people will suffer." Tom wanted to know the names of the "great people." He wanted to know who was giving Fay orders. He wanted to know who was running the German spy network in America.

Fay refused to answer. He said Tom could beat him, do whatever he wanted, but he was not talking. He said he had family in Germany. If he gave up his superiors, they'd never survive.

Tom clenched his fists. He had no qualms about methodically hammering away at Fay until the German agent changed his mind. This was war.

But he hesitated; and in the long, pregnant moment, he managed to rein in his frustration. His perspective shifted, too.

Bang him around enough, and sure, Fay would eventually give him names, Tom thought. Every man has his breaking point. But there'd be no guarantee that the spy wasn't dissembling, throwing out false leads simply to stop the punishment. Coerced confessions, Tom knew, were rarely satisfying, rarely effective. They didn't reveal the truth, only another version of the old lies.

Tom unclenched his fists and called for the guards. Take him back to his cell, he ordered. This was only the first session. There would be others, Tom assured himself. He'd get the names of the "great people."

TOM WAS WRONG. THE NEXT day the feds arrived and took over the case. The unforgiving Robert Lansing had replaced the fidgety, peace-loving Bryan as secretary of state, and the mood in Washington had begun to change, too. The Justice Department had been ordered to grab control of select "showcase" espionage trials in the hope that the publicity would help to persuade the nation—as well as a still very reluctant president—that war with Germany was inevitable. A year later Fay would confess and, after being convicted of violating piracy statutes for his role in conspiring to blow up munitions ships, be sentenced to eight years in the federal penitentiary in Atlanta.

Tom never had an opportunity to interview Fay again. The haughty Justice Department, unwilling to cooperate with the New York Police Department, rejected all his requests.

And despite Fay's arrest, the fires continued. The day after Fay was caught in the woods, a blaze raced through the *Rio Lages* as the steamer crossed the Atlantic. A week later a fire started in the hold of the *Euterpe*. The next victim was the *Rochambeau*, followed by the *Ancona*, and then the *Tyningham*. "Never in the history of the port," Tom would remember, "had so many fires occurred in a single year."

Glumly, Tom had to concede that while Fay's arrest had prevented scores of Allied ships from foundering at sea, it had done nothing at all to stop the outbreak of fires that had originally provoked his investigation. His hunt, he despaired, had led him down another alley. "It was high time," he declared, "we got back into Main Street."

Fay, he had come to accept, "was not the one we wanted most." He was not the German agent orchestrating the waterfront campaign against Allied shipping. He was not one of the "great people" leading Germany's secret attack on America. And when Tom tried to put a name and a face on the master spy, he found himself recalling the image of a dapper man-about-town strolling down a midtown street outside the New York Yacht Club with the rigid, parade-ground bearing of a German officer.

CHAPTER 41

———

The windowless back room of the Hofbrau House was dark and narrow, only big enough for a single long table. But von Rintelen felt at ease in this tight, shadowy space.

At the German Club there was always the annoying possibility of running into von Papen and Boy-Ed. Berlin had ordered that von Rintelen keep the two diplomats informed of his activities, but he drew the line at socializing with them.

He also felt uneasy about Martha Held's. There were too many strangers, too many drunks. And he didn't trust the pretty women; he had little doubt they'd sell the secrets they overheard to the highest bidder. The entire establishment, he felt, was operationally insecure.

Sitting at the table in the long back room of the Hofbrau House, a stein of beer in his hand, he felt comfortable. He could have a conversation without being constantly on guard. He could, as he put it, play the wily spider, continuing to "spin my threads."

And so one Saturday afternoon, after a planning session with the Executive Committee, he was in no hurry to go. Everyone else had left except for Erich von Steinmetz, and the two men continued drinking and talking.

It was a meandering discussion, two professionals sharing war stories. The beer, the camaraderie, the mutual respect, the implicit recognition that they could talk candidly to one another—all worked to keep the conversation going. And this time when von Rintelen pressed his friend to tell him about the "important, top secret mission" that had brought him to America, von Steinmetz felt there was no longer any reason to hold back.

Still, von Steinmetz did not tell the whole story. Von Rintelen suspected that the agent had omitted anything that would reflect poorly on his own conduct in the field. But he heard enough that afternoon to begin thinking about the secret war against America in an entirely new way.

THE SOFT WARTIME ROUTE FROM Germany to New York favored by the kaiser's spies was overland to Scandinavia, then a berth on a ship heading across the Atlantic. But an apprehensive Erich von Steinmetz, according to the account he had shared with von Rintelen in the back room, had chosen a less direct, and intentionally more covert, itinerary. He made his slow way east traveling by foot, horseback, and train through the enemy wilderness of Siberia.

Upon his arrival at the bustling Russian port city of Vladivostok, von Steinmetz went shopping. He bought a brunette wig, a wardrobe of dresses, and pots of makeup. Then he went to work transforming a tall, middle-aged naval officer into an apparently convincing woman.

Disguised as a hefty Frau Steinberg, he purchased a ticket on a steamer heading across the Pacific to San Francisco. From there, still playing the broad-shouldered widow, he boarded a train traveling east to New York. Throughout the entire long, uneasy journey, from Berlin to a hotel on Forty-Fifth Street in Manhattan, a small dark suitcase rarely left his hand.

It was the extraordinary contents of this valise that had caused him to take such nerve-racking and inventive operational precautions. At all costs, his Abteilung IIIB masters had instructed, their sharp words more a threat than advice, this treasure must be kept out of enemy hands.

It contained what the spy liked to refer to simply as "cultures." Each of the corked vials was, however, a deadly weapon. The glass tubes held bacteria for glanders, anthrax, and meningitis. Von Steinmetz had come to attack America with germs.

BIOLOGICAL WEAPONS WERE NOT NEW to warfare. The Hittites had turned plague victims loose in enemy cities. Persian archers, recorded Herodotus, had shot arrows tipped with manure into enemy ranks. A British captain had traded smallpox-tainted blankets to Indians during the French and Indian War. In the Civil War, both Union and Confederate horse soldiers accused each other of sneaking into cavalry corrals and poisoning mounts with viruses. And in Berlin, at 27 Hannoversche Strasse in a redbrick former stable, scientists at the Military Veterinary Academy had discreetly been stockpiling supplies of glanders and anthrax cultures since 1907, with the resigned expectation that one day the Fatherland would need a bioweapon.

That time had come. As terrorized battlefield soldiers on both sides in World War I choked on harsh, suffocating waves of chlorine and phosgene gases, as troops charged through sheets of mustard gas that blanketed the ground with an oily residue that burned on contact like the fires of hell, the increasingly desperate Abteilung IIIB flung aside one more civilizing restraint. The decision was made to launch a secret campaign of germ sabotage in America.

The primary targets were horses.

The war, it had become frustratingly apparent to the German general staff, was destined to sputter forward as a battle of attrition, a long-running stalemate where supplies would be as crucial to victory as the soldiers in the field.

Horses were a particularly vital resource; an estimated 6 million would serve. The animals galloped through storms of flying bullets and exploding shells in cavalry attacks. They trudged through knee-high rivers of mud and pounded over rutted, rocky terrain, pulling ammunition wagons, field kitchens, and ambulances.

This was rough, perilous service. Exhaustion, disease, bullets, shells, and gas caused hundreds of thousands of equine deaths. The four-legged combatants, like the two-legged soldiers, were being killed off at a horrific rate. Yet as the war dragged on, hardened generals on both sides conceded that the loss of a single warhorse was of greater tactical concern than the loss of a single soldier. The path to victory, the generals knew, was on horseback.

In Germany, 715,000 horses were mobilized during the first weeks of the war. After two years of fighting, an estimated half million of these animals, victims of battles and attrition, were not in the field.

The German army, which depended on horses and mules to haul artillery pieces and supplies, replaced some of this stock by conquest. More than 375,000 animals were summarily commandeered from the occupied territories, another 140,000 from the Ukraine.

But this was not sufficient. The general staff's great fear was that if the fighting kept on, the day would inevitably come when the army would run out of horses to pull the supply wagons, and the Fatherland's brave troops would be left stranded on distant battlefields without cannons, bullets, and food.

For the Allies, the reserves of horses at the start of the war were far less than those in the Central Powers' stables. Britain's entire horse population consisted of not more than 80,000 mounts. The French possessed perhaps five times that number.

Yet the Allies could buy what they did not have from America. It was costly; the British Remount Department would ultimately spend £36.5 million on the purchase and delivery of North American horses and mules to the front. Still, endless herds of animals were available from the United States. A 1910 census counted 21 million horses on farms throughout the country.

These animals were suddenly as valuable as oil. Ranchers made fortunes shipping horses across the Atlantic. The demand was constant. Even tired, stumpy mounts were drafted as warhorses. They arrived at the front lines at the rate of 1,000 animals a day. By the war's end, more than 1 million American-bred horses had been sold to fight in Europe for the Allies.

Germany, too, could buy all the American horses it could afford. But the nation was victimized by the same problem that affected all American supplies—it could not transport the animals across the ocean. The powerful British navy controlled the sea. The kaiser's U-boats were a menace, but the submarine fleet was too small to be effective. Submarines couldn't succeed in opening up the Atlantic sea lanes for German trade. Germany was stymied.

Enter Nicolai. Resourceful, imaginative, and coolly pragmatic, he proposed to the general staff a spy's strategy to undermine the Allies' advantage. Abteilung IIIB would dispatch an operative to America to poison the corralled animals as they waited to be shipped overseas.

Of course, he acknowledged, it was quite possible, perhaps even inevitable, that Americans would die too as the viruses spread to humans. But they would be casualties of war. That the war was still undeclared and the victims civilians were minor concerns, dismissed as not really worth considering.

PSEUDOMONAS MALLEI WAS THE SPECIES classification for the glanders bacteria; the Latin word *mallei,* meaning "mallet" or "hammer," was chosen by Aristotle, who had witnessed the pounding the infection delivered. It attacked the nasal passages, searing them with deep ulcers that spread through the horse's upper respiratory tract. Long, hard ropes of burning nodules appeared under the skin. Fever quickly spiked to 106 degrees. And after a tortured few days the animals, if they were lucky, would die. Many, though, lingered painfully for agonized weeks.

The effects of the bacteria, however, did not concern von Steinmetz. Now living the long night of an agent working behind the lines, he was simply eager to proceed on his mission. Just days after checking into his hotel, he took his suitcase and rode the elevated train line to the Bronx.

Under the cover of darkness, he hurried about the network of stables and corrals adjacent to Van Cortlandt Park that held hundreds of horses soon to be sent overseas. His battle plan was direct: he'd insert a stick coated with the curdled, liverish yellow glanders bacteria into the nostrils of every third horse, and then hope the infection would spread to the others.

He worked with precision, full of focus and concentration. Still, it was a tense, dangerous assignment. Unaccustomed to foreign objects being jammed up their nostrils, the horses kicked, neighed, and stomped in rageful self-defense. By the time von Steinmetz was done, he was exhausted and shaking.

The next evening he went down to reconnoiter the West Side docks. A few desultory guards patrolled the waterfront corrals with clockwork regularity; it would not take much ingenuity to time their rounds and work around them.

The previous night, however, had left him unnerved; the roar of high-pitched neighs was still echoing in his memory. Jittery, he decided it would be more secure to insulate himself. He hired a pier superintendent to find an interned German sailor who, out of loyalty to the kaiser as well as for a hefty fee, would go off and do the dirty work.

The following evening von Steinmetz gave the superintendent the sticks coated with glanders. The superintendent, in turn, instructed the seaman: "Shove them up the nose of every third or fourth horse in the stockades and along the ships of the waterfront."

For days von Steinmetz waited to see headlines announcing the mysterious plague ravaging the warhorses. He read the papers with great care, then went over each page again, fearing that he had missed the article. But the story never appeared.

Perhaps, he came to decide, the horse breeders had conspired to keep the outbreak secret. A glanders epidemic would be bad for business. Not even the desperate British buyers would want to buy a horse that might infect the entire stock.

Yet he needed a definitive answer. After a week spent pacing in puzzlement about his hotel room, von Steinmetz realized he would have to investigate the matter himself. He took the elevated line back to the Bronx and walked to the stables.

The horses were healthy. A trip the next day to the waterfront corrals provided similar intelligence. The horses sauntered about with playful energy, their eyes bright, their coats shiny.

What had gone wrong? von Steinmetz wondered in sudden panic. He knew his Abteilung IIIB superiors would demand an explanation; and he also knew his life depended on whether they believed him.

With his anxiety mounting, his fate hanging in the balance, he decided to make a bold move. It was utterly reckless, but at the time von Steinmetz felt he had nothing to lose. If he couldn't provide Nicolai with a satisfactory explanation for his failure, he'd be executed. At least if his new scheme went bad, the Americans would give him a trial before they hanged him for espionage.

Posing as a scientist, he brought the remaining germ cultures to New York's Rockefeller Institute, a renowned scientific research facility. Blithely, he explained that he had obtained the cultures for "experimental purposes." He now wondered whether the organisms were still viable.

The Rockefeller scientist asked how long von Steinmetz had had the cultures. He spoke absently, without suspicion. He had already taken a sample and started to prepare a slide for examination under the microscope.

Von Steinmetz answered truthfully: it had been four months, maybe longer.

The scientist stopped his preparations. There was no longer, he said, any need to look at the specimens. He explained that after a month glanders cultures lose their potency. They become harmless.

Von Steinmetz sighed with relief. The mission had been a failure, but he had the explanation that would save his life.

IN THE DAYS THAT FOLLOWED, von Rintelen found himself playing the conversation with von Steinmetz back over and over in his mind. It was all very new to him, even strange, and he found it difficult to grasp.

In time, however, he grew certain that von Steinmetz had been involved in an operation of immense strategic importance. It didn't matter that it had not succeeded. As a military man, he could see that its potential effectiveness was enormous. It could change everything: germ warfare could sneak up on the enemy, quiet, unseen, unsuspected, until it struck with lethal force. Once targeted, a terrorized America would never find the resolve to fight in a European war.

His heart was pounding with excitement as he drafted the cable to Nicolai. It was imperative, he urged the spymaster, that he send an operative to America to take up von Steinmetz's aborted mission.

CHAPTER 42

———

There had been much to keep Holt busy during his final term at Cornell. He taught two classes of undergraduate French while also finishing, in marathon writing sessions that had him going without sleep for days, his doctoral thesis.

Life at home was no less exhausting. He was now the father of two children, the older only a little more than two years old. To his wife's great joy, he had accepted a professorship to teach Romance languages at Southern Methodist University in her hometown of Dallas, Texas. He'd start in the fall, and they had somehow managed to find time to plan the dream house they'd soon start building close to campus on a lot they'd purchased sight unseen for $600.

Rippling with restless, manic energy, Holt also kept up his hobby—collecting stories on murder and insanity. He maintained a thick scrapbook crammed with neatly clipped reports. "The Rare Case of the Insane," "Suffers for Brother's Crime," "Admits Killing Stepchild," "Slain in Defense of Woman"—he'd found hundreds of similarly themed articles while obsessively going through newspapers and magazines from all over the country.

And still, with all that was crowding his professional and personal life, Holt, the curious and loyal friend, had made time to read Hugo Munsterberg's new book, *The War and America*.

His former Harvard colleague's book was a revelation. It was a proudly combative argument that insisted on nearly every page that Germany occupied the moral and legal high ground in the European war. The book was dedicated "to all lovers of fair play," and in chapter after unyielding chapter it continued to reiterate that America's prejudicial treatment of Germany was "a baffling injustice."

The professor's irrefutable proof of America's "anti-German sentiment" was the nation's continued shipments of arms and munitions to the Allies. "It is a sin against the spirit of fair play," he argued, that Allied soldiers went into battle firing American bullets while the British blockade prevented the Fatherland's troops from receiving supplies.

Holt read these words and felt as if Munsterberg were once again talking directly to him, urging him on. Years ago the psychologist had provided Erich Muenter with the secret faith that he could get away with murder. Now the Harvard professor's words were a call to action for Holt, the man Muenter had become.

Since the outbreak of the war, Holt's emotions had been with the Fatherland, but in only an instinctive, native son's way. The professor's book reinforced these airy sentiments with girders of steely intellectual rigor. Holt now understood that this was a crucial moment in history. An epic battle between good and evil raged in Europe. A German defeat would be a blow to the future of civilization.

The tighter the professor's argument gripped his thoughts, the clearer it became that once again Munsterberg was imploring him to make a contribution. It was incumbent on men like him, men who dared to have the necessary moral courage, to act. It was his duty to force America to realize its mistakes. He would restore fair play in the world.

When the term ended in June, Holt gave his wife nearly all the money he had saved, almost $400, and sent her and the children off to Dallas. They would live, it was agreed, with her father until he joined them. In the meantime, he would go to New York. He needed to do, he explained, "some special research."

With only $20 and some loose coins in his pocket, he took the train to Manhattan. He had no plan, and no resources. Yet he was confident that he had embarked on a secret road that would lead to glory.

PART V:
THE WALK-IN

CHAPTER 43

————

A walk-in always put those in the spy trade on edge. One fear was that the stranger volunteering his services was too good to be true. He might be a double, an operative sent by the opposition to infiltrate and gather intelligence. Another concern, also quite probable, was that the amateur showing up at the door, his head full of big ideas and grandiose schemes, would be impossible to control. Every professional had heard too many hand-wringing stories about how a single loose cannon had brought down an entire network.

As a consequence, the general rule was not to recruit anyone who made the initial approach. Yet when this would-be asset had something tantalizing to offer, rules could be broken. When the balance between risk and opportunity was not clear, a decision had to be made about which way to jump.

That was the dilemma dividing the case officers of the Abteilung IIIB network in New York when Frank Holt approached them. During the weeks when Tom was grappling with the enigma of von Rintelen, trying to understand whether the suave financier was who he claimed to be, they were tugging at their own riddle.

Holt had presented a bold plan. It was nothing less than a way of putting a definitive end to the American munitions and supply shipments.

For the past year, the network's attacks had been sporadic, their effectiveness short-lived. Cigar and rudder bombs targeted single vessels; no sooner had one ship gone up in smoke than another sailed off in its place.

This operation would be much more ambitious. With a single daring act, it would destroy the enemies' ability to outfit their armies. It would cut off the unending flow of money that paid for the Allies' orders. And at a time when von Rintelen had already railed to associates that "Morgan ought to be put out of the way," it held the promise of not just retribution but a wish fulfilled.

There were nevertheless many reasons to reject the walk-in's proposal. Holt would fail, and once captured he'd trade the valuable secrets he had acquired while serving the cause—names, locations, tradecraft—in return for leniency. Or Holt would succeed, and the audacity of his act would so infuriate the American president that Wilson would at last find the resolve to lead the nation into war. Either way, the consequences for Germany would be disastrous.

There was, however, a way of limiting the risk. Keep the walk-in at arm's length—*semiconscious* was the specific jargon in the secret world—and deniability would be possible. Supply him with money, guns, dynamite, whatever resources he required. Even share a bit of operational guidance. Then let him go off and do the rest on his own.

The walk-in's fanaticism would be an operational blessing. There was no need to wind Holt up; he couldn't get any tighter. One conversation, and it was obvious Holt was a time bomb set to explode. His crazed zeal, in fact, painted the entire mission with a natural cover: Holt was the perfect fall guy.

People would see only the marionette prancing about wildly onstage; the strings of the puppet masters would go unobserved. Blame would fall on the unbalanced lone gunman; there'd be no compelling reason to look any further. When the operation was considered in that shadowy light, the decision to go forward was an easy one.

Or that was what Tom, trying to put all the disparate pieces together in the aftermath of headline-making events, would later imagine had happened. He had spent a detective's rigorous lifetime boiling cases down to the hard facts, the times when, he said, "two and two makes four." But this was another sort of investigation entirely. The web of conspiracy had been woven too tightly. The entirety of the plot could never be known, and, Tom grudgingly conceded, it would therefore be "valuable in speculating on what probably happened." "A flight of imagination," he went on, was required to fit the tangible pieces into a fully assembled puzzle.

As for the initial pass, Tom could only speculate on how it had played out. One theory got its inspiration from an undercover sting Barnitz had run.

That June, Madison Square Garden hosted a week of pro-German rallies. On almost every night that same month speakers also crowded Herald Square, bellowing passionately about the Fatherland and providing earnest justifications for the kaiser's decision to go to war. When Felix Galley, hoarse and exhausted, finally stepped down from his soapbox one evening at Herald Square and headed up Broadway on his way home, a man from the crowd followed.

It was unnerving, footsteps echoing on the sidewalk, a solitary presence trailing behind him in the darkness. Galley prepared himself, ready for a fight.

Yet when Harry Newton caught up, he burst out with a fervent declaration: "I want to help Germany win the war!" To prove his commitment, he was prepared to dynamite the Brooks Locomotive Works in Dunkirk, New York. And that was for starters. He was also ready to place bombs in the federal building and police headquarters. Would Galley, he implored, introduce him to a German official who'd know how to make use of his services?

Galley agreed to consult "the chief." But he was secretly shocked by the intrigues the stranger had suggested; and Newton's jittery intensity had only added to his sense that this was someone to avoid. Galley was a loyal supporter of the Fatherland, yet the chief he rushed to speak to was the chief of police.

The case was passed on to Tom, who assigned Barnitz to investigate. Playing the role of a burly, formidable German agent, Barnitz met with Newton in the man's narrow, white-walled crib of a room at the Mills Hotel No. 3 on Thirty-Sixth Street.

"I'm in a hurry," Barnitz, the busy spy, began brusquely. He immediately offered the walk-in $5,000 if he'd "smash the Welland Canal or blow up the Brooks Locomotive Works." Newton was gung ho. In fact, he revealed, he already had the necessary equipment. He'd left a suitcase packed with bombs he'd built in the baggage room of the New York Central Railroad.

"Fine," said Barnitz. "You are under arrest."

Holt's initial approach could have gone down very much like that, Tom suspected. A sidling up to a speaker at the Garden or Herald Square, and a whispered name passed to the would-be agent. Only instead of Barnitz, the sit-down would have been with a genuine Abteilung IIIB hood.

Although, Tom also hypothesized, it was no less possible that the walk-in had simply marched into the German Club on Central Park South or, for that matter, the German consulate on lower Broadway and announced that he wanted to offer his services. Someone would've passed his name on to Koenig.

Within days, the security chief would've sent word to the prospect scheduling a meeting at any of a dozen clandestine spots he used around town—say, for example, the Turkish Bath up in Harlem. Once the higher-ups had made their decision, Koenig, dusting off one of his many aliases, would have run the asset, pushing him forward, guiding him as he went off on his mission.

But while many of the particulars remained beyond Tom's grasp, it was undeniable that days after a nearly penniless Frank Holt arrived from Ithaca and checked into a thirty-cents-a-night room at the Mills Hotel, he embarked on a well-financed, operationally sophisticated mission of murder and destruction that shook America.

CHAPTER 44

———

Later, after much detective work, Tom succeeded in reconstructing many of the events that kept Holt busy as he moved around New York during the final three weeks of June 1915. Each new revelation left him convinced the case "was becoming more interesting every minute." Still, he also couldn't help feeling that for all his efforts he had uncovered only part of the tale, the iceberg's proverbial tip. And what remained forever submerged, he believed, concealed a powerful corollary story. The substantiated facts, however, were these.

On June 8, Holt checked into the Mills Hotel No. 3 (the same low-cost barracks, Tom noted with interest, where Barnitz had bagged the would-be saboteur and where the German passport scam had, for $20 a head, recruited its stooges). He'd arrived alone, having walked from the train station carrying one small valise and a typewriter. The hotel was crowded, nearly all its 1,875 rooms booked, but the clerks would remember Holt.

Three days into his stay, the letters started arriving. The Mills was the sort of down-and-out establishment where the occupants usually didn't get mail, so when the envelopes addressed to Mr. Frank Holt began coming in, sometimes three or four delivered throughout a single day, the clerks took notice. Someone—or several persons, for all the clerks knew—was staying in constant touch with this guest. Then the police came.

During his years at Cornell, Holt had played the mild-mannered, bookish academic. His time in Texas too, as well as at the succession of colleges where he'd taught, had passed without any public outbursts of anger. But during his second week in New York, his discipline snapped. All the control he'd previously summoned to help conceal the secrets of his past was abandoned. Never a man known to throw a punch, let alone the first blow in a fight, Holt suddenly began pummeling another guest.

Critical comments about Germany were the ostensible provocation. There had been only a few words, but they ignited a blazing rage. Holt was all over the helpless man, punching and kicking wildly. The police were called, and when the victim refused to press charges, they let Holt off with a stern warning.

But an incident report was filed. And it was the evidence many authorities would later cite to demonstrate that during his stay in New York Holt's carefully constructed persona had begun to unravel. Or it could just as well have been, Tom found himself suspiciously thinking, a deliberate attempt by the enemy secret service to get it on the record that Holt was a violent pro-German lunatic.

Yet while his mood might have been unsteady, Holt's attention was focused. He spent those three weeks in June busily obtaining supplies and conducting reconnaissance for his mission. The professor worked with the skill and the resourcefulness of a professional, and money was suddenly no object.

He went to Jersey City, where he found a hardware dealer who sold guns. How a Cornell professor found his way across the Hudson to a New Jersey gun shop and how he got the money for the trip, not to mention the gun and ammunition, were never clarified. He studied the glass case filled with rows of rifles, but a .38-caliber Iver and Johnson revolver caught his eye. Does it come with a guarantee to "work every time"? he asked the clerk.

John Menagh frowned. Revolvers don't come with a warranty, he grumbled.

Nevertheless, Holt purchased the gun along with a box of cartridges. Then he decided that he'd better buy another revolver, too.

The .38 was the last handgun in the store, so Menagh suggested he go across the street to Joseph Keechan's pawnshop. There he bought a used .32-caliber revolver. Adding a new alias to his growing list, he signed "C. Hendricks" on the sales slip.

The next day, Holt was out in the Long Island North Shore farm country, poking around a bucolic community then known as Central Park but soon to be incorporated as the town of Bethpage. Only now the previously destitute college teacher was calling himself Mr. Patton, driving a black Ford, and giving the impression to Louis Ott, a local real estate broker, that he was a man of means.

His physician, Patton explained gravely, had ordered him to move to the country for his health. He was looking for a quiet place, off the beaten track, where he could rest.

Ott found him a secluded two-room bungalow, far from the main road and hidden by a stand of tall trees. Just what I'm looking for, Patton decided at once. He paid a month's rent in cash. He would still keep his room at the Mills, but the bungalow would be his operational headquarters, a place where he could lie low, hide his weapons, and plan his attacks.

But first he needed dynamite. He made inquiries in New York, and when those were unproductive, his hunt took him to New Jersey and then on to Pennsylvania. He finally found a company on Long Island that could sell him the explosives he needed, he volunteered to the salesman, to "get rid of some tree stumps." He asked that the shipment be freighted to the train station at Syosset, a town near Central Park; he'd pick it up at the railroad freight office.

Railroad safety regulations required that explosives must be carried on special trains, ones without passengers or other freight. It could take a few days, the salesman advised. Maybe more.

Still, the next day, and then every day for the following week, Holt went to the station on Jackson Avenue to inquire if a shipment for

Henderson—the new name he was using—had arrived. And each day the freight agent, George Carnes, would tell him sorry—nothing for Henderson. But the persistent Henderson wouldn't take no for an answer, and would invariably ask Carnes to check again.

It got so irritating that one morning Carnes barked back, telling Henderson to calm down and relax or get out of his office. And when something finally arrived for Henderson, it wasn't the dynamite but a big black trunk shipped from New York and weighing thirty-six pounds, according to the shipping invoice.

Henderson seemed glad it had arrived, but he let Carnes know that he was still waiting for the explosives he needed to remove an ugly stand of tree trunks. "It'll come when it comes," Carnes told him.

So he waited. He nailed a bull's-eye target to a tree behind the bungalow and began practicing with the revolvers. He was good with guns, and the target's inner circles were soon perforated with holes. And when he wasn't shooting or pestering the freight agent, he went off and did reconnaissance.

LIKE A GOLDEN ARROW POINTING the way, East Island on a bright June day was a shining narrow peninsula of land jutting straight out toward the shimmering blue waters of Long Island Sound. The Gold Coast town of Glen Cove was famous for its great estates, mansions as big as the Ritz surrounded by fields of shaved green lawns. But most locals would enviously agree—especially those who were weekend sailors— that Matinicock Point, the estate house situated at the center of East Island, was special.

It wasn't that the house was particularly large, although as with nearly every estate on the Gold Coast, there was enough room to bivouac a battalion. Nor was its architecture distinguished, or even graceful. It was a squat, dormered two-story redbrick mansion, its front door flanked by a fatuous pair of Ionic columns. And if you believed the old saw that people choose houses that reflect their personalities, at first glance you'd guess that this was a banker's home—solid, uninspired, and forbiddingly dull.

But what rescued Matinicock Point, what transformed a stolid redbrick fortress into something more lively and unique, was the boldness with which it had been sited. It rode the tip of the peninsula like a figurine carved on the prow of a pirate's ship. Every room not only looked out on the water but offered open vistas that conspired to make the sound—its whitecaps, its roar, the pounding rhythm of its waves—a nearly palpable presence. It was breathtaking.

Matinicock Point was J. P. Morgan's home. In mid-May he'd take up residence, commuting to Wall Street by automobile or steam launch across the sound; and, except for a precious few days at the family camp in the Adirondacks, he would stay on Long Island until the annual August trip to his farm in the English countryside. His oldest child, Junius, had married that spring, but his three younger children and his wife, Jane, had settled into Matinicock Point for most of the summer.

Holt spent days surveilling the estate. In an inspired bit of cover, he posed as Thomas Lester, a representative of the *Society Summer Directory*, even flashing an embossed card with his name and title to confirm his identity. Gold Coast matriarchs, with snooty humor, called the *Society Directory* "the Good Book" and kept it by their phones. It listed the names, addresses, and telephone numbers of the only families with whom one would need to speak, along with other necessary information such as club and university affiliations. As a result, its representative was greeted with courtesy and offered the sort of discreet information that would never normally be shared with an outsider.

Lester politely knocked on mansion doors throughout Glen Cove and, without pressing too hard, succeeded in gathering a good deal of intelligence about Morgan, his family, and even his servants. It was such resourceful fieldwork that Tom, mulling over it all after the fact, had to admire Holt's skill. At the same time, he also wondered how a college professor with no apparent knowledge of the smart set had the inspiration to pass himself off as a *Society Directory* representative, down to the impressively embossed card.

TWO CRATES ARRIVED AT THE Syosset station for "C. Hendricks" on June 28, holding 120 pounds—two hundred sticks—of 60 percent dynamite. The standard formulation contained 40 percent nitroglycerin, but this batch was considerably more powerful. Holt was elated to discover that at last his shipment had been delivered. With great care, he loaded the wooden boxes into his Ford and drove off.

Another crate arrived the following day, packed with blasting caps and fuses. But when Holt banged on the locked freight office door at 6:00 p.m., the crotchety Carnes roared that the office was closed. He should come back tomorrow.

Holt refused to leave. He begged that he really needed to get the crate. He even apologized for all his incessant pestering.

Carnes couldn't see why there was so much rush to blow up a few tree trunks, but it'd be easier to get things done and over with than to keep on arguing. He opened the door and gave the man his crate. It was only as Hendricks was driving off in his Ford that Carnes noticed he'd signed the receipt "Hendrix." Which was odd, but then again, he told himself, everything about that fellow was odd.

Holt spent the next two days in New York. The clerks at the Mills later told Tom that he'd leave by nine in the morning and wouldn't return until after dark. Did he walk the streets aimlessly? Was he gathering up his courage? Did he meet with his control? Tom could only guess.

But Tom did establish that on Thursday, July 1, Holt arrived in Glen Clove on the 3:00 p.m. train from Manhattan. He found a taxi and instructed the driver, Matthew Kramer, to take him to the Morgan estate.

Kramer had grown up in the town and was proud of knowing everyone, including all the grand families. There was little he liked better, in fact, than letting people know how deeply he was tied into the gilded community. And talking helped to break up the tedium of sitting behind the wheel of his cab. When his passenger started asking questions about Mr. Morgan, Kramer was only too happy to let him know that he was speaking to the right man.

The taxi driver cheerily confided that this was going to be a big holiday weekend up at the house. On Saturday the *Resolute*, Morgan's yacht, would be racing the *Vanitie* in the America's Cup trials. And then that night there was a party in honor of Junius, Morgan's oldest son, and his new bride. There were lots of people coming, he said knowingly. Even the British ambassador.

As Kramer talked on, the plot took final shape in Holt's mind. The timing, he had to realize, couldn't be better. The July 4 weekend offered the perfect opportunity.

When the taxi reached the causeway that connected East Island to the mainland, he told the driver to stop. From his seat, Holt had a clear view past the tall wrought-iron gate and the manicured lawn to the redbrick mansion. He stared at the house in silence. Morgan lived like a king; and he'd die like one, too.

At last he gave the driver the address of the bungalow in Central Park, and ordered Kramer to take him there.

The next morning Holt left on the 7:09 train to Penn Station. He had hired the young son of a local livery operator to wheel a large brown trunk to the train, while he carried two small suitcases, one in each hand as if for balance. Once he reached Manhattan, he arranged for the trunk to be sent to a storage warehouse on Fortieth Street, just off Seventh Avenue.

Then he boarded a train to Washington, D.C. His mission had begun.

CHAPTER 45

————

At the end of the long checkerboard-patterned first floor of the U.S. Capitol Building, adjacent to the mahogany door leading to the vice president's office, were two tall arched windows that looked out across the city toward the Washington Monument. A deep alcove stretched beneath the windows, and it was there that a telephone switchboard had been wedged. It serviced a row of phone booths, their elegant raised paneled doors carved from the finest walnut, reserved exclusively for the members of the U.S. Senate. A senator could give the switchboard operator a number anywhere in the country, and within minutes she'd make the connection.

On the afternoon of Friday, July 2, the Senate was not in session, and the switchboard was covered with a canvas drop cloth. Tourists, though, were allowed to walk through the Capitol. As Holt rambled through the hallways, a suitcase in his hand, he walked past a door whose gold-leaf lettering announced, "Office of the Vice President." This would do, he decided.

He surveyed the hallway and saw the covered switchboard across the way. He knew he had to act now, or he would never find the nerve. He glanced to see if he was being observed, and when he was certain no one was watching, he quickly shoved the suitcase beneath the canvas, placing it directly under the switchboard. Unless someone lifted the canvas, then got down on his hands and knees, they'd never notice a thing, he reassured himself. Still, at about 4:00 p.m., as he hurried as best he could with his gimpy leg down the long stone Capitol steps, his heart was pounding.

Inside the suitcase was a bomb.

AFTER ARRIVING AT UNION STATION the previous day, Holt had wandered until he found a boardinghouse. He checked in, immediately went to his room, and then made sure the door was locked. For further security, he wedged a chair against the door. He didn't want the landlady bursting in while he was assembling his bomb. Its core was three sticks of dynamite.

When he was done, he reread the letter he had drafted during his long evenings in the Central Park bungalow. He had made five copies, one to President Wilson and the others addressed to the four principal Washington newspapers.

Satisfied with what he had written, he put the five envelopes into the inside pocket of the pin-striped brown suit jacket he'd be wearing tomorrow. Then he cleaned up carefully. He still needed to plant the bomb, and he wanted to make sure the maid tomorrow morning found nothing that would prompt any concerns while he was on his way to the Capitol.

All had gone off as he'd planned. Even better, in fact. No one would ever notice the suitcase; finding a switchboard covered by a drop cloth had been a genuine bit of luck. Walking down the block from the Capitol, he passed a mailbox. He pushed the letters one at a time through the slot. In case anyone was watching, he tried to act as if he were mailing off nothing more significant than a payment for an outstanding bill, which was precisely what he believed he had done— paid America back for its great unfairness.

Holt returned to the boardinghouse, retrieved his suitcase, and checked out. Then he walked the city, waiting.

He expected to hear the blast crashing through Washington at any moment. The wait was excruciating. And the steady, even hum of city noise was a constant reprimand. How can I have failed? What has gone wrong? he wondered, close to panic.

He knew he shouldn't return to the Capitol Building, but he couldn't restrain himself. At 10:30 on the hot, quiet night he was pacing back and forth on the Senate terrace, his eyes fixed on a pair of tall, arched windows.

Growing tired, he found a bench at a nearby trolley stop, where he sat with his back turned to the road, all his shivery attention on the Capitol. He watched and listened, but the domed building remained swathed in an immense silence.

At 11:23 p.m. the bomb exploded, violently shaking the Capitol Building to its foundations. The roar reached across the city. Sitting at his desk in the basement of the Senate, Frank Jones, a thirty-five-year veteran of the Capitol police, was thrown from his chair. "It sounded like several cannons going off," he said. "I thought the Capitol dome had toppled."

Inside, plaster rained down from walls and ceilings, gaping holes were punched through stone walls, doors were blown off their hinges, crystal chandeliers crashed to the floor. The East Reception Room was in shambles. No one had been killed, but a message had been delivered: America was under siege.

Holt had seen it all happen. He was sitting on the trolley bench when the huge noise burst into his ears like a victory trumpet. As a curious crowd gathered, he walked off, tingling with a great, proud excitement.

It was three blocks to Union Station, and he covered the distance in time to make the 12:10 a.m. train to New York City. The conductor showed him to a berth in car 27, but sleep was impossible. Alone in the darkness, he listened to the sounds of the powerful train racing down the tracks, taking him to his destiny.

A photograph taken in the aftermath of the explosion
that rocked the U.S. Capitol on July 2, 1915.

AND THEN IT WAS SATURDAY, July 3.

In Manhattan, Holt transferred to the Long Island Rail Road,
boarding an Oyster Bay line train.

It was 8:30 on the quiet holiday weekend morning when he stepped
off the train at the Glen Street station. He wore a stiff-brimmed straw
hat on his head, and in his hand he carried a suitcase. It was filled
with newspaper clippings about the war in Europe—and two sticks of
dynamite. In his brown suit coat were the .38- and 32-caliber revolvers, one in each pocket. An inside breast pocket held another stick of
dynamite.

At the station, he hailed a Glen Cove yellow cab. He told the driver, Arthur Ford, to take him to the Morgan estate.

It was a two-mile drive.

In Washington, he expected the president and the newspaper editors would soon be reading his typewritten letter.

"Unusual times and circumstances call for unusual means," it began:

> Would it not be well to stop and consider what we are doing?
>
> We stand for PEACE AND GOOD WILL to all men, and yet, while our European brethren are madly setting out to kill one another we edge 'em on and furnish them more effective means of murder. Is it right?
>
> We get rich by the exportation of explosives, but ought we to enrich ourselves when it means the untold suffering and death of millions of our brethren and their widows and orphans?

And there was a handwritten postscript:

> We would, of course, not sell to Germans if they could buy here, and since so far we only sold to the Allies, neither side should object if we stopped.

It was signed, "R. Pearce."

Now that he had their attention, he hoped that they would read his words and understand that he was right. Men like him, those who were special, had a responsibility to make other people—even the president of the United States or the richest man in the world—listen. It was his natural duty. He could not turn away.

The taxi drove through the open gate toward the big brick house. It stopped in the circular driveway across from the front door.

"Oh, I forgot," Holt told the driver, hesitating for a moment before he got out. "I have to get my card."

He opened his suitcase and searched for the card that identified him as Thomas Lester of the *Society Summer Directory*.

He found it, and put it in his jacket.

Ford, watching, wondered: Was that a revolver sticking out of the passenger's suit pocket?

But before he could ask, Holt had left the car.

He walked up the three short brick steps to the front door and rang the bell.

CHAPTER 46

P hysick, the butler, was immediately wary. As soon as he opened the door and took quick measure of the man in the rumpled brown suit, holding a battered suitcase, he knew something was not right.

"I want to see Mr. Morgan," the caller said, and handed the butler a business card.

Physick glanced at the card identifying the stranger as Thomas Lester, a representative of the *Society Summer Directory*. But he was still not persuaded. The hollow look in the man's eyes was reason enough to remain on guard.

"What is your business with him?" the butler asked, his curtness deliberate.

"I can't discuss that with you," he answered. "I am an old friend of Mr. Morgan. He will see me."

Physick did not appreciate the insistence in the man's tone. It was inappropriate, and certainly not how a gentleman would conduct himself. "You must tell me the business you have with him," the butler repeated firmly.

So it had quickly come to this, Holt decided. During his weeks of planning, he'd liked to imagine that he'd be swiftly ushered in for an audience with Morgan; and that as they sat face-to-face the financier would be not merely persuaded by but impressed with the powerful logic of his argument. Morgan would appreciate that he was talking to an equal; a friendship would blossom. And violence would not be necessary.

But even as the vision took shape in his mind, he also knew it would never become a reality. He had prepared for rejection: guns were in his pockets, and his suitcase was packed with dynamite. He had offered an alternative, but they refused to listen. Now he would do whatever was necessary to complete his mission.

Holt pulled the .38-caliber revolver from his jacket and charged into the front hall. "Where is Morgan?" he demanded, the gun trained on the butler.

"In the library," Physick lied. He knew his employer was at the other end of the big house, in the breakfast room dining with his houseguests, including Sir Cecil Spring-Rice, British ambassador to the United States. When he led the armed intruder down the hallway to the library, it was a diversion. It was all he could think of to protect the household.

The library double doors were open, and Holt rushed in, waving his gun. It was a spacious room, and with the curtains drawn and the dark mahogany paneling it seemed bathed in perpetual night. Adjusting his eyes to the shadows, he surveyed the space.

It was empty, he quickly discovered. He had been tricked!

In the same moment Physick bolted, taking advantage of the gunman's confusion. He ran down the hall in the opposite direction, toward the breakfast room, his feet slipping on the well-polished marble floor, his frock coat constraining his movements. Terrified that any second a bullet would slam into his back, he ran as fast as he could down the mansion hallway, all the time shouting at the top of his lungs, "Upstairs, Mr. Morgan! Upstairs!" It was imperative to warn his employer. Mr. Morgan needed to lock himself in an upstairs bedroom. "Upstairs, Mr. Morgan! Upstairs!" he repeated as he fled.

As Physick approached the breakfast room, it occurred to him that it would be a mistake to enter. He'd be leading the intruder straight to Mr. Morgan. Instead, he hurried down a narrow staircase that led to the basement servants' hall. He'd recruit an army of footmen and valets to subdue the gunman.

Holt tried to pursue the butler, but his deformed leg made running impossible. And then, before he could understand how it had happened, the butler had vanished. He looked down the long hallway, but he might as well have been peering down the wrong end of a telescope. The house was vast and empty. With his gun drawn, he moved forward with caution. He felt completely exposed, and very alone.

"WE WERE AT BREAKFAST IN the room on the ground floor, when the butler was heard shouting from the main entrance by the library to Mr. Morgan to go upstairs quickly," Sir Cecil would remember. "We did not know what was the matter, whether it was fire or burglars, and the whole party left the table and ran up the rear staircase, which was nearest to the door."

Morgan led the way. He was a man who always took charge. His authority was instinctive, and a lifetime of experiences had proved that he had the power to shape events to conform to his will. He was not frightened, but he was annoyed. It wouldn't do to have any sort of disturbance—fire? burglars?—in *his* house. Especially this weekend, with so many guests, and Junius's party tonight.

Rosalie McCabe, the ancient nurse who took care of the youngest children, was standing at the top of the stairs. She had also heard the butler's shouts and wondered what was happening.

"What has gone wrong up here?" Morgan demanded petulantly. "What do you want me for?"

"Nothing has happened up here that I know of," she answered at once. She wanted to make it clear that she was not the one responsible for disturbing her employer.

Perhaps, Morgan wondered, it had all been a mistake. He'd need to give Physick a good talking-to. But even as his anger started rising, he knew that this sort of thing wouldn't be like Physick at all. Something must've occurred. He told Sir Cecil to take a few of the guests up to the attic floor and check the servants' rooms. He would inspect the second-floor bedrooms with the others.

JANE MORGAN, THE FINANCIER'S WIFE, saw him first. She was standing outside her bedroom on the second floor with her husband when she turned. *And there he was.* He was coming up the main staircase. He had a revolver in each hand and a wild look in his eyes. And right behind him were her two youngest children.

Minutes earlier, as Holt was wandering through the downstairs hall, he'd heard voices. He pulled open a door and found Frances and Henry Morgan in the playroom. He pointed a pistol at them. "Come with me," he ordered. He led them out of the room, and told them to follow as he started up the staircase.

Jane Morgan came from old Boston stock, and she was by nature a quiet woman, happy to read her books and grow award-winning roses while her husband stormed the citadels of finance and politics. But this man had her babies! She let out a small shriek and, sheer instinct pushing her, moved toward him.

The instant he heard his wife's cry, Morgan turned and saw the intruder. The man held two revolvers, and both were leveled at his wife.

He pushed her out of the line of fire and charged at the gunman.

"Now, Mr. Morgan, I have you," said Holt.

Morgan was not deterred. He hurled his 220-pound body at the intruder.

Holt fired once. Then again. The noise echoed through the house.

The first bullet entered Morgan's abdomen. A red stain quickly began to spread across his white linen waistcoat. The second bullet passed through his left thigh. A river of blood gushed down his leg.

Holt pulled the trigger two more times. There were two distinct *click*s, and after each one it was as if time had stopped as Morgan waited for the inevitable explosion. But on each occasion the caps did not detonate.

Despite his wounds, Morgan fell on Holt. Bleeding profusely, he wrestled with the thin, spindly gunman, his full weight pressing against the intruder like a massive boulder. Both of Holt's hands were pinned to the floor, and his grip on the revolvers loosened.

Morgan twisted one of the guns from Holt's hands. His wife and the elderly nurse worked frantically to pry away the other.

"I have a stick of dynamite in my pocket," Holt managed to shout.

He might have been warning that he was still a threat. Or perhaps he was begging for some restraint; if they treated him too roughly, the house could come tumbling down around them.

But events were now rushing by so quickly that no one was paying any attention. Morgan's clothes were soaked with blood. It looked as if he was dying. Then suddenly there was Physick, accompanied by the members of the household staff, charging up the staircase.

The gardener had a shovel, a valet had a broom, and the butler had armed himself with a large chunk of coal. As the man who had introduced himself as Lester lay pinned to the floor, Physick kept pounding and pounding the rock-hard lump of coal into his head until at last the gunman lost consciousness.

MORGAN WAS CARRIED TO HIS bed, and as soon as he was settled in, he demanded a phone.

He dialed the number of his Wall Street office. "I've been shot in the stomach," he announced in a weak voice. "Get the best doctor you can."

The first doctor to arrive at Matinicock Point, though, was a local man, Dr. William Zabriskie. He had little experience with shooting victims, and his examination of Morgan left him very concerned. The hip wound, he quickly decided, was only an annoyance. The bullet had passed through the thigh muscle and apparently exited. The other bullet, however, had penetrated the lower part of the abdominal cavity, and that was a genuine danger. If it grew infected, the prognosis was dire. Yet since there was no hospital in Glen Cove, he decided the most reasonable course would be to wait for the arrival of the New York specialists.

Matinicock Point, meanwhile, became an armed camp. The partners at J. P. Morgan & Company did not know if the assassin had accomplices, or if he did, whom they were working for, and whether they would attack again to complete the botched job. Police officers from all over Long Island and New York were summoned to protect the estate. A shotgun-toting officer stood at every entrance to the main house. Private detectives patrolled the driveway. A squad of burly armed men stood in front of the now tightly locked entrance gate. Charles Price, the gatekeeper, toted a large repeating rifle and made it clear to curious neighbors that they should stay away. "There are scores of men with shotguns up there on the grounds. They are men who are not taking any chances."

When the pair of New York doctors arrived, they found that Morgan's condition was stable, but an extensive examination brought new concerns. The first bullet had traveled through the abdominal cavity and apparently lodged in the financier's spine. They would need to probe for the bullet, a dangerous, life-threatening procedure.

Since the two-hour ambulance ride to New York risked exacerbating Morgan's condition further, it was decided to perform the operation in Morgan's bedroom. The doctors went into his private bath to scrub. But minutes later, one of the doctors hurried back into the room. He ordered the butler to summon all the servants.

"I need your help," he began fervently. "I need you to find the bullet. If we can establish that it exited, then a probe won't be necessary." He knew that they had already conducted a search, but, nearly begging, the doctor asked them, please, to look again.

Twenty minutes later the bullet was found. It had passed through Morgan, ricocheted off a wall, and lain hidden in the dark floral design of the carpet on the second-floor landing.

That night, the relieved doctors issued a statement to the many reporters who had gathered outside the front gate: "A further examination of Mr. Morgan's wounds shows that the bullets did not involve any vital organs. The condition of the patient continues excellent." The crisis had passed.

As for the gunman, he had regained consciousness. Dr. Zabriskie treated the cuts on his skull and forehead and, after washing away the blood, found they were superficial.

Erich Muenter *(center)* after his capture. On his left is chief constable Frank McCahill, who arrested him at Matinicock Point.

"Who are you?" the doctor asked as he applied antiseptic to the wounds. "The butler says your name is Lester."

"I am a Christian gentleman," was the cryptic reply, the words spoken with pious conviction.

Before the doctor could ask another question, the local justice of the peace and the chief of constables hurried into the room. They snapped handcuffs onto the assassin's wrists. Then they led him out the front door and into a waiting police car.

A THICK WHITE CLOTH BANDAGE was wrapped around Lester's head like a turban. One eye had been blackened. The other was a narrow slit. But as soon as Lester was brought into the Glen Cove jail after his arraignment, he informed the arresting officers that he wanted to draw up a statement. They brought him ink and a sheet of paper, and he started to write:

> I, F. Holt of Ithaca, N.Y., formerly professor of French of Cornell University, make the following statement: "I have been in New York ten days, and made a previous trip to Mr. Morgan's a few days ago. My motive was to try to influence Mr. Morgan to use his influence in the manufacture of ammunition in the United States and among millionaires who are financing the war loans, to have an embargo put on shipments of ammunition so as to relieve the American people from complicity in the deaths of thousands of our European brothers."

As he wrote, he hoped this would appease them. He would give them this much: I am not Thomas Lester but rather a college professor named Holt. And they would not bother to dig for other, more deeply buried secrets.

CHAPTER 47

———

Some old athletes live forever in their glory days, preferring the memories of their youthful triumphs to the present. Tom was not one of them. But on a single afternoon each year he'd relive the moment seventeen years earlier when as a rookie he won the hundred-yard dash at the annual Police Field Day. Now, though, Captain Tunney would stand at the finish line, the celebrated past champion awarding the gold medal to this year's young winner.

He had risen on the morning of the meet at the Gravesend Bay track, July 3, looking forward, he'd recall, "to a day of relaxation and pleasure." He felt he needed it. For months he'd been grappling with mysteries whose solutions remained just beyond his grasp. The ship fires, Koenig, Fay, and now von Rintelen—they all were, he was growing convinced, tied together, strands of the same conspiracy. But the old track star didn't need to remind himself that he was a long way from the finish line. Or that only winners received gold medals. Nevertheless, "it was a holiday, with another to follow, and I proposed to enjoy it," he remembered.

He rode a streetcar from his Prospect Park home across Brooklyn to the track, reading the newspaper on the way. A front-page bulletin reported last night's Capitol bombing. There were few details—the morning edition went to press at 1:00 a.m.—yet he gave the story a professional's attention. He wondered what group was responsible, and what sort of device had been detonated. But once he was at the park, it was a sunny summer's day, and there were old friends from precincts around the city, and many other things to talk and think about.

At about noon the runners were warming up on the track, and Tom decided he'd better make his way to the finish line. "Duty calls," he joked to the circle of detectives he'd been talking to, finishing his beer with one long swallow and excusing himself. He was headed across the grass when an officer found him. "Captain," the officer announced with urgent excitement, "the PC needs to talk to you. He's on the phone."

"Mr. Morgan has been shot by a German," Commissioner Woods revealed as soon as Tom got on the line. He wanted Tom to get to Glen Cove at once. "Find out the man's motives and any accomplices he had," Woods ordered. "Keep in touch with me." He hung up without another word.

BY THE TIME TOM ARRIVED at Glen Cove at about three that afternoon, the sleepy little town had shaken itself anxiously awake, and rumors were spreading quickly. Many residents had grown convinced the Gold Coast was under siege.

Sir Cecil Spring-Rice had reported that only hours after the attack on Morgan, he had been motoring to a neighboring estate when a "low, long, dark-colored touring car" filled with six men had tried to abduct him—but Paddison, the Morgan chauffeur at the wheel, had bravely outrun the assailants. A garage owner claimed that "two young Germans" were asking questions about Morgan. Someone else notified the police about a bicyclist "with a German accent." And F. Worthington Hine, the owner of the Keystone National Powder Company, which manufactured much of the munitions being sent overseas, had spotted two strangers sprinting across the lawn of his estate. When he called to them, they turned and ran. Joined by Donald Bane, the son of the president of the Seaboard National Bank, he hurried to his car and gave chase. He sped down the road, only to lose control at the first sharp turn and crash into the brick wall of a neighbor's estate.

There was no proof that these incidents were tied to the shooting, or that German agents were involved in them. People might have simply been on edge, willing to jump to unsubstantiated conclusions. In the end, no arrests were made.

But by the afternoon dozens of reporters were milling around the entrance of the tiny Glen Cove police station. When they saw Tom, they converged on him in a ravenous pack. At Gravesend, while he searched for an available car, Tom had spotted Detective James Coy from his squad and recruited him to come along. Coy spoke German, and Tom thought an interpreter might come in handy. But now Coy might have been a blocker on a football field as he roughly cleared a path through the scrum of reporters shouting questions at his boss.

Inside, the station house was a hive of noisy activity, officers and civilians scurrying about feverishly. Tom took it all in with a critical eye. It looked as though the country cops were in over their heads.

He was led into the office of Frank McCahill, the constable in charge. Heavyset, with a red drinker's face, McCahill quickly confirmed Tom's initial suspicions. Never had anything like this before, the constable confided, a desperate note in his voice. A maid pinches the silver, we can handle that. But an assassination, Germans running all over the place, that's out of our league.

Tom asked McCahill to tell him all he knew. He spoke evenly, hoping his calm would help settle the constable.

McCahill pulled himself together to give a broadly accurate account of the attack. Then he handed Holt's one-page statement to Tom.

With some embarrassment, he added that it was already out on the wires; both the Associated Press and United Press had somehow gotten hold of it.

Tom did not think this was a problem. Since it was out there, he told McCahill, there was no telling what would turn up. It might even be a blessing, he suggested. Then Tom focused all his attention on Holt's words.

He read slowly, as if he was trying to uncover something hidden in each sentence. But all he found, he decided when he reached the end, was an assassin who was smart enough to understand that silence would be impossible. Holt had attempted to gain control of the dialogue, volunteering what he wanted them to focus on. Tom knew he needed to learn the rest of the story.

"I'd like to talk with the prisoner," he said finally.

THERE WAS NO INTERROGATION ROOM, and Tom thought commandeering McCahill's office would be a rudeness that might make any future cooperation with the locals problematic, so the interview took place in a corridor. Two camp stools were placed in the hallway; Holt sat on one, and Tom across from him on the other.

With the thick bandage still wrapped around his head, one eye blackened, the other now swollen shut, and handcuffs on his thin wrists, Holt looked very vulnerable. Tom began by asking the prisoner his name, age, and profession; he hoped to establish a perfunctory rhythm that would keep the conversation moving forward. But once the frail, slight man started talking, Tom realized he was entering a world of madness, and he would have to journey through it patiently before he could discover what lay at the end.

"What did you try to kill Mr. Morgan for?" Tom asked.

"I didn't intend to kill him," Holt corrected prissily. "I want to persuade him to use his influence to stop the shipment of ammunition to Europe."

"Well, you chose a pretty strong means of persuading him, didn't you?" Tom joked, all deliberate lightness. "What was the dynamite for?"

"I was going to show him what was causing all the trouble—explosives."

The explanation made no sense at all, so Tom simply let it go. Instead, he tried to learn where Holt had bought the dynamite. But this was territory into which the prisoner adamantly refused to enter. "No amount of questioning would bring an answer," Tom would later explain.

He decided that Holt had drawn this line because crossing it would reveal his accomplices. If Tom tried to push him across it, he feared, Holt would retreat completely. Besides, Tom had the sticks of dynamite that had been found in Holt's suitcase and jacket pocket. They could be traced, and the resulting intelligence fed back to the prisoner. If Holt felt the authorities already had most of the story, he'd be more likely to cooperate and fill in the blanks.

For now, Tom offered Holt a compromise, and the prisoner grabbed it. Without any hesitancy, he revealed the names of the shops in New Jersey where he'd purchased the guns and the bullets.

"These facts gave me something to work with," Tom rejoiced. Earlier, Coy had reached out to Barnitz, and the sergeant had assembled the entire team in the Centre Street offices, waiting for the captain's instructions. Tom asked McCahill to bring the prisoner back to his cell while he went off to find a phone. It was time to set his squad off on the hunt.

THIS MUST BE MY TENTH time, Robert Boardman, chief of detectives in Washington, D.C., wearily told himself as he once again picked up the letter signed by "R. Pearce" and forced himself to reread it. The bewildering statement had been delivered earlier that day to newspapers throughout the city, and so far it was the only clue he had in the Capitol bombing.

His boss, police chief Raymond Pullman, had left the night before to go to some sort of field day the New York cops were holding, but Pullman had already called twice—at long-distance rates!—to let him know that the whole department was counting on him to solve the bombing. The implication was clear: if Captain Boardman didn't make some tangible progress soon, a new chief of detectives would be found who could. But all Boardman could think to do was to reread the damn letter.

When he finished his twelfth run-through without discovering even a hint of a clue, Boardman had had enough. He decided he needed a break; perhaps a short rest would cause something to come bubbling up into his thoughts. Absently, he glanced at what had been left on his desk while he was preoccupied with the Pearce letter. Seeing the statement that had come in over the AP wire from the man accused of attempting to assassinate J. P. Morgan, and with nothing better to do, he started to read.

"If Germany should be able to buy munitions here," Holt had written, "we would, of course, positively refuse to sell her."

Quickly, Boardman reached for the Pearce letter. And there it was, just as he remembered it: "We would, of course, not sell to Germans if they could buy here, and since so far we only sold to the Allies, neither side should object if we stopped."

The two statements had to be written by the same man!

Elated, convinced not only that his job was now safe but that he could be in for a promotion, he telegraphed Chief Pullman in New York: "Ascertain from F. Holt, in custody at Glen Cove, N.Y., for shooting J. P. Morgan, his whereabouts Thursday and Friday, as he may have placed the bomb in the Capitol here Friday night."

THE INVESTIGATION MOVED FORWARD. TOM had telephoned his men the serial numbers of the revolvers, and detectives were on their way to New Jersey to question the store clerks. At the same time, another team was trying to find out the sales history of the recovered sticks of dynamite marked "Keystone National Powder Company. 60 per cent. Emporium, Pa."

And now Woods had just called to tell Tom that the Washington police suspected Holt could have been involved with yesterday's attack on the Capitol.

Tom needed to formulate his next move. He walked by Holt's cell and stared at the prisoner lying on his bunk. "The man was getting tired: he had had a hard day, had been considerably battered, had been interviewed, photographed, harried with questions, his ankles and wrists ached, his head throbbed, and his mind, which though alert and active, was none too stable, and showing signs of exhaustion." Tom decided the moment had come for "a formal examination."

Erich Muenter being arraigned in court in Glen Cove, Long Island, where he was charged with the shooting of J. P. Morgan Jr.

The session convened at once, and this time it was in McCahill's office, where his assistant, two deputy sheriffs, two patrolmen, a detective from nearby Mineola, and a stenographer joined Tom. But it was still Tom's show. He asked the questions, and a smirking Holt continued to hold him at bay.

Question. Where were you born?

Answer. Somehow my brain is in such a shape that I can't remember—Wisconsin, I know. I don't know what it is that affected me—something inside of me—maybe it is the shock I got from that.

Q. You speak with a German accent. Were you born in Germany, or in any of the European countries—tell me the truth.

A. Now listen. That has been said before—that I speak with a foreign accent. That is because I speak several languages. I speak French, German, Spanish, and all that. That is the cause of that, you see?

Q. We will eliminate the trouble of asking you questions if you will tell us the town or city in which you were born.

A. Yes. Now I'm trying to think. (*A pause.*) I will have to disappoint you.

The thrusts and parries continued while Tom, with masterly control, inch by precious inch, subtly turned the questioning in a new direction. He needed to follow up on the lead that had come from the Washington detective. Could Holt have placed the bomb in the Capitol? Or was he just one of the plotters, part of that conspiracy too? Tom desperately wanted answers. But he knew if he blurted out his questions, Holt, disdainful, deliberately vague, an infuriating smirk on his face, would hold him off. Instead, Tom had to lead Holt slowly along to this destination. The prey could not realize he had stepped into a trap until it had sprung shut.

Q. How many times have you been in Philadelphia?

A. No time.

Q. You came to New York from Ithaca?

A. Yes.

Q. Do you mean to truthfully answer my question by saying that you have not been to Philadelphia at any time since you left Ithaca?

A. At no time.

Q. You have a clipping of a Philadelphia newspaper in your possession. Where did you get that?

A. I think I got that out of a Philadelphia paper of course, that I found lying around.

Q. Were you not in Philadelphia when you purchased that paper?

A. I did not purchase that. I saw that lying around somewhere, probably in the Mills Hotel.

This was the moment, Tom decided. A leap had to be taken, and now was the time. There was no pause, no alteration in his voice, nothing to signal that this wasn't the most casual of questions.

Q. Where did you sleep last night?

As soon as the question was asked, Holt realized he had been led into a corner. Desperate, he tried to create a distraction, his tone haughty and superior.

A. Now, I will tell you. A reporter from the Associated Press asked me about this Washington business, and he was trying to connect me with that. I suppose that is what you are trying to do.

It was Tom's turn to be indignant; and he let his genuine anger goad him on.

Q. I am not trying to connect you with anything. I want truthful answers. I am very frank and honest with you. I will fairly investigate every answer that you make.

Tom sensed that Holt was drained. The walls he had erected were tumbling down, and even the madness offered no more sanctuary. The prisoner let out a long, thin sigh, and surrendered.

A. I think it is just as well to say that I wrote that R. Pearce letter.
    I was in Washington yesterday and came back on the train.
I think it is just as well to say it.

Tom's demeanor betrayed no sense of triumph. He continued in his deliberate, thoughtful way to press for details about the Washington attack. But McCahill listened to only a few more of Holt's valiant attempts to pass off what he'd revealed as really nothing extraordinary at all before he rushed out of the room to send a telegram to Captain Boardman in Washington:

Frank Holt placed dynamite in Capitol building at 4 p.m. yesterday. Left Washington on midnight train for New York. Will wire particulars later.

AT HALF PAST SEVEN THAT night, Holt was moved to the county jail in Mineola. Tom had insisted. It was just a precaution, he told McCahill. And only later did the constable realize he had never asked the broad-shouldered New York police captain who he feared might come looking for the prisoner. Only later did he realize Tom had suspected a larger plot.

Front page of the *New York Tribune* on Sunday, July 4, 1915, after Holt's attempted assassination of J. P. Morgan Jr.

CHAPTER 48

————

In the course of a long and busy career, a veteran detective would handle so many investigations that once a case was solved, it'd be shoved into a file and quickly forgotten. But for most officers, unsolved cases could not be so easily dismissed. These mysteries would linger, churning away restlessly below the surface and rising up at odd, unexpected moments. And as Holt settled into his first night in the Mineola jail, a Cambridge, Massachusetts, police detective, Patrick Hurley, found himself suddenly thinking about a nine-year-old case.

He had been reading the description in the evening paper of the man accused of trying to assassinate J. P. Morgan when a single phrase unlocked his memory as if it were a key. The assailant was described as having "a shambling walk." These were the exact words he had used back in 1906 when he'd sent out the description of Erich Muenter, a Harvard instructor who had fled after poisoning his wife.

But even as Captain Hurley relived the anger and frustration he had felt at the time over Muenter's getting away with murder, he chided himself for jumping to conclusions. There must be thousands, maybe even tens of thousands, of people who had loose-jointed, shambling gaits; tuberculosis of the bones, the detective had discovered back when he was actively trying to track down the fugitive professor, was not an exceedingly rare condition. Still, he had a hunch.

He reread the newspaper description of Frank Holt, and he might as well have been holding up a mirror to the image in his mind. Every detail corresponded to his memory of Muenter: five feet ten inches tall; dark hair; long, thin face; high forehead. And a shambling walk.

That night he dispatched an express telegram to Chief Constable McCahill in Glen Cove. "Reason to believe," he wired, "Frank Holt is fugitive Erich Muenter wanted by Cambridge Police for murder." He advised that he would send a photograph of Muenter in the morning.

IN TOM'S WORLD, INDEPENDENCE DAY came, but it was not the holiday Sunday he'd been anticipating. He was up early, and soon on his way back to Mineola to interview Holt again. He had spent a fitful night assembling an inventory of his concerns, and on the ride out to the Long Island jail he found himself replaying them in his mind.

Yesterday, Holt had given him an account of how he'd made the bomb used in the Capitol blast. He'd taped together three sticks of dynamite, hollowed out a depression at the end of one of the sticks into which he'd fitted matches, and then placed a corked vial filled with sulfuric acid above the matches. When the acid ate through the cork, drops fell onto the match heads and caused a flame, which ignited the dynamite. It would have been an impressive device, Tom realized even while he was listening to the prisoner's earnest recitation, except for one thing: it would never have worked. During his years with the bomb squad, Tom had picked up a good deal of hands-on knowledge about the manufacture of bombs, and he had no doubt that everything Holt had told him was a lie. Sulfuric acid would take weeks to eat through a cork, and even then the drops of acid would not cause matches to burn. Holt, Tom was convinced, didn't know the first thing about making an explosive device.

But if Holt hadn't made the bomb, then who had? Were the bomb makers the same individuals who had given him the dynamite—and the money to fund his travels? And was there additional dynamite hidden away somewhere? They had recovered three sticks from his jacket and suitcase, and Holt said three sticks had been detonated at the Capitol, but Tom had "a feeling that Holt had bought more explosives."

In fact, little of what Holt had said made any sense—unless he was trying to cover up the fact that he had not been alone. Tom had tried to pursue that possibility yesterday, but Holt had been dismissive. "I think that can be easily figured out that I could not have anybody else with me," he had snapped at Tom in his now familiar superior voice. But after the long, restless night's calculations, Tom still found himself returning to the same provocative conclusion: "I felt confident that he had accomplices."

As soon as Tom arrived at the jail, he was handed a message to call Sergeant Barnitz. The Jersey City gun shop clerks, the sergeant reported, had found the sales slips. Holt had given his name as "Henderson" and his address as Syosset, Long Island.

Armed with this new information, Tom was escorted into a room where Holt was already seated. The prisoner seemed to have aged a decade or two overnight. He had not shaved, and his jailers had taken his suit as evidence, replacing it with a blue one that could easily have fitted a man twice his size. The sleeves stretched past his fingers, and the jacket swam about his thin, childlike chest. Tom saw his advantage, and swiftly attacked.

Why had he given this particular fictitious name and address? Tom demanded. He hoped Holt would be impressed that they had uncovered this intelligence after only hours on the case. Perhaps he would appreciate the resources aligned against him, and begin to cooperate.

Holt merely shrugged. The name Henderson had simply "popped into my head." As for the address, he had happened to see Syosset on a railroad timetable and the location had stuck in his mind. It was all—he sighed—of no consequence.

Tom returned to the dynamite. Where had he gotten it? How much did he have? Where was the rest of his cache?

In the course of Holt's own long night, Tom later suspected, the prisoner had worked out what he would say when these questions would inevitably be raised. Tom had kept tapping at them during the first day's session, and Holt had to realize he would not give up until he received answers. So Holt had devised a strategy to keep Tom off balance.

He announced that he would answer those questions on July 7.

Why July 7? Tom asked. What happens in three days?

But Holt would not yield. "Everything will be revealed on July 7," he repeated with a small, tight smile.

Tom had no doubt that Holt was enjoying the power his riddle had given him. He was a prisoner, handcuffed, beaten, humiliated, but now he had turned the tables on his interrogator: Frank Holt was once again in control.

Tom, exhausted, despairing, found himself silently conceding that Holt suddenly had an advantage. Either July 7 was more madness, a meaningless date provocatively tossed out to tantalize the authorities, or it was something more sinister. But what? Was it the date when his accomplices—German agents? antiwar activists?—would have completed their escape from America, and their existence could be revealed? Or was it the date of another round of attacks? Another assassination? Another bombing?

Either way, it was a mystery that Tom had to solve. He told the jailer to take the prisoner back to his cell. He needed time to think.

What would happen on July 7? He kept turning the question over and over, but he was unable to latch onto a persuasive answer. He called Barnitz, then Woods, but neither had a solution. So Tom decided to go for a drive. Perhaps, he hoped, escaping from the dismal jailhouse with its tight, airless spaces would free his mind. He drove for hours around the Long Island countryside. He had dozens of theories, and yet not a single one in which he had any faith.

When he returned to the jail, he discovered that the already complicated case had in his absence taken off in a whole new and completely unexpected direction. McCahill, following up on the telegram from Cambridge, had brought the Nassau County district attorney to the jail. The DA, in a stroke of luck, had studied German at Harvard with Muenter, and after a long look he decided that the prisoner was indeed his old college acquaintance. While in Chicago, the police had shown a news photograph of Holt to the two spinster sisters of the fugitive professor, and they offered an unqualified identification: he was the brother who had vanished. "The news will kill our mother," they worried.

It was a case, Tom was beginning to understand, in which the peeling away of one secret served only to reveal a new one. "This Pearce-Lester-Holt-Henderson-Muenter was becoming more interesting every minute," he decided with a new appreciation of the deceptively frail and downtrodden prisoner. "Wife-poisoner, dynamiter, gunman—what next?"

AS THE NEW WEEK UNFOLDED, Tom and his men scurried about, trying to discover what would be next. They needed to know what was going to happen before they were caught once again by surprise.

Tom went to Syosset to interview the freight agent. The conversation led him to the bungalow in Central Park. While there, he spoke with the boy who had pushed a wheelbarrow carrying a heavy trunk to the train for Holt. The stationmaster went through his records and found that the trunk had been shipped on to New York. He had a shipping number, but there was no record of where the trunk had been delivered.

Then all at once the mystery of the missing trunk took on a new urgency. The Aetna Powder Company reported that its books showed a C. Henderson as having ordered two hundred sticks of

60 percent dynamite, plus another separate order for two hundred sticks of 40 percent dynamite. A total of four hundred sticks had been sold to Holt. Tom felt the explosives could be in the trunk. But he no idea where the trunk was. And July 7 was Wednesday—two days away.

Desperate, he played the only card he had: he went to see Holt. But when he repeated his questions about the dynamite, Holt remained obstinate. "I will tell you Wednesday," he said infuriatingly.

Tom's patience had worn thin. He had tried everything with Holt, and it had all been futile. The prisoner gave only what he was prepared to give. Holt was playing Tom, and the realization of his own helplessness stung his pride.

"Look here," Tom at last exploded. "That dynamite is in the trunk. It's liable to go off any minute and kill a lot of people. You better tell me quick where you left that trunk."

And just like that, Holt agreed. "All right," he decided. The trunk, he said, had been sent to a warehouse near Fortieth Street and Seventh Avenue.

Sirens blaring, Tom and his men drove like madmen to the warehouse. The only person on duty in the evening was a watchman, and he had no knowledge of how items were stored. With an indifferent shrug, he told Tom that they were just going to have to search until they found a trunk with a number matching the one on the shipping invoice.

The warehouse was eight stories high and spread out over an entire city block. Led by Barnitz, six of Tom's men began the daunting search. They went one floor at a time, starting at the bottom and determined to work their methodical way up. Tom, meanwhile, went to call headquarters to report that they might have located the dynamite.

The desk officer had a message for him. "Commissioner Woods just called and wants you to call him at the Harvard Club."

"Get that trunk as fast as you can and find out exactly what's in it," the commissioner said as soon as he came to the phone. "Washington just called me to say that Governor Colquitt down in Dallas just wired them. He says Holt's wife got a letter from Holt dated July 2 that he's put dynamite on a ship now at sea. It will sink on the seventh."

So that's what would happen in two days: a ship would blow up! But which ship? And, just like Holt's last operation, where the Capitol bombing preceded the assassination attempt on Morgan, would this explosion be the opening salvo in a two-part attack? But Tom understood that those questions would need to wait. First he needed to find the dynamite. And if something happened while they were opening the trunk, there'd be no need to call in a report to Woods. Sitting in the Harvard Club on Forty-Fourth Street, the commissioner would be rocked by the blast.

More than two hours later they found the trunk in a dark corner of the fifth floor. There were a dozen other trunks on top of it, and they took care snaking it out of the pile and then carrying it down four flights of steep stairs. They wanted to open it in the well-lit ground-floor office.

With a single, precisely aimed swing of an ax, Barnitz snapped off the lock. Tom lifted the cover slowly.

Inside were, they counted, 134 sticks of 60 percent dynamite. The Glen Cove police had recovered 6 sticks.

Which meant 60 sticks of 60 percent dynamite were still missing.

As were the 200 sticks of 40 percent dynamite.

Tom suddenly understood why Holt had decided to reveal the location of the trunk. Once again, he had provided only a small corner of the entire story. He had held on to the rest, guarding it. The location of the 260 sticks—enough TNT to take down a skyscraper or a factory or police headquarters—remained a mystery. Tom's only hope would be to return to Mineola tomorrow and once again try somehow to get Holt to talk.

New York commissioner of combustibles Owen Egan displays Muenter's
trunk of explosives in the aftermath of Tunney's discovery.

He called the commissioner at the Harvard Club to report the discovery of the dynamite, and the disturbing fact that 260 sticks were
unaccounted for.

Woods listened, then invited him to come to the club. He said he
expected that Tom could use a drink.

Twenty minutes later, a welcome beer in front of him, Tom was seated in
the high-ceilinged lounge across from Woods and Scull. Their talk was fixed
on Holt. He remained a mystery, but they were determined to tug persistently
away at the few sparse facts they had. The three police officers wanted to believe that a solution was possible if they put their minds to it. As they kept at it,
a white-coated waiter came over and said the commissioner had a call.

Woods got up, and Tom continued the meandering, inconclusive
conversation with Scull.

In a moment Woods returned. The color had drained from the
commissioner's face, and he appeared shaken. Then Woods spoke in a
grave voice: "Holt is dead in Mineola."

CHAPTER 49

———

There were two versions of Holt's death, and each was official—at least for a while.

Both accounts started with Jerry Ryan, the guard assigned to watch the prisoner during the evening shift. Ryan had arrived at 8:10 on the night of July 6 and taken up his post in a straight-backed wooden chair. From his seat, he could look directly into Holt's cell.

Holt immediately started talking to the guard. Tomorrow, July 7, was going to be "The Day," he said. He was looking forward to it so much that he doubted he'd be able to sleep. "Oh, I want to sleep so bad," he told the guard.

Ryan watched the prisoner tossing about fitfully in his bunk and couldn't help feeling sorry for him. No matter what the man was accused of, he at least deserved a good night's sleep.

Ryan told him to stop thinking about tomorrow. Get some sleep, he advised kindly.

"I shall do everything I can to get some sleep," he said.

"Then I'll do all I can to keep things quiet for you," said Ryan.

Ryan was soon relieved to see that Holt was sleeping.

The door of the cell remained open. Warden William Hults had insisted. In case Holt tried to commit suicide, the warden wanted Ryan to be able to rush in without having to waste lifesaving time unfastening the three separate locks that normally secured the cell door.

At 10:35, Ryan heard a noise coming from another cell. He decided to go off and investigate. He thought, he later explained, another prisoner needed assistance.

He left Holt unguarded, and his cell door remained unlocked. He didn't even bother to close it. Ryan figured it'd be an unnecessary precaution. He wasn't going far, and anyway Holt was sleeping soundly.

The next thing Ryan heard was a powerful explosion. He was certain it was a gunshot. A pistol. Or maybe a rifle. He couldn't be sure; he knew only that the gun's blast was sharp and distinct. He immediately called to another jailer to get Dr. Cleghorn. Holt had shot himself, he yelled as he ran back to the cell.

Holt was lying facedown on the concrete floor outside the cell. A pool of blood spread around him.

When Dr. Cleghorn came, the two men turned the body over on its back. "He must have had a gun because I heard an explosion," Ryan told the prison physician. Cleghorn examined the corpse. Holt's skull had been badly damaged, but he identified two specific wounds. He decided they were bullet holes. "It looks as though he had blown his nut off," the doctor said.

This was the story the commissioner had shared back at the Harvard Club. Before Tom left, Woods had also divulged that Holt had not shot himself: a German had shot him. Tom grimly realized that "the international consequences of the case, which had been hovering just out of reach for the past four days, now seemed certain. And if Holt had been shot by a German, it was more than likely that he had been killed to prevent a further confession which would implicate the imperial German Government."

On the urgent late-night ride that evening back across the Queensboro Bridge to Mineola, as Barnitz pushed the car as fast as it would go, Tom, his heart thumping wildly in his chest, mournfully anticipated what would happen next. The nation "would certainly not brook the violation of its Capitol and the assassination of one of its chief figures by a German agent." War would be inevitable.

But in the next day's clarifying light, Tom was told to accept an entirely different story. Holt had not been shot at all.

It seemed, according to the account prison officials now gave to the newspapers, the prisoner had scrambled up the crossbars of his cell and then dived headfirst twenty feet to the concrete floor. It was suicide. Cleghorn had been mistaken about the bullet wounds; apparently they were injuries Holt had received during his capture at Morgan's home. And Ryan, after talking to the warden and giving the event some more thought, now said he was willing to accept the theory that the prisoner had committed suicide by plunging to his death; the noise he'd heard wasn't a gunshot but the impact of Holt hitting the concrete floor. Anyway, the coroner had already given his permission for the body to be embalmed. The inquest was scheduled for tomorrow, but coroner Walker Jones had told the press he had no doubts it would be "perfunctory."

IN THE DAYS FOLLOWING HOLT'S death, Tom waited for the press to start asking questions about whether the professor had acted alone and to investigate further the confusing circumstances surrounding his death. And for a few gratifying days there was a flurry of thought-provoking stories.

"Muenter's Acid Bomb Myth," read the tabloid headline on an article suggesting that a Cornell language teacher did not have the expertise to fabricate the sophisticated device that had been detonated at the Capitol Building. A subsequent supporting story in the *New York Times* reported: "Experiments conducted in the laboratory of the George Washington University by Professor Charles E. Munroe have failed to show that a bomb such as Erich Muenter, alias Frank Holt, said he used to blow up the Capitol would have exploded."

Other articles focused on the still-missing dynamite and the questions this raised. The *Times* provocatively wrote that "the police are ready to believe that Muenter got two lots of dynamite, one in person and the other through a confederate. They are ready to believe also that if he bought two lots his plots were being financed by others, as his own funds are known to run low."

And when Commissioner Woods was asked if Muenter had accomplices, he was prominently quoted as conceding that "it would be very dangerous to say no to that question. . . . There would be no development in this case so startling that it would surprise me."

Meanwhile in Mineola, Jerry Ryan, who had been assigned to guard the prisoner, was once again equivocating. "I refuse to be made the goat in this," he told reporters. "I have never decided," he went on dramatically, "whether Muenter jumped to his death, or was shot, or shot himself." And a follow-up article in the *Times* observed that "there was a window facing the cell. . . . An assassin would have to fit through two sets of bars."

In response to Ryan's statement and the *Times* story, the town's board of supervisors met with district attorney William Smith and then issued a widely reported statement: "The District Attorney is doing everything in his power to investigate and find out who is directly responsible for the act and will lay the whole thing before Sheriff Petitt . . . and if the facts warrant, further action will be taken and the persons responsible dealt with according to the law."

Tom read this and rejoiced. At last, he felt, there was going to be an official investigation into whether Muenter had been shot, and if so, how a gunman could have entered the jail.

But no sooner were his hopes raised than they were dashed. The next day a stern District Attorney Smith stated that the board of supervisors was "creating false impressions." He was not investigating a possible shooting. "What is all the fuss about?" he asked with a dismissiveness that Tom found infuriating. "There is no question that there has been negligence. We all know that."

And just as the promised Mineola investigation had come to a sudden halt, so did the appearance of probing stories in the press. Articles about Muenter, the circumstances of his death, the existence of possible accomplices, were apparently no longer newsworthy. It was all very strange. It was as if, Tom couldn't help feeling, the reporters had been told to let the story die, to stop raising questions.

Tom wondered if the editors were simply following orders. Perhaps, he speculated, the wealthy, well-connected men who owned the papers had been informed that a more aggressive pursuit of this story could very well have an irreparable consequence: the nation would have no choice but to go to war. Was it patriotism, some shared concept of what was in the national interest, that had led to the apparent embargo on what had previously been a provocative, headline-making story?

Tom had no answers. Yet he found himself acting more and more like a man in mourning. And when he thought about it, he realized he was grieving the loss of his case: it would never have a satisfactory conclusion. When Woods had given him command of his special task force, the commissioner had warned that some secrets might never be revealed. The circumstances surrounding Holt's death, he now suspected, were among them.

He felt utterly helpless. But he knew for certain that once the coroner ruled that it had been a suicide, "there went our case."

Which left him with only his suspicions.

He wondered where Holt had gotten the money for his mission, funds to travel to Washington, to Philadelphia, to rent a bungalow, to buy four hundred sticks of dynamite. He wondered who had suggested to the college professor that he pose as a representative of the *Society Summer Directory*. Who had made the bomb, provided the mysterious black Ford that Holt drove across Long Island? Where were the missing 260 sticks of dynamite, and would they become the core of new bombs? Had Holt traveled alone to Washington, to Glen Cove? Had someone helped plan his mission? And Tom couldn't stop wondering if Holt had been killed to make sure there would never be any answers to these questions, to keep the conspiracy a tight, guarded secret.

"If Holt was a German agent," Tom soberly conceded, "he died with his secret." Tom's sense of shame was palpable. It was his case, and he had allowed it to come completely apart. The conspirators—and he knew with all his well-honed cop's intuition that Holt had accomplices—had fled. They had sent their patsy off on a mission, and while Holt had paid for it with his life, they had escaped.

But there was nothing Tom could do. Or so he thought until two events helped to channel his disparate suspicions—and a living, breathing target became centered in his crosshairs.

First, his squad received a reliable report that "a woman appeared at the offices of J. P. Morgan on July 2, and attempted to warn the financier." She had come to inform him of "something that was going to happen the next day." Morgan did not see her.

Tom tracked her down, but he could not get her to state categorically that she'd had prior knowledge of the shooting. She said that it was too late to change things. It didn't matter anymore, she argued.

Yet it mattered to Tom. So he kept at it. And it didn't take him much digging to establish that the woman spent a good deal of time in the company of Franz von Rintelen.

Then, on July 7, an explosion occurred in the hold of the *Minnehaha*, a steamship carrying munitions to France. The boat was in mid-ocean, and the blast was so intense that it had ripped out a section of the upper deck.

Holt's prophecy had been fulfilled. And its realization riveted Tom's attention. Was it just an accident, pure luck, that Holt had succeeded in targeting a boat leaving New York during the first week in July, carrying war supplies? Since the fires had started, that sort of information had been carefully guarded. Another question: How had Holt, a stranger to the waterfront, succeeded in getting his bomb aboard the ship?

Tom had no proof, or at least not the sort of evidence he could take to the district attorney. But he no longer had any doubts that Holt had not been alone. He had joined up with a well-organized network of conspirators—the very group that was responsible for the ship fires. And Tom felt with equal certainty that Holt's handlers had received their orders from the man he'd seen walking down the block from the New York Yacht Club with a professional soldier's stiff-backed formality.

Tom made up his mind to do something. Ever since the British Section V station chief first told him about von Rintelen, Tom had suspected that Gaunt had a good deal more information than he was sharing. Tom, who had given the matter some thought, also had a notion about how the British had managed to know so much. It was, he'd deduced, the only answer that made sense.

He went to Guy Gaunt and asked for his help.

A WHITE-COATED ATTENDANT HURRIED ACROSS the sunlit breakfast room of the New York Yacht Club on the morning of July 19 and handed Franz von Rintelen a sealed envelope. Tearing it open, von Rintelen saw that there was no name, only an unfamiliar telephone number—and instructions to call it as soon as possible.

He left the room immediately to make the call, and was surprised to hear Karl Boy-Ed, the naval attaché, at the other end of the line. Boy-Ed curtly told von Rintelen to meet him in half an hour on a street corner.

As soon as von Rintelen arrived, the naval attaché handed him a cable from Berlin. It had already been decoded, and von Rintelen read:

To the Naval Attaché at the Embassy. Captain Rintelen is to be informed unobtrusively that he is under instructions to return to Germany.

Von Rintelen was shocked. He had previously instructed headquarters in Berlin not to use his name in any cables, and not to send him messages through the embassy. He believed that communications between Wilhelmstrasse and Washington were not secure.

And why would they want him back now, just when his schemes were making genuine progress? "The Irish were relying on me, our strikes had begun to boom again, and we were still placing bombs on the transports. All this would now come to an end," he would complain years later, the frustration and puzzlement still raw in his mind. Why, he wondered, had they sent this telegram?

But he had no choice but to obey. He was an officer in the German navy. Once again using the Swiss passport in the name of Emile V. Gaché, on August 3 he boarded the SS *Noordam* sailing from New York for Rotterdam.

Nine days later the *Noordam* approached the English coast. There would be a few days' routine delay as British sailors boarded the ship to check passports and inspect the cargo. Von Rintelen was not apprehensive; he took the inspection in stride. Still, "nobody who had done what I considered it my duty to do in America, and was in possession of a forged passport, would have been anxious to converse with British officers opposite the white cliffs of England," he later admitted.

The first day's inspection passed without incident. On the morning of the second day there was a knock on his stateroom door. The steward didn't wait for von Rintelen to answer before he called through the door, "Some British officers wish to have a word with you."

The steward sounded uneasy. But von Rintelen was not disturbed; he was confident he could talk his way out of any problem. He pulled himself out of the tub, put on his silk bathrobe, and opened the stateroom door.

There were two officers and ten sailors. The sailors had their bayonets leveled at his chest.

"You are Mr. Gaché?" a British officer asked.

"Yes. What can I do for you?"

"We have orders to take you with us."

"I have no intention of disembarking here. I am going to Rotterdam," he insisted bravely.

"I am sorry. If you refuse, we have orders to take you by force."

It was at that moment, staring at the bayonets, that von Rintelen understood that the telegram had not been sent from Berlin. It was a forgery, sent by someone who had knowledge of the German diplomatic code—someone who had led him into a trap. And as he was marched off the boat, surrounded by armed soldiers, he could not help suspecting that the long arm of Tom Tunney had reached across the Atlantic and finally taken hold of him.

PART VI:
TONY'S LAB

CHAPTER 50

———

In retrospect, the only concession that Heinrich Albert would make was that perhaps he should not have been so concerned about saving money. But as the infuriated Abteilung IIIB spymasters judged it, the German commercial attaché's entire conduct on that hot July afternoon in the summer of 1915 was a series of blunders, colossally poor decisions, and a total disregard for even the most elemental tradecraft. And as for economy, avoiding the $1.75 taxi fee was really not much of a savings, considering that it jeopardized a $40 million network.

At the very least, they argued, Albert, as paymaster for the German secret service in America, should have had a heightened sense of operational security. Especially after the sinking of the *Lusitania*.

TEN WEEKS EARLIER, ON MAY 7, 1915, a German U-boat off the south coast of Ireland shot a torpedo without warning into the Cunard passenger liner *Lusitania*. The bow of the fastest and largest steamer traveling the Atlantic, a gilded floating palace, began to dip precariously; the big gleaming boat started to heave; and then quite quickly it disappeared under the dark, rolling waves. The toll: 1,198 lost, including 124 Americans.

The nation was shocked. Germany had unleashed a cold-blooded attack against defenseless citizens, including women and children, of a neutral country. In retaliation, the outraged American press hurled volleys of indignant adjectives at the Hun: "savage," "villainous," "barbaric," "unspeakable," "homicidal." Even Edward House, the Texas militia honorary colonel who held court in the smoke-filled back rooms of Washington because of his role as the president's closest adviser, predicted the country would soon be firing off more than mere words. "We shall be at war with Germany within a month," he confidently stated.

An illustration made for the *New York Herald* and the *London Sphere* shows the RMS *Lusitania* as a second torpedo hits behind a gaping hole in the hull.

Germany responded stiffly to the uproar. The government ex-pressed "deepest sympathy at the loss of American lives," but at the same time noted uncompromisingly that the *Lusitania* was a blockade runner. The bulk of its freight was contraband: 4,200 cases of Rem-ington rifle cartridges, 1,250 cases of empty shrapnel shells, and a large shipment of foodstuffs. Von Bernstorff's stance was even more defiant. With a cold and unforgiving logic, he wrote that "the victims of the submarine campaign were far less numerous than the women and children killed by the English blockade, and . . . death by drowning was no more dreadful than slow starvation."

Six days after the sinking, President Wilson officially responded to the attack. His diplomatic note to the kaiser's government was another of his desperate attempts to tread the thin tightrope that stretched over the chasm between war and peace. The former professor pedantically lectured "that if a belligerent cannot retaliate against an enemy without injuring the lives of neutrals . . . a due regard for the dignity of the neutral powers should dictate that the practice be discontinued." Yet the commander in chief of the U.S. armed forces presented neither an ultimatum nor a threat if his request was ignored.

But even as the president struggled to, as he desperately put it, "do nothing that might by any possibility involve us in the war," he continued to read the dispatches from New York police commissioner Woods about the activities of German spies and saboteurs in America. The confidential summaries of Captain Tunney's reports filled him with a high-minded moral outrage. It had become increasingly obvious that Germany was fighting an undeclared war on American soil. And the death of American civilians on the *Lusitania* worked further to close the divide in his mind between the war in Europe and the war at home. National security, Wilson decided, required that a covert counterattack must be mounted against Germany's agents.

The day after he sent his patient, circumspect diplomatic note to Berlin on the *Lusitania* sinking, behind the scenes Wilson took more authoritative action. He instructed secretary of the treasury William McAdoo, whose department ran the Secret Service, to begin surveillance of German and Austrian embassy personnel.

"We rented an apartment," William Flynn, the head of the Secret Service, revealed years later, "and the telephone man led the wires in and hooked them up so that we had a telephone matching every telephone in the two embassies. When a receiver was taken down in the embassy a light flashed in the Secret Service apartment. When a phone bell rang in the embassy, one rang in our apartment. Four stenographers worked in relays, all expert linguists."

While in New York, the Secret Service eavesdroppers piggybacked on the wires Tom was already running. And teams of federal agents joined the ranks of Tom's watchers, supplementing the number of pavement artists following the suspected members of the German network about the city.

A horrified nation had clamored for action, but only in the shadows, in the heavily veiled secret war, did a new operational phase begin.

ALBERT WAS NOT CONCERNED. THE sinking of the *Lusitania* neither put him on alert nor suggested any need for greater caution. His disdain for an enemy led by a president who had ludicrously proclaimed in a recent speech that he was "too proud to fight" convinced him that there was no need to be suspicious. Or edgy. He was as safe in the streets of New York as he would be on the streets of Berlin.

To a small, if ultimately not very consoling, degree, his analysis was correct. Albert was not the watchers' target, or at least not the primary one. On July 24, 1915, it was George Sylvester Viereck, an American who was editor of the *Fatherland,* an unflinchingly pro-German newspaper, who was being followed.

When Viereck, a dandy with a bushy blond pompadour who had boasted that he'd gathered up the violets strewn on Oscar Wilde's grave and lovingly preserved those treasures in a glass jar, entered 45 Broadway in lower Manhattan, the Secret Service agent on his tail became concerned. In this building were the offices of the Hamburg-American Line, and there was no telling if Viereck would come out alone or with another potential suspect. W. H. Houghton decided he'd better not take any chances. He called over to the agency's operational headquarters on the top floor of the nearby Custom House and asked Frank Burke to join him.

Burke refused. It was Saturday and a scorcher; besides, he had plans to go to a baseball game. But Houghton insisted, and at three o'clock a resigned Burke was at his side when Viereck left the building. The editor was accompanied by another man—tall, older, his face bearing the dueling scars of a Prussian officer, a brown briefcase held as portentously as a sheathed saber at his side. Even more intriguingly to the agents, Viereck treated this unknown individual with smarmy deference. It was only later that the agents would deduce that they were staring at Dr. Albert, the German commercial attaché.

As the four men stood in separate pairs on the downtown city street, two seemingly small decisions were made that would have enormous consequences. The first was Albert's. He decided that there was no need to hail a cab to take him to his suite at the Ritz-Carlton uptown on Madison Avenue. Locked in his office safe he had $7 million in cashable drafts that he'd recently received from Berlin, but the skinflint banker in him thought a $1.75 taxi ride would be too unseemly an extravagance. On this hot afternoon, accompanied by Viereck, he walked to Rector Street and then up the long flights of stairs to the Sixth Avenue El train.

At the same time, the two federal agents quickly improvised a plan. They'd follow the two men; if the targets went off in different directions, Houghton would stick with the editor, while Burke would tail the man with the bulging brown briefcase.

At Twenty-Third Street, Viereck got off the train alone. Houghton gave his fellow agent a small, almost imperceptible nod, and then followed.

As the El continued uptown, the midsummer's humid heat washed over Albert and the steady, lulling motion of the moving train rocked him like an infant in a crib. He started to doze, and from his seat across the aisle Burke watched with amusement. He had been warned by Captain Tunney that some of these Germans were "slippery fish." They'd be on to you the moment you picked them up. Perhaps, but this one, whoever he was, didn't have a clue. He was sleeping.

The train ground to a stop at the Fiftieth Street Station, jerking Albert from his nap. Abruptly awake, he saw that the doors were open and this was his stop. He hurried from the train. In his groggy haste, he left the bulging briefcase on the adjacent seat.

Burke stared at it. He had no intimation that it contained anything of consequence. For all Burke knew, it held the man's lunch. He simply saw the briefcase lying there and, in an instant, made up his mind. He took it because he could. With the briefcase tucked under his arm like a football, he started to make his way to the rear door of the train.

Don't run, Burke told himself. Don't attract attention. But then he turned and saw that the man with the dueling scars had returned. He was rushing down the length of the car, his eyes darting wildly over each seat, an obvious panic lurching through him.

Burke dashed out of the car and hid behind a pillar, a commuter ostensibly lighting a cigar. He watched as the man whose briefcase he'd taken hurried, frantic, down a flight of stairs to the street. Full of a false calm, determined to act as if it were the most natural of journeys, Burke joined the bustle of people walking toward the other end of the platform. He continued along, not too fast, not too slow, and then descended the stairs.

On the street, an uptown trolley was passing, and Burke jumped onto the running board. He was silently congratulating himself when he heard the shouts. "Stop! Thief! That man has my briefcase!" He turned and saw the man with the dueling scars chasing frantically after the trolley. He was running swiftly, gaining on the slow-moving streetcar. Burke realized that when the streetcar pulled up at its next stop, the man would be waiting to jump on board.

"That guy's a nut," Burke told the conductor. He pointed to the agitated man trailing after the car, his pleading words made indistinct by the din of the city traffic. With just a glance, the conductor immediately confirmed the passenger's assessment: a lunatic was chasing his trolley. He had caused a disturbance on the train, too, Burke added.

The conductor hurried to the front of the car and told the motorman not to stop. A madman was after them.

The trolley continued uptown. Albert gave pursuit, his arms waving imploringly, his hoarse shouts insisting that the streetcar stop. But as Burke watched, the frantic man became an increasingly distant figure, and after several more blocks he had vanished from sight altogether.

After a while, Burke got off and, making sure no one was on his tail, switched to a downtown trolley. He rode it all the way to the carbarn, the briefcase—his furtive treasure—hidden beneath his suit jacket.

As soon as he got off, Burke found a telephone and called his boss, William Flynn. The two men rendezvoused at the Secret Service office in the Custom House down by the Battery.

It was Flynn who opened the briefcase. Inside were files crammed with papers, and fortunately, most were in English. He started to read, but as he quickly realized what he had, he stopped, too excited to continue. He knew what he had to do.

He sent a wire to Secretary of the Treasury McAdoo, who was at his summer home in North Harbor, Maine. "Must meet immediately on matter of utmost urgency," he wired. Without waiting for a reply, Flynn boarded a train to Maine that evening, the briefcase handcuffed to his wrist. Burke, now armed, accompanied him.

Albert, in the meantime, had gone to the German Club on Central Park South. Pulling himself together, reclaiming the bearing of a haughty diplomat, he sought out Boy-Ed and von Papen and confessed to a carefully edited version of the afternoon's events.

A thief, he said with as much dignity as he could muster, had stolen his briefcase. It contained, he feared, documents that would be embarrassing to the imperial government if they fell into the wrong hands. What should they do?

Boy-Ed wanted to know if Albert was certain the culprit was a mere thief.

Yes, Albert assured him. He was convinced that no one else would be interested in his briefcase.

Boy-Ed agreed. He too was certain the enemy had no idea about the commercial attaché's clandestine activities. They decided the loss of the briefcase was just an annoyance, the sort of inconvenience that could happen to anyone riding a New York subway. The thief would discover the files inside, curse his bad luck, and then toss them into the trash.

Still, an aide was sent to the offices of the *New York Evening Telegram* to place a classified ad:

Lost: On Saturday, on 3:30 Harlem Elevated Train, at 50th St. Station, brown leather bag, containing documents, deliver to G. H. Hoffman, 5. E. 47th St., against $20 reward.

THE MEETING WAS IN THE White House's Oval Office, but it was all Secretary McAdoo's show. He did the talking, while the president, Colonel House, and Secretary of State Lansing listened in mute attention.

With the precision of an accountant reciting a series of numbers, McAdoo reeled off the contents of Albert's briefcase. The documents spoke loudly for themselves. Each one was another incriminating footprint on a trail that led straight to the front door of the German embassy.

One set of papers detailed how Germany, using an American industrialist as a powerless proxy, had set up a munitions manufacturing plant in Connecticut. The Bridgeport Projectile Company had been incorporated for $2 million, and the plan was for it to buy up at exorbitant prices all the available raw materials and explosives necessary to fabricate bullets and shells—and in the process prevent firms that sold to the Allies from being able to fulfill their orders. It had already contracted with the Aetna Powder Company, one of America's largest manufacturers of explosives, to purchase its entire output up to January 1916. At the same time, the firm was eagerly seeking out munitions orders from British purchasing agents—orders that would promptly disappear into filing cabinets and never be delivered.

Bridgeport Projectile had also announced that it would pay unrealistically high wages, a policy designed to provoke envious workers at other plants to strike unless they received equal compensation. And Bridgeport was to be just the first factory in a nationwide attempt by Germany to gain covert control of the munitions industry: front men for Dr. Albert had made a $17 million bid on the Union Metallic Cartridge plant.

Another document was entitled "Steps Taken to Prevent the Exportation of Liquid Chlorine." Liquid chlorine was used in the making of poison gas, and American factories had previously been sending fifty-two tons of the chemical each month to the Allies. There was also a record of the $1.4 million that had been paid to the American Oil and Supply Company to buy up large quantities of carbolic acid, used in the manufacture of medical supplies, which would otherwise have been shipped to the Allies. And there was the outline of a plan to tie up all the American production of toluol, a key ingredient in the manufacture of TNT.

Then there was a series of documents that detailed payments made to encourage strikes and ensure the publication of pro-German stories in American newspapers. Journalists, union chiefs, cotton growers in Texas, Irish American organizations, German American groups—all received monthly stipends to do imperial Germany's bidding.

The briefcase was crammed with over one hundred separate documents; Albert had apparently thought there was no need to lock them in his office safe. McAdoo's presentation took some time. Predictably, when the treasury secretary finished, a mournful President Wilson looked as if he wished Burke had never taken the briefcase; if the government were to pursue legal action against the participants in these sordid schemes, he realized, the indictments and then the trials would push an already enraged nation closer to war. At the same time, the president was shocked and despairing. Wilson had always considered von Bernstorff to be a gentleman, but Germany's commercial attaché would not, he understood, have entered into these agreements without the ambassador's acquiescence.

Lansing raised a more practical issue. The United States, he said forcefully, cannot use these papers in court. It cannot be known that a government agent stole the property of a fully accredited diplomat. The nation would lose its standing in the international community.

At once Wilson was relieved; a seemingly unavoidable decision could be postponed. And suddenly he was in a hurry. He had no time to discuss the matter any longer. He turned to House and, quite peremptorily, told him to deal with the matter. Then he picked up a memo from his desk, his attention drawn to some other great issue.

House, however, was not prepared to let the matter rest. He felt personally betrayed by von Bernstorff, whom he had considered a friend. The Texan in him wanted revenge.

He brought the papers to Frank Cobb, the editor of the *New York World*. As long as the editor never revealed his source, he could print them all, House said.

On August 15, 1915, a banner headline appeared on the *World*'s front page: "How Germany Has Worked in U.S. to Shape Opinion, Block the Allies and Get Munitions for Herself, Told in Secret Agents' Letters."

The revelations caused a sensation. Newspapers all over the country picked up the *World*'s scoop. The schemes detailed in Albert's briefcase were reported on front pages across America. As for Albert, he issued a wordy, convoluted, legalistic denial of any wrongdoing that was sensibly ignored. Instead, inevitably, he became famously known as the "Minister Without Portfolio."

Von Bernstorff ran. It would be wiser to hide until the scandal passed, he decided, than to bluster through a response. Besides, the count had too much pride to embarrass himself with excuses when he knew there were none.

The Secret Service informed the State Department that the German ambassador had taken refuge in the Adirondacks, where "he has been buried for the last ten days with his inamorata." But while the federal agents simply viewed the randy diplomat with prissy disdain, Guy Gaunt, who knew a bit about peccadilloes, decided to make some mischief.

He got hold of a photograph taken of von Bernstorff in the Adirondacks. The married ambassador, a leer on his face, was in a bathing costume, his right arm wrapped around the waist of one adoring bathing beauty, his left snuggled beneath the breast of another.

Count von Bernstorff on vacation; photograph published in *The Sketch* on October 25, 1916.

Gaunt had the photo enlarged and then passed it on to the Russian ambassador, who had the compromising photo tastefully framed and, with a wicked vindictiveness, placed it prominently on his mantel. It attracted a good deal of snickering attention from the Washington diplomatic corps. When von Bernstorff returned from his self-imposed exile to resume his duties at the embassy, the photo began to appear in newspapers all over the country. Gaunt's complicity in its distribution was never suspected.

The kaiser, though, had no interest in how the photograph came to be reprinted in the American press. He was simply enraged. He had not rebuked Albert for riding on a subway with a trove of secret documents, but a strongly worded cable was sent to the head of his American spy network. His actions, the ambassador was bluntly informed, had embarrassed the German imperial government.

STILL, WILSON'S PATIENCE WAS INEXHAUSTIBLE. He now wearily conceded to House that "the country is honeycombed with German intrigue and infested with German spies. The evidence of these things are multiplying every day." Yet he refused to speak out against Germany's covert activities in America, remaining reluctant to take any actions or make any statements that would push the nation closer to war.

House, though, was alarmed. Prepared to jeopardize his invaluable friendship, he spoke bluntly, abandoning all his previous deference. The president was endangering the nation, he charged. The consequences of not directly confronting the German threat to the homeland would be grave and immediate: "Attempts will likely be made to blow up waterworks, electric lights and gas plants, subways and bridges in cities like New York."

The president was unmoved. Do not "oversimplify matters," he warned sternly.

As for Tom, he had dismissed the revelations in the Albert papers as a sideshow. They were, he said curtly, "fiscal shenanigans." The scandal that had become known as "the Bathing Beauties Episode" was, similarly, just gossip. He had larger concerns. He had been fighting a war where blood and smoke were real, where ships were bombed and great men were targeted for assassination. It had been his maverick's mission to defend the homeland, and the many battles in his long undeclared war had left him with a stubborn dread. He lived with the certain knowledge that an uncompromising enemy would unleash previously unimaginable acts of terror against an unsuspecting America. He feared what was yet to come.

CHAPTER 51

Anton Dilger.

D
r. Anton Dilger was coming home. The thirty-one-year-old physician had been born on an 1,800-acre farm spread across the green rolling hills of Virginia's Shenandoah Valley. His father had ridden as a lieutenant in the Duke of Baden's horse artil-

lery and after immigrating to America had brought further honor to the family by winning the Medal of Honor for his service as an artillery captain in the Civil War. His mother, also a German immigrant, was the granddaughter of one of Germany's most eminent physicians, Dr. Friedrich Tiedmann, celebrated in medical annals as "the great physiologist of Heidelberg." Hoping to emulate his maternal grandfather, Dilger had gone to Germany as a teenager to study medicine.

With impressive speed, the industrious Dilger launched a brilliant career. He passed his medical examinations at the University of Heidelberg in 1908 and then followed this up with graduate study in microbiology at Johns Hopkins in Baltimore. A year later he returned to Heidelberg to take an assistant surgeon's appointment in the university's vaunted surgical clinic, and at the same time he began research on his thesis. Just two years later, in 1911, this thesis, "Concerning In Vitro Tissue Cultures: With Special Consideration of the Tissues of Adult Animals," was published, garnering modest professional acclaim from the specialists in this newly emerging medical arena. When the war broke out, he left his practice in Heidelberg and, although still an American citizen, worked as a volunteer surgeon at a German field hospital. But now he was coming home.

It was early in October 1915, and as the Dutch passenger liner *Noordam* steamed into New York Harbor in the shadowy early-evening darkness, Dilger stood on deck. Tall and athletic, his thick jet-black hair brilliantined and combed straight back, with intense brown eyes and a perpetual smile on his handsome, chiseled face, Dilger carried himself with an easy, comfortable grace reminiscent of a leading man on the silent screen. A bit of a dandy, partial to well-cut vested suits and shirts that allowed him to flash the solid gold cuff links he'd received as a present from the king of Bavaria for his medical services, Dilger was well aware of the figure he cut. He was a charmer, too, convivial by nature and chivalrous in his affections.

In his hand he clutched a small black case that, if any of his fellow passengers inquired, could have passed for a doctor's medical bag. The bag was lined with a thick soft padding, and inside, wrapped for further protection in dark velvet like precious gems, were four glass test tubes, all firmly stoppered with a cork plug.

Two of the vials had a large capital *B* marked on the glass—an abbreviation for *bos*, the Latin word for "ox" or "cow." Each contained a brown gelatinous culture, the bacteria from which he would breed *Bacillus anthracis*: anthrax. The other vials were marked with a capital *E*, the first letter of *equus*, Latin for "horse." Inside were the cultures for *Pseudomonas mallei*, the microbe that causes glanders in horses and mules.

Abteilung IIIB had sent Dilger to America. Nicolai, encouraged by von Rintelen, had recruited the young physician to carry out von Steinmetz's aborted mission. Dilger was returning to the land of his birth to spread a plague of destruction.

THE HOUSE WAS PERFECT. IT was a cozy two-story brick cottage with a fireplace in the entry parlor and an ample living room that, if private matters needed to be discussed, could be closed off by a cherrywood sliding door; the two upstairs bedrooms opened onto a shaded roof terrace that could discreetly serve as an observation post to monitor the arrival of any unexpected visitors—the police? Secret Service?—coming up the road.

The location, too, could hardly have been improved upon. It was on Thirty-Third Street, a quiet block just off Connecticut Avenue in Chevy Chase. This was a new, fast-growing neighborhood near the nation's capital where developers were busily constructing comfortable family homes on what just a decade or so ago had been country fields. People were always moving in, delivery wagons constantly pulling up to front doors. No one would pay any attention to another new arrival, give a second thought to the loads of crates being delivered, or grow curious about the stream of craftsmen showing up to get a new home in order.

It was a suburban neighborhood, but it was not remote. The tram-line conveniently connected Chevy Chase with downtown Washington. The White House was only six miles—a pleasant fifteen-minute ride—away from the little house on Thirty-Third Street. And this, too, was what the Abteilung IIIB spymasters taught: hiding in plain sight was the shrewdest of covers.

Most appealing of all, what had convinced Anton Dilger to rent the house after only a brief walk-through, was the basement. It was about twenty-five feet square, a bit small perhaps, but well lit; there was an over-head electric bulb, and two rectangular casement windows let in daylight. And, an invaluable boost to operational security, it had its own private entrance. Just below the kitchen, a basement door opened into the backyard. Agents could arrive in the middle of the night to make pickups without any nosy neighbors growing suspicious.

Dilger asked his older sister, Em, to move up from the family farm in Virginia to live with him. With tactless candor he told the forty-eight-year-old woman she had wasted too many years living an isolated, lonely life in the country. In Washington, he pointed out, there'd be new opportunities. Besides, there was nothing to keep her at the farm; both their parents were dead.

Appealing shamelessly to the affection he knew Em felt for the brother she still called "my little Anton," Dilger said he truly needed her. She could keep house and serve as hostess when anyone came calling. And, although he wisely left this unsaid, her presence would discourage gossip. Washington was southern and conservative; the neighbors would feel more comfortable knowing that a spinster sister was keeping a watchful, almost parental eye on her good-looking bachelor brother.

Also left unmentioned was what he'd be doing. His sister had no idea that her brother was a German agent.

Accompanied by Em, Dilger moved into the house on Thirty-Third Street on a crisp October day in 1915. He listed his name and new address in the Washington, D.C., directories and gave his occupation as "physician." But Dilger had no license to practice medicine in America, and he had no intention of accepting patients. Instead, he went to work turning his basement into a germ warfare laboratory.

IN HEIDELBERG, DILGER'S LABORATORY HAD been spacious and gleaming, full of the most modern medical equipment. It was inspired by a visit he made to the impressive facility in Berlin where Dr. Robert Koch had done the pioneering work in bacteriology that had won him the Nobel Prize. While still a graduate student, mastering the techniques he'd need to propagate pure cultures of bacteria for his thesis, Dilger had always aspired to work one day in his own well-equipped lab. The lab in Heidelberg was the fulfillment of this dream, a research center where he'd be able to conduct the organ-transplant experiments that would one day save lives and earn him acclaim.

He had more modest ambitions for the lab in the small, square basement in Chevy Chase. Here he needed no sophisticated equipment. This room would have a single purpose: to produce germ cultures—deadly, highly effective killing machines.

Just as he had recruited his sister to help set up his household, Dilger enlisted his older brother to assist in the lab. Family, the Abteilung IIIB maxim had it, offered the most reliable guarantee against betrayal.

Carl Dilger was neither a medical doctor nor a scientist, but he was amply suited to help. He had worked at the Heurich Brewery in Washington and then set up his own brewery in Montana that had, until it went bust, produced a thick, creamy German lager. He had acquired the brewer's patient talent for propagating yeast and fermenting vats of beer; the lab technician's skill necessary for growing germ cultures would come easily to him. And when Dilger confided the nature of his secret mission, Carl had no misgivings. He was eager to assist the German terrorist plot.

But first they needed to turn an empty white-walled basement into a medical laboratory. The two brothers visited medical supply stores in the area and, freely spending Nicolai's money, ordered an incubation oven, a sterilizing machine, cases of petri dishes, and dozens of glass vials. Shipments of guinea pigs arrived, and so did small wire cages. Under Anton's direction machines were set up, shelves and worktables built, and guinea pigs housed in their cages. The two brothers worked in unison and with great smoothness; it was almost as if they were young boys again, doing chores on the farm.

For Carl, who was thirty-six and had not had a paycheck for a while, the opportunity to earn a weekly salary, even if he was taking orders from his younger brother, brought with it a renewed sense of accomplishment. For Anton, the activity involved in setting up the lab killed any lingering doubts he had about the ethics of his lethal work.

As a doctor, Dilger had pledged to do no harm. In Berlin and on his journey to Washington, there had been unsteady nights when he struggled with the distance his new life as a terrorist would take him from his heartfelt, life-affirming vocation. But the long days working with his brother, as the basement room was transformed into what they both proudly called "Tony's lab," brought him a new appreciation for the practical challenges he would soon be facing. These thoughts overwhelmed the occasional stabs of uncertainty. His focus centered only on the mission. He was ready to initiate the next stage of his attack on America.

A SINGLE BREATH COULD BE dangerous. Even lethal. Dilger worked with extreme care, each movement assured and deliberate. Wearing surgical gloves, he removed the stopper from the vial labeled "B" that he had brought from Berlin, containing the gelatinous culture for *Bacil-*

lus anthracis, the anthrax microbe. A stale odor filled the small white-walled room. He knew it was the smell of death.

He stood the vial upright in a test-tube rack and began sterilizing a thin wire loop by holding it over a high flame. When the wire had cooled, he inserted it into the vial. It was a slow, painstaking procedure. Steady, he told himself. A rushed movement, a sudden jerk of his arm, would have disastrous consequences.

The petri dish marked "I" had already been prepared with a dark, soupy mix of beef broth and blood. This was the growth medium.

With great delicacy, he removed the wire from the vial and then ran it lightly through the rich, fertile soup in the petri dish. In time virulent new anthrax microbes would germinate. In about a week, petri dish I would contain enough germs to start a toxic plague.

Propagating the germs in the second set of vials, marked "E," for *equus*, was trickier. These contained *Pseudomonas mallei*, the glanders microbe. Working with Carl, Dilger had earlier prepared the growth medium—ragit-agar glycerin. This was a dried culture produced by a German chemical firm, and it had to be mixed with boiled water and then left to gel. The process took several days, and there was always a concern that the delicate mixture would be contaminated. Dilger had taken great care to make sure the gel had hardened in a completely sterile environment.

Using another preheated metal loop, he inserted the glanders microbe into the chemical gel. Incubation would take possibly a week—this was not an exact science—and the temperature would need to be constantly monitored; too much heat or sunlight would kill the bacteria. If all went well, in a few days a yellowish paste that resembled curdled milk would form on the surface of the glycerin mix. After several more days it would molt into a brighter yellow, and then turn a muddy brown: the glanders germ.

For now, all Dilger could do was wait. One afternoon Em had several neighbors from down the block come by. They sat in the sun-filled living room, where she served coffee in the heirloom china cups she had brought up from the farm in Virginia, and a large plate filled with cookies she had baked that morning. Her brother told amusing stories about his years in Germany. As they talked and laughed, in the basement the lethal germs silently grew to life.

CHAPTER 52

———

Little Bremen was what people had taken to calling Hoboken, New Jersey, and with good reason. Its port was home to two major German steamship lines, packs of German sailors stranded by the British blockade prowled its waterfront, street-corner newsboys hawked German-language newspapers, the bars echoed with rowdy choruses of "Ach! Du Lieber Augustine," and on Sundays Lutheran ministers delivered sermons in German to crowded congregations. In its proud and boisterous way, this town on the Hudson River felt as much a part of the Fatherland as the one on the banks of the Weser. And it was in Hoboken, as von Rintelen was interned in an English prison camp (later he would be extradited to the United States and spend the remainder of the war as a prisoner in the federal penitentiary in Atlanta) and Dilger set up his base six miles from the White House, that Tom now decided to refocus his exasperating, seemingly unending search for the ship bombers.

It was another strategy Tom had settled on largely by default. In the days after Fay was caught red-handed in the Jersey woods and the initial optimism that the case would soon be reaching a climax had proved false, Tom found himself going back over old ground. "We resumed patrolling the river in various disguises," he recalled with weary frustration. When that uncovered "absolutely nothing to excite suspicion," in his desperation he "returned to our sugar theory and the Chenangoes." But this second go-round was not an iota more productive than the first. Once again, the inquiries were time-consuming and futile.

Searching for an entirely new investigative street to travel, Tom decided to try Hoboken. Without any hard evidence to bolster his suspicions, he felt it was a city bristling with the wildest sort of pro-German sympathies. He had walked its beery streets, hearing German openly spoken without shame wherever he went, and in his mind he could see the legions of restless sailors and their officers goose-stepping to their battleships if they were given the chance.

He settled on a plan, but even he would be the first to concede it was simply a fishing expedition. He chose Detectives Barth, Corell, and Senff, three men who had grown up in immigrant households and whose German was as good as their English, and sent them across the river to Hoboken. They were instructed to troll the restaurants, saloons, and hotels where the officers and petty officers from the German ships gathered to pass their vacant time. As for bait, Tom told the detectives to dangle the vague suggestion that they had ties to the German secret service.

Don't egg them on with contrived cloak-and-dagger stories, Tom warned. Hints, he knew, would be more enticing than even the most exciting lies. Let them decide to swallow the hook. The secret world was an exotic playground, especially to men far from home with nothing but more humdrum days in their future. "A nod here, and a wink there, a whisper and a wag of the head"—that'd be all it would take, Tom told his undercovers. "Fish about," he said with a playful confidence, all the time silently praying it would be as easy as he had promised.

IT ALMOST WAS. BARTH HAD been cultivating a petty officer for nearly a week. He met him in a Hoboken bar, and over the nights that followed Barth drank an ocean of beer and listened with feigned interest to a long saga that kept returning with a drunken logic to the petty officer's unrequited love for his older brother's wife. In the rare pauses in the petty officer's tale, Barth would fill the silence with subtle hints that he lived a secret life and that his orders came directly from powerful men on Wilhelmstrasse.

They had just drained one more tankard dry and were waiting for the next round to be brought to the table when the petty officer leaned in close. It was the night of the sixth day of this new friendship, and a weary Barth assumed he was about to hear another whispered fantasy about what the petty officer would like to do with his brother's wife. Instead, he heard an altogether different sort of revelation.

The petty officer confided that he knew someone else who'd been doing secret work for Germany. He asked if Barth would like to meet him.

THE ARRANGEMENTS TOOK SEVERAL DAYS. Barth suggested one place to meet, only to learn the next evening that the petty officer's mysterious German friend considered anywhere in Hoboken unsafe even for a clandestine sit-down. The agent, the petty officer explained, believed the city was crawling with undercover policemen. Ridiculous, Barth responded with what he hoped was convincing indignation. Any cops around here, he said, he would've spotted them.

But after some perplexing back-and-forths that left Tom wondering if the petty officer was simply playing with his detective, they finally settled on a restaurant in Manhattan. Hahn's was on Park Row, the kind of place that German immigrants were quick to establish anywhere, with steaming wursts, platters of pickled herring, and heavy beer on tap.

Barth approached the table, and before he could sit, the man next to the petty officer rose. With exuberant formality, he pumped the detective's hand as if they were celebrating the signing of a treaty. To

Barth's wary eye, he didn't have the sinister demeanor of a German agent. Tom, in fact, would later describe him as "a funny little old man who looked like a cartoon of the late Prussian eagle."

He introduced himself as Charles von Kleist. And although Barth's instincts offered him no hint of the enormous prize within his grasp, this was the same Captain von Kleist who had worked hand in hand with von Rintelen.

For a sullen Barth, the meal played out as a disappointment. The old man kept telling blatantly absurd sea stories, and the petty officer kept ordering more rounds of beer. Barth sat there saying very little and wondering how he was going to justify the cost of the lunch to Captain Tunney.

It was after dessert had been served that von Kleist fixed Barth with another of his wide, happy smiles. He was very glad to meet a real agent, he said respectfully.

Why is that? Barth asked. He was just playing along; days ago, or so it seemed to the bored detective, he had lost any real interest in the conversation drifting about the table.

Von Kleist explained that he had a grudge against a man in Hoboken who claimed he was a member of the German secret service.

"You can't be too careful of those fellows," Barth said with knowing authority. "There are a lot of fakes around. What's he done to you?"

"This Scheele, he has a laboratory, where he has been doing work, making some things. I was his superintendent now for a long time, and he owes me several hundred dollars, but he does not pay me. I think Captain von Papen ought to know about it."

"So do I," said Barth, his sympathy unflinching. "I'll see that it gets to him."

The detective waited a moment. He didn't want to sound too eager. He wanted to make sure his voice did not betray the excitement he was feeling. "What was it you were doing over there?" he asked innocently.

Von Kleist proceeded to tell him. He spoke laboriously, with a

Prussian exactitude. As he saw it, he was a wronged agent reporting a formal grievance to a superior.

Dr. Walter T. Scheele, von Kleist began, had been employing him in his laboratory in a factory at 1133 Clinton Street, Hoboken. The ostensible business was the manufacture of agricultural chemicals. The real business was the manufacture of bombs. Ernst Becker, the chief electrician on the *Friedrich der Grosse*, and Carl Schmidt, its chief engineer, fabricated containers out of sheet metal on the liner. The seamen would deliver them to the laboratory, and he worked with Scheele to fill them with explosives. Then Becker would take them away and distribute the bombs to the men who planted them on the ships. It was a very effective operation.

"But what good does it do me," he complained, "if I don't get any pay?"

"You wait," assured Barth. "I'll get you fixed up. I know a man. I'll have him meet you. If what you say is true, you certainly have something coming to you. Wait till I get this other man."

Von Kleist reached out and once again pumped the detective's hand effusively. He was very pleased. He said he knew his new friend would be able to help.

WHAT SHOULD TOM DO?

Barth's report brought the promise of the end of his long quest.

But, he reminded himself, he had been fooled before: first by the lighter captains who had turned out to be common thieves; and then by Fay, who had proved to be a different sort of saboteur. How could he be certain the ship bombs were being manufactured in the Hoboken lab? Or that the sailors on the *Friedrich der Grosse* were also involved? What proof did he have besides the story told by an old man, who, Tom had subsequently discovered, was famous all over Hoboken for telling tall tales?

He considered raiding the Hoboken factory and seeing what that would yield, but he also wondered if von Kleist had told the entire story. If Tom acted now, would he be hauling in only minor players while the key operatives escaped and the bombings continued? It certainly seemed possible that the old sea captain had embroidered his role in the conspiracy. Perhaps, in fact, the whole operation was another of his yarns. And Tom's raid would be one more embarrassment, one more dead end. He'd find nothing but vats of agricultural chemicals.

In the end Tom decided that Barth, in an inspired moment, had provided him with an opportunity. It was a way to get the confirming evidence his tidy mind needed before making any move. Barth had promised von Kleist he "knew a man." Well, Tom would make sure the sea captain got to meet him.

ONCE AGAIN THEY GOT TOGETHER at Hahn's, only now Barth brought with him a Herr Deane, a big man with a hard, no-nonsense face. An unlit cigar was stuck in the corner of his mouth as if he had been born with it.

"Herr Deane doesn't speak German," Barth announced jovially. "But he's a good man nonetheless."

A trace of suspicion crossed von Kleist's face.

"We have to use all kinds of people to fool these stupid Yankees, see?" Barth quickly confided, a professional sharing a bit of tradecraft.

Von Kleist relaxed, flattered that an Abteilung IIIB agent would share operational secrets with him. He never suspected that Herr Deane was Detective Sergeant Barnitz.

As the meal continued, von Kleist once more laid out his angry case against Scheele. He was determined to convince Herr Deane to persuade the people at the top to pay him the money he was due. "If you want any more proof, I'll show you," he volunteered. "Come to my house."

They took the ferry to Hoboken, and von Kleist found a shovel in his ramshackle garage. He started digging in a muddy corner of his yard while the two detectives watched in silence. They exchanged bewildered looks as the old man's hole grew deeper. They had no idea what was buried.

Von Kleist lifted a box out of the ground. Dusting the dirt off the top, he said, "This is one of them—and I have filled dozens like it."

He opened the box.

Inside was an exact duplicate of the cigar bombs that had been found on the *Kirkoswald*.

CHAPTER 53

———

"Let's go for a ride," Barth suggested. Now that the two detectives had seen the cigar bomb, he was eager to get von Kleist out of Hoboken and back to New York, where they had the authority to make an arrest. But he didn't want to spook his prey. Barth wanted the old man to go back willingly across the Hudson. And he wanted von Kleist to keep on talking.

"We can go down to Coney Island and have supper," he said. "The hotel has opened up, and we'll talk things over," he went on, taking care to soft-pedal every step of the way.

This was better than von Kleist had expected. Not only was Herr Deane going to get him the money Scheele owed him, but his two new friends were going to treat him to a meal at the Shelburne. He had never been to the restaurant in the Brighton Beach hotel near Coney Island. It wasn't the kind of place he could afford. But he hoped there'd be the strong salty smell of the sea wafting through the dining room, and with the evening ocean breezes coming in from the Atlantic an old sailor could pretend he was back at the helm with the deck pitching and rolling beneath his feet. Let's go, he agreed eagerly.

The three men had made their ravenous way through huge steaks, and Herr Deane was about to light up an after-dinner cigar when, match in hand, he paused. "How about," he said to von Kleist as if the idea had just occurred to him, "I write out a statement of the services you told me you performed for this Scheele? This is just for the sake of regularity, you understand. I have to have a written report to give to the chief, or else you won't get yours. You can sign this as your formal statement."

Von Kleist suspected nothing. Herr Deane was his champion. He'd sign the statement, and the chief would read it and then set things right. "All right," he agreed.

Herr Deane pulled out a memo pad and a pencil and started to write. With impressive accuracy, he recounted everything just as von Kleist had told it. When he was done, the old sea captain quickly read the three handwritten pages and then signed his name at the bottom of the final page with a flourish.

"How long do you think it will be before I could get some money?" he asked.

"Oh, don't worry about that part of it," Barth said reassuringly. "I tell you what we'll do. We'll all go up to see the chief now. I want him to meet you anyhow, and you can supply any more facts that we may not have put down."

The three men drove back into Manhattan, chatting all the way. It was only as Barth pulled the car up in front of the domed headquarters building on Centre Street that von Kleist realized he had been deceived.

"I see now why you have been so good to me," he said with forlorn resignation.

EVERY INTERROGATION WAS BUILT AROUND a strategy of deceptions. Tom sized up the docile old man and decided that he'd proceed with unflagging geniality. He'd flatter von Kleist with respectful curiosity and an almost deferential responsiveness. He'd lull the saboteur into thinking he had been apprehended by stolid, by-the-book policemen, and not very astute ones at that.

Captain Charles von Kleist.

Tom began at precisely the point where he had ended with Robert Fay. He displayed the *Kirkoswald* bomb and said it had been found on board the ship when it had docked in Marseille.

"Yes," von Kleist agreed obligingly, "it was supposed to explode within four days, but it didn't explode in twelve."

"How many did you make?" Tom asked. His tone was blunt and professional. He was very conscious that it would be a mistake to reveal his realization that his long, winding investigation had at last gotten on track. Or his growing sense of triumph.

"I don't know how many," the prisoner said. But, as if to apologize for his faulty memory, he quickly added, "The ones that were put on the *Inchmoor* and *Bankdale* went off all right. And there were two fires on the *Tyningham*. I gave one box of thirty of them to two Irishmen from New Orleans, O'Reilly and O'Leary. They took them down there to set fires to ships with them."

Tom paused for a moment to consult the statement Barnitz had written and von Kleist had obediently signed. Ernst Becker, the chief electrician on the *Friedrich der Grosse*, had played a key role in the operation. It was worth a try, he decided. "Did you give the rest to Becker?" he guessed.

"Yes. And he gave them to Captain Wolpert. Wolpert is the superintendent of the piers of the Atlas Line over in Hoboken. Captain Bode, he is also a superintendent, for the Hamburg Line."

Tom was experiencing an incredible night. The prisoner was talking easily, providing confirming details, giving up names. All Tom's previous mistakes, all the false scents, no longer mattered. "Will you tell me everything about the plot, from its beginning up to the moment?" Tom asked.

Von Kleist said he would. He was now going to help the United States, he pledged.

Captain Otto Wolpert *(center)* stands on the right of Ernst Becker.

Only Tom could not believe it was going to be this easy. He suspected that despite all the evidence of von Kleist's eager cooperation, the prisoner was holding back. There was more the old man knew, and more he wasn't telling.

So Tom told von Kleist he had to make his report to Chief Woods. He'd return when he was done.

VON KLEIST SAT ALONE IN the room. As the minutes slowly passed, the gravity of his predicament pressed down on him. He now inhabited a much darker world than he had only hours ago. He needed, he realized, to get word to his friends in the network. He needed to warn them.

He also needed their help. With nowhere else to turn, he convinced himself that they were his salvation. With their assistance, somehow he might extricate himself from an impossible future.

His troubled thoughts were suddenly interrupted as the door to the room opened. A man in a work shirt and overalls, a ladder in his hands, entered. Von Kleist watched as the workman set up the ladder and began to change the overhead lightbulbs.

He worked in silence, paying no attention to the prisoner.

Von Kleist, by nature, was gregarious. And his harrowing situation only reinforced his need for a moment's diversion. Without thinking too much about it, he struck up a conversation with the janitor, asking him about his job, what it was like to work in police headquarters.

When the worker responded, von Kleist realized his words carried a slight German accent.

"*Sie sind Deutsch, nicht wahr?*" he asked excitedly.

"*Ja,*" said the janitor. He was German.

After all the solitary time he'd spent searching for a bit of clarity, for a clever way to spring himself free from the trap he'd walked into, von Kleist suddenly understood he had been presented with a fortuitous opportunity. Speaking in German, he asked the workman if he'd be willing to do a fellow countryman a favor.

"*Ja,*" the man responded enthusiastically.

"Deliver these notes for me, will you?" von Kleist went on, a revitalized man. "I can't get out of here, and I would like to send word to some people."

Fearful that at any moment Captain Tunney would return, he quickly scribbled four terse notes. The messages were identical: "Run! I'm in custody." He addressed one to each of the conspirators whose names he'd earlier revealed, and then handed the four slips of paper to the workman. They'll reward you, he promised.

The workman put the notes in the pocket of his overalls and then shook the prisoner's hand as if to seal the arrangement. He closed the door behind him as he left the room.

For the first time since he had been led into police headquarters, von Kleist was beginning to think that not all was lost. He had warned his compatriots, and they would not let him down. Germany would repay his loyalty and service by finding a way to get him out of this mess.

Then Tom came into the room. And with him was the workman— only now he was wearing a policeman's uniform. "I'd like to introduce you to Detective Senff," Tom said.

At that low moment, von Kleist knew there was no escape. He had no choice but to tell all he knew. Nothing could save him.

IN THE EXULTANT DAYS THAT followed, Tom refused to rest or even pause for a moment to enjoy his victory. He immediately swooped into action. One team of men burst into the offices of Atlas Line and Hamburg-American Line in New Jersey and invited the superintendents "to come to headquarters to consult with us in a little waterfront investigation we're carrying out." Senff snared Becker, the chief electrician on board the *Friedrich der Grosse,* by posing as a messenger. He delivered a whispered warning in German: "Von Kleist wants to see you. Trouble." Becker grabbed his hat, and a dutiful Senff led him off to meet von Kleist—at police headquarters. With guns drawn, Tom led his men in a charge up the gangplank of the *Friedrich der Grosse*. He took into custody the engineers who had made the bombs and the sailors who had delivered them to the ships embarking for Allied ports. They raided the factory in Hoboken, climbed through the trapdoor into Scheele's secret laboratory, and discovered a dangerous trove of explosives and chemicals. Scheele, though, had run. It would be another two years before he was arrested by the Cuban police in Havana and extradited to New York.

But the other conspirators were in custody, and most of them were talking. Becker, thin, ghostly pale, and surprisingly young, confessed that he had fabricated several hundred bomb containers, including the ones found on the *Kirkoswald*. He said Carl Schmidt, the chief engineer, had helped, and that they had delivered them to Captain Wolpert in his offices at the Atlas Line.

The Hamburg-American Line piers in Hoboken, New Jersey.

Otto Wolpert, however, was less cooperative. He was a large, burly man with bright red hair and beard, and a drinker's flushed face that was only a shade lighter. Tom realized he would need to push him into a confession.

"Captain Wolpert," he said, "don't you think you're doing Germany more harm than good by doing this sort of thing?"

"Damn it!" Wolpert exploded. "But you've got to do what those bullheaded fellows tell you, haven't you?"

"Did you know Robert Fay, Captain?" Tom asked. He wanted to throw out his nets as widely as possible and see what he would trap.

"Yes. I met him one time in Schimmel's office with Rintelen."

Tom had no idea who Schimmel was. But he filed the name away while he chased after bigger prey. "You mean *von* Rintelen?" he challenged.

"No!" shouted Wolpert, his face now as red as his beard. "Not *von*, damn him—*Rintelen*!"

And Wolpert's anger gave a new fluency to his words. He started talking, part confession, part vengeful payback to the man he felt was ultimately responsible for his arrest. He freely shared details about von Rintelen's many activities. He even revealed that, using the alias Hansen, von Rintelen had accounts in a variety of New York banks that continued to fund the network.

In time, Wolpert's meandering yet exhaustive account mentioned a lawyer whom he had seen once or twice with von Rintelen—Bonford Boniface. Wolpert had no specific knowledge of Boniface's role in the network, but Tom was eager to pursue any connection to von Rintelen. The unanswered questions that surrounded the assassination attempt on J. P. Morgan and, no less perplexing, the events surrounding Holt's—or should he say Muenter's?—death continued to eat at him. His orderly mind demanded answers. He wanted to know for sure who else had been involved. He needed to hear his suspicions about von Rintelen's role in the conspiracy confirmed. He told his men to bring in Boniface.

To Tom's great disappointment, Boniface quickly made it clear that he knew nothing about the events surrounding the attempt on J. P. Morgan's life. He had never discussed the incident with von Rintelen, he insisted. Tom wasn't sure if he believed him, but he was willing to let the matter go for now. Instead, with no intimation of the sinister territory he was about to enter, Tom matter-of-factly turned the interrogation in another direction.

When his men arrested Boniface, they had discovered two letters on the lawyer's desk. One was postmarked Buenos Aires, and the other was from Holland. Both were signed "Karl Schimmel." The text of the letters was banal, but Tom couldn't help wondering if this was the same Schimmel whom Wolpert had mentioned, the man in whose office he had met Fay. He wanted to know what role Schimmel played in the network.

Boniface talked freely, his lawyer's mind already calculating the deal he'd negotiate with the district attorney in return for even further cooperation and testimony. He told Tom he had provided Schimmel with a weekly list of all steamships leaving New York for Europe.

Tom asked where had he delivered the reports.

In his office. At 51 Chambers Street.

For the past three weeks, every day had been filled with endless interrogations; and in the course of this long ordeal, the wide-ranging activities of the German spy network in America had been fleshed out. Yet at this point in the process, with the mystery of the ship bombings solved, the chase had lost some of its urgency. An exhausted Tom had taken to poking about aimlessly. Now he followed his investigative instincts, and then waited to see what would turn up.

Tom asked whom Boniface had seen in Schimmel's office.

The lawyer said that von Rintelen had been there once. But Boniface didn't know what his business was.

Anyone else?

Boniface volunteered two names: Captain von Steinmetz and Herman Ebling.

What did they do? Tom asked. These were new names to him, and he doubted that they could be significant. The question had shot out reflexively.

Boniface hesitated.

Suddenly alert, Tom sharply ordered him to continue.

Von Steinmetz, Boniface stated with newfound gravity, had smuggled anthrax and glanders germs into America. Ebling had worked for him. They had inserted germ-coated sticks into the nostrils of horses that were about to be shipped overseas. They had hoped to cause an epidemic, but the cultures were weak. They didn't work.

Germany had launched a germ warfare attack in America. Tom was stunned. All of his worst fears were suddenly becoming real.

Where was von Steinmetz? Ebling? he demanded.

Boniface said he didn't know.

Are they going to try again? Has a new shipment of germs been smuggled into the country? Tom pressed.

Once again, Boniface said he didn't know. Then he hesitated.

Tom fiercely told him to answer the question.

Boniface now spoke with the perfect calm of a man who has come to accept that the impossible is indeed true. He said that before von Rintelen had left the country, the agent had cabled his superiors. He had urged them to launch a new germ attack.

CHAPTER 54

———

Dilger was happiest when he was working. It had always been that way, whether it was in his Heidelberg surgery or in the field hospitals. He would throw himself into the task at hand and quickly become absorbed. And so that afternoon when he was in the basement lab monitoring his incubating cultures and heard the knocking on the front door, his instinct was to ignore it. He wasn't expecting anyone; it was probably just a salesman or a neighbor. If he stayed in the lab, the visitor would go away.

When the pounding on the door continued, an exasperated Dilger decided he'd better investigate. He peeled off his rubber gloves, carefully washed his hands, and then hurried up the stairs.

He opened the door to a big, rough blond man, with the trapped look of a seaman in dry dock and a thief's darting eyes. His outfit was exotic and marked him as a foreigner: a tweedy gray hiking suit with a jacket that ended at his ample waist; a green fedora with a small feather stuck in the band; and sturdy black boots that reached up nearly to his knees. On guard, Dilger said hello.

The man answered in German. "I'm Captain Hinsch," he said. "I think you have some packages for me."

Captain Frederick Hinsch, German operative and commander of the *Neckar*.

At once Dilger relaxed: this was one of von Rintelen's men. In Berlin, he had been told about the Baltimore network the secret agent had assembled. Its control—and paymaster—was Paul Hilken, who although in his early thirties was still, Dilger had been warily advised, very much his father's pampered son.

The senior Hilken was head of the local office of the North German Lloyd shipping fleet as well as Baltimore's honorary German consul, and he freely used his wealth and position to cushion his son's life. He had sent the youth to Lehigh University and then on to study graduate engineering at MIT, had bought him and his new wife a sprawling house in Baltimore's posh Roland Park section, and, until the war broke out and the company's shipping business came to a halt, had been grooming him to become the managing director of German Lloyd's New York office.

When von Rintelen decided to expand his sabotage operation south to the busy port of Baltimore, he had summoned the younger Hilken to the

Ritz Hotel in Philadelphia. Hilken had been apprehensive; his father had already revealed that Captain von Rintelen was a spy. Father and son had also already agreed that it would be foolish for the young man to jeopardize his comfortable life by signing on for secret duties. However, the wily von Rintelen, first with charm and then with patriotism, won him over.

The operation needed, the secret agent explained in a hushed voice as the two men sat opposite one another in the Ritz's wood-paneled writing room, someone who knew about business, who had the respect of the community. The survival of Germany's frontline soldiers depended on men loyal to the Fatherland who had the courage to prevent shipments of American shells and bullets from reaching the enemy. And von Rintelen, without laboring the point, shrewdly hinted at another opportunity he was offering: here was the chance to escape a doting father's broad shadow, to become his own man. Hilken signed on. He announced that he would do "all in my power to assist Germany."

Baltimore-based German operative Paul Hilken photographed here in Baltimore with Captain-Lieutenant Paul König *(left)* of the Imperial German Navy, who served as the commanding officer of the merchant submarine *Deutschland*, circa 1916.

Von Rintelen, a born talent spotter, had quickly sized up that power: the soft, well-connected young man would function effectively as the network's banker. But, as he explained with careful tact to Hilken, a different set of skills was required in the field. He needed to find an agent who could recruit assets from the Baltimore waterfront, a hard case who could keep the undisciplined stevedores and sailors in line, a man whose very menace was a constant warning that betrayal would be a death sentence. Hilken promptly said he knew such a man.

The meeting took place a month later, in May 1915, in Hilken's home. As the maid set the table in the dining room with the heavy silver for Sunday lunch, in the basement office Hilken introduced von Rintelen to Frederick Hinsch.

Captain Hinsch was a burly old salt. He said he was in his early forties, and even if it clearly wasn't true, no one was prepared to contradict him. He commanded the *Neckar*, a German Lloyd cargo ship, and had just steamed out of the port of Havana when the war started. For nearly a month, he'd found good sport in fearlessly dodging British warships, but then there was engine trouble and he was forced to take sanctuary in Baltimore Harbor. The *Neckar* had now been tied up at Pier 9 for over a year, and each day had been a stiff sentence for its landlocked captain. He was bored, restless, and dangerous.

Von Rintelen, whose survival depended on his snap judgments, quickly took the seaman's measure and happily decided that young Hilken had been right. Hinsch, he appraised, "was made of good stuff." And Hinsch proved it. For months he had engineered the planting of cigar bombs on ships leaving Baltimore.

Standing at the open door, Dilger understood that the time had come for his mission to move forward to the next operational stage. The orders he had received in Berlin were clear: Deliver the deadly vials to Hinsch. The captain would direct the actual attacks.

"I've been wondering when you'd show up," he told Hinsch.

DILGER POURED TWO BEERS IN the kitchen, and they carried them into the front salon. As the captain took a seat on the sofa, Dilger slid the cherrywood door shut in case his sister returned home unexpectedly from her visit to relatives in Washington.

The men drank their beers and talked about the war. Dilger spoke of his nephew Peter, who had been killed in France. His father, he recounted proudly, had ridden with the Duke of Baden and then served in the Union Army. Hinsch said that many of his old shipmates, merchant officers, were now in the imperial navy. But in all their earnest talk about the fighting and Germany's prospects, both men left unsaid a thought they could not bring themselves to articulate: they were soldiers in a different sort of war, and what they were setting out to do would forever change how wars were fought.

Their glasses drained, Dilger led the way down into the basement.

On the shelves in two neat rows were the dark vials containing the cultures he had grown. The vials in the front row were labeled "1"; this was, he told the captain, anthrax. The vials marked "2" contained the glanders germs.

Hinsch looked at the inventory with a critical eye. "Always keep 24 to 36 bottles on hand," he instructed. From now on, he said, you can expect that either I or one of my men will come at least once, maybe twice a week to pick up the cultures.

Dilger assured Hinsch that he could keep them well supplied.

Hinsch questioned him about the quality, and there was an unmistakable challenge in his words. Dead bacterial cultures, he added pointedly, had caused von Steinmetz's mission to fail. He wanted to be certain he and his men wouldn't have a similar experience.

Dilger explained that he was a doctor. He knew what he was doing.

Then he pointed to the cages filled with guinea pigs. The small animals lay there, inert and listless. They had been fed pellets laced with the germs, he explained. "They will be dead soon," he said.

Hinsch was satisfied, so Dilger began to pack the cultures. He put the two-inch-long vials into two round wooden medical containers. The vials had been stoppered with corks, and as a further precaution he cushioned the interior of the containers with a layer of cotton. As he wrapped the wooden containers with brown paper and then tied them with string, he gave Hinsch instructions.

No one should touch the germs, he warned sternly. Always wear rubber gloves. That was most important, he said. Your life will depend on it. He asked if Hinsch understood.

Hinsch said solemnly that he did.

Dilger continued. The bacteria in the vials marked "2" should be inserted directly into the horses' nostrils or emptied into their feed or water troughs. The "1" cultures should ideally be administered to the horses like shots with syringes.

Make sure, Dilger added, that the package is always kept upright. If it falls, if the vials break, do not in any circumstances open the wooden containers. The contents are lethal. Bury them underground immediately.

There was one final bit of business. Hinsch pulled out his wallet and counted out several thousand dollars, the money in hundred-dollar bills. He had received it from Hilken, who had taken the funds out of an account von Rintelen had opened in New York to subsidize the Baltimore network. For expenses, the sea captain explained as he handed Dilger the money.

Dilger led the way up from the basement, and Hinsch followed. In the captain's arms were two packages wrapped in plain brown paper. He held them carefully; he understood that his life depended upon their not being damaged.

They said their good-byes at the front door. Hinsch had parked his Model T Ford on Thirty-Third Street, and he carried the packages to the car. With great delicacy, he positioned them on the floor by the passenger seat.

He drove off slowly down Livingston Street, trying not to stare at the packages lying only a foot or so away on the car floor, all the time praying that the road to Baltimore would not be bumpy.

HANSA HAUS LOOKED AS IF it had been plunked down in bleak downtown Baltimore as the scenery for a production of a Hansel and Gretel fairy tale. The building had been lovingly modeled after a sixteenth-century courthouse in the ancient German town of Halderstadt, and was quaintly decorated with half-timbered corbels and rows of brightly colored armorial shields. The first two floors were home to the city's German consulate and the local offices of the German shipping lines. Its dormered attic was the operational headquarters of Baltimore's Abteilung IIIB spy network.

Hinsch parked the Ford on Redwood Street in front of Hansa Haus. As had been arranged, Ed Felton was waiting on the street to meet him.

Felton was a black stevedore whom the captain had recruited months ago. Hinsch had been paying him between $150 and $200 a week—the size of the payments depended upon the number of dockhands Felton assembled—to place the cigar bombs on ships carrying supplies to the Allies. He was devoted to Hinsch, completely loyal. In turn, the captain felt that "Ed Felton was a smart fellow, always on the job from morning to night." That was high praise in Hinsch's demanding world.

Hinsch directed Felton to take one of the packages from the floor of the car. Be very careful, he told the stevedore. Don't drop it.

When they were in the attic, Hinsch told Felton to put the package on a wooden table in the center of the room. He placed his own down gently next to it. Then he made sure the door was locked. Finally, he turned to Felton.

He said that he had a special mission. He wanted Felton to assemble a group of dockhands, men he could trust. There'd be extra pay. But they had to understand that they could never discuss what they were doing. If they did, they'd have to answer to him. And, he warned, they wouldn't like that. He asked Felton if he understood.

Yes, said Felton gravely.

The packages, Hinsch revealed, contained germs. The plan was for Felton and his men to travel to the port cities where horses were corralled before being loaded onto French and British transport ships. They were to go to Newport News, Baltimore, Norfolk, and New York. They were to poison as many horses as they could; Hinsch would show Felton how it was done, and Felton would then instruct his men. They were to spread the poisonous germs in cities all along the East Coast.

CHAPTER 55

————

Three hundred and fifty thousand! That was the estimated number of people, Tom had learned, who rode the New York subways each day. For the past uneasy year he had lived with the fear of a bomb going off in a subway station or on a crowded subway car. If the German secret service's goal was to convince America that it would be more prudent to focus on troubles at home than to sail off across a wide ocean to take up arms in a foreign war, a mysterious explosion on a New York subway would be horribly persuasive.

Tom had shared this nightmare vision with Woods and Scull, and they agreed it was a disheartening possibility. Scull, in fact, had traveled down to Washington to meet with Franklin Polk. With bombs going off nearly every day in factories and on ships, the administration's chief adviser on intelligence matters did not have to be pressed into believing that an "unexplained" explosion on a subway was a very real threat.

Polk met that day with Colonel House, and the result was the colonel's anxious letter to the president, predicting a devastating attack by German agents on the New York subways—the letter that President Wilson, still determined to stay out of the war, had stiffly chosen to ignore.

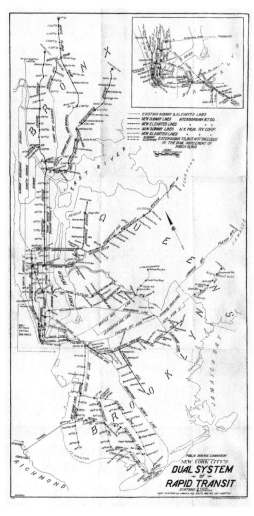

A Dual System of Rapid
Transit map, dated
between 1913 and 1919,
that shows New York
City's existing subway
lines, the new IRT
line, and some planned
extensions not yet built.

But this new threat to the subways, to the people of New York, was
much greater. Now the number 350,000 took on an even more ominous prominence in Tom's thoughts. When Tom learned that Germany had already instigated a failed biological attack and that no less
an adversary than von Rintelen had urged his superiors to try again,
he'd been left shaken. The prospect of anthrax germs being released in

a crowded subway car, of a virulent disease spreading through the city, had sent currents of alarm, anger, and disgust charging through him. An entirely new scale of mayhem could soon be unleashed.

Still, what could he do? He increased the number of guards at all the city's horse corrals, but he also understood that this was small security when measured against the power of a terror he did not entirely understand. He intensified his search for von Steinmetz, only to discover to his frustration that the spy had returned to Germany. He had men combing the waterfront for Ebling, but even as he pressed that hunt, he knew that a lowly dockhand would not be privy to any intelligence regarding a new plot. Lengthy, troubled discussions with Woods and Scull inevitably ended with all three men gloomily acknowledging their helplessness should a terror attack take place.

This time when Scull brought the unsettling news about germ warfare to Polk, Polk didn't even bother to go to his ally House. Regardless of the messenger, he had no faith that the president would listen to the news and then act decisively.

With so much in the balance, Polk instead went on his own to see von Bernstorff. His outrage seething through his diplomat's manners, Polk warned the German ambassador that an attack on the New York subways would not be "mysterious." The nation would know who to blame. The ambassador protested vehemently, insisting that Germany would never be party to or condone such activities. Polk had expected this response, but at least, he told himself, he had the small satisfaction of doing what little he could.

In the end, though, it all came down to Tom. Polk, Woods, and Scull counted on Captain Tunney to prevent the outbreak of a plague that would creep in deadly silence across America, spreading from horses to people with its own mystifying virulence. He had apprehended the men behind the ship bombings, and the fires had abruptly stopped. He would once again protect the homeland.

Tom, though, didn't know where to begin. This was a new, baffling sort of investigation, totally unlike the ship fires. In that case, he had been called in *after* the ships had started burning. The crime had been committed. But now he was being sent off to stop something *before* it even happened. And he understood why: in the aftermath, it would be too late. The death toll would be unthinkable.

Yet just as he was searching unsuccessfully for an angle of attack, he suddenly received help. It came from the most unexpected source: President Woodrow Wilson.

THE PRESIDENT, ALTHOUGH THIS WAS unknown to Tom, was in truth only the final link on a long, rattling chain.

The instigator was a patriotic waiter on the roof terrace of the Ritz-Carlton in New York. He was serving dinner to von Bernstorff; Constantin Dumba, the Austro-Hungarian ambassador to the United States; and a third guest whom he recognized as John Archibald, a well-known American reporter. As the waiter was clearing the plates, he saw Dumba cautiously pass a sheaf of papers to Archibald.

The next day the waiter reported this exchange to the Secret Service. The federal authorities had long been suspicious of Archibald. For many years before the war he had been based in Berlin, and the articles he now published in papers throughout the country were decidedly pro-German. It was suspected that he was on Albert's payroll, and that both von Bernstorff and Dumba used him as a courier to deliver confidential documents to Germany. When they discovered that Archibald was scheduled to sail, just days after the rooftop dinner, to England while en route to Germany, the Secret Service notified Guy Gaunt, the British intelligence station chief based in New York. Immediately, Gaunt wired his superiors in London.

When Archibald's ship docked at Falmouth, British sailors searched his suitcase. It was crammed with papers the reporter had intended to deliver to the officials at Wilhelmstrasse.

The documents—one hundred and ten of them—were a remarkable and varied inventory of Germany's covert acts against America. There were plans to foment strikes at Bethlehem Steel Company plants; canceled checks to saboteurs and propagandists; reports signed by von Papen and Boy-Ed, detailing the progress of sabotage operations; and summaries of Boy-Ed's arrangements with Huerta, as well as von Papen's visits to Mexico and the American border towns to organize the local German community for "self-defense." There was also a mean-spirited letter from von Papen to his wife, in which the military attaché took snippy aim at "these idiotic Yankees."

Archibald was formally charged as "an enemy courier," and the gleeful British authorities delivered this packet of goodies to Walter Page, the American ambassador. Page, who'd been futilely urging the president to bring America into the war on the Allied side, quickly sent them on to Washington. By the time Wilson read the pages, however, they were public knowledge. Wary that Wilson's agile mind would find some convoluted new reason not to respond to this damning evidence, British intelligence had forced the president's hand: they published the documents in a parliamentary white paper. Gaunt then made sure they were brought to the attention of the American press.

Just months after the contents of Albert's briefcase had made news, the new revelations about Germany's covert activities in America once again caused banner headlines. An already enraged public grew further incensed. And even the president's slow-simmering temper started to boil.

He was, after all, still exchanging unsatisfying diplomatic notes with Germany over the *Lusitania* attack. And it had become increasingly difficult to ignore the secret reports he had been receiving from the New York police. Each brought a new grievance to what had become a devastating list: von Rintelen's many plots, Fay's rudder bombs, the ship fires, Germany's scheme to restore Huerta to power, the attempted assassination of J. P. Morgan, and the failed attempt to poison warhorses.

When a seething Colonel House suggested that America send home "the obnoxious underlings," this time Wilson agreed.

On December 3, 1915, Secretary of State Lansing summoned von Bernstorff to the State Department. The president, he stated with taut formality, considered Captains Franz von Papen and Karl Boy-Ed personae non gratae. Their recall was demanded.

Four days later, Wilson addressed Congress. He seemed changed, more forceful, a newfound resolve fortifying his words. Yet, as was so often the case with this sensitive, thoughtful man, his candor was disarming. The address was a public apology. He spoke not simply as the president of the United States but as an aggrieved man, frankly acknowledging that his own stern morality had prevented him from suspecting that other people lived by a less rigorous code:

> There are citizens of the United States, I blush to admit, born under other flags . . . who have poured the poison of disloyalty into the very arteries of our national life; who have sought to bring the authority and good name of our Government into contempt, to destroy our industries wherever they thought it effective for their vindictive purposes to strike at them, and to debase our politics to the uses of foreign intrigue. . . .
>
> A little while ago such a thing would have seemed incredible.
>
> Because it was incredible, we made no preparations for it. We would have been almost ashamed to prepare for it as if we were suspicious of ourselves, our own comrades and neighbors!
>
> But the ugly and incredible thing has actually come to pass and we are without federal laws to deal with it. . . .
>
> Such creatures of passion, disloyalty must be crushed out.

Berlin promptly responded to the president's words with a bewilderment as hollow as it was contrived: "Apparently the enemies of Germany have succeeded in creating the impression that the German government is in some way morally or otherwise responsible for what

Mr. Wilson has characterized as anti-American activities. . . . This the German government absolutely denies."

At the same time, the Foreign Office took private solace in the fact that von Bernstorff had not been recalled. "You are in no way included in this episode," Lansing told the ambassador, according to the cable von Bernstorff sent to the Foreign Office. "We should look upon it with extreme regret were you to leave us." The president, it seemed, still had the wishful notion that the ambassador could help him persuade the kaiser to negotiate a peace settlement.

But von Papen and Boy-Ed had no choice but to make preparations to leave. On a snowy evening in mid-December, von Papen had a farewell dinner with Paul Koenig at the German Club on Central Park South in New York. He thanked Koenig for running the bureau. "It is a comfort," he told his security chief, "to know that you will still be at work when I am gone."

Von Papen's words, however, were premature. A team of Tom's watchers had followed Koenig through the snow-covered streets to the club. The next morning, when Tom read their surveillance report, he started thinking. The president had already moved against the two military attachés; the long-running investigative strategy predicated on Koenig's somehow providing the leads needed to document their roles in the network had been superseded.

It was more important—vital even, Tom told himself—to discover what Koenig knew about Germany's germ warfare program. Perhaps he had information about where Ebling was hiding. Did his files contain the proof that a new biological attack had become operational? Tom desperately needed answers to these large questions.

The time had come, Tom decided, to arrest Paul Koenig.

CHAPTER 56

———

Anyone who interferes with Germans or the German Government will be punished!" Koenig growled as Tom's men raided his office. Barnitz responded to the threat by snapping a pair of handcuffs firmly onto his wrists.

Once in custody Koenig, as Tom had predicted, was uncooperative.

He bellowed curses and stared down probing questions with a defiant silence. Tom was beginning to wonder if the arrest had been precipitate, if continuing the surveillance on Koenig would have been more productive than this unsatisfying interrogation. But that was before Barnitz, a self-satisfied grin on his face, rushed into the room.

The detective held a small black loose-leaf notebook. There were hundreds of pages, all neatly typed. It had been found in Koenig's West Ninety-Fourth Street apartment, in a locked desk drawer. When Koenig saw it, he burst out with a savage, desperate volley of protests. "That's private property," he shouted. "You have no right to touch it. I insist you return it to me at once." Yet even as he screamed the words, Koenig realized that it was too late.

The notebook was, Tom would soon say, "unquestionably one of the richest prizes of the spy hunt in America."

It was an operational history of the Abteilung IIIB's network in America, and at the same time it was the intriguing personal diary of a self-styled master spy. The pages, all in fluent English, meticulously documented Koenig's varied activities from August 22, 1914, when, according to the notebook, he became "a German military spy," until his farewell dinner with von Papen.

Compiled with a comparable thoroughness, there were also pages of carefully thought-out rules and regulations. Some involved tradecraft: "A street number in Manhattan named over the telephone means that the meeting will take place five blocks further uptown than the street mentioned. Pennsylvania Railroad Station means Grand Central Depot. Kaiserhof means the General Post Office in front of P.O. Box 840. Hotel Ansonia means café in Hotel Manhattan (basement). Hotel Belmont means at the bar in Pabst's, Columbus Circle."

Others involved personal security: "In order to safeguard the secrets and affairs of the department prior to receiving a caller, hereafter my desk must be entirely cleared of all papers except those pertaining to the business in hand." Or "All persons related to me, however distant, will be barred from employment with the Bureau of Investigation. This does not apply to my wife."

Then there were "Health Rules": "I have decided to refrain from chewing tobacco in the office as it disagrees with my health thereby interfering with my work." "I shall drink no more whiskey."

But it was what Koenig called his "D-cases" that Tom kept returning to over and over again. These were operations conducted by the *Geheimdienst,* or secret service division, and they made up a catalog of the network's most covert missions. The problem, however, was that they were recorded in a code known only to Koenig. The specifics were disguised by aliases, false locations, random numbers, and seemingly meaningless phrases.

SECRET SERVICE DIVISION.

List of Aliases Used by XXX.

	D-Cases.	
Sjurstadt	#250	Watson
Markow	#260	von Wegener
Horn	#277	Fischer
Portack	#279	Westerberg
Berns	#306	Werner
Scott	#309	Werner
McIntyre	#311	Bode
Miller	#314	Reinhardt
Harre	#315	Kaufmann
Kienzle	#316	Wegener
Wiener	#316	Wegener
von Pilis	#316	Bode
Burns	#325	Reinhardt
Stahl	#328	Stemmler
Coleman	#335	Schuster
Schleindl	#343	Wöhler (Paul)
Leyendecker	#344	Heyne
Feldheim	#357	Winters
Warburg	#362	Blohm
Van de Bund	#358	Taylor
Lewis	#366	Burg
Hammond	#357	Decker (W.P.)
Uffelmann	#370	Schwartz
Hirschland	#371	Günther
Neuhaus	#371	Günther
Ornstein	#371	Günther
Witzel	#371	Wöhler
Plochmann	#375	Breitung
Archer	#289	Mendez
Bettes	----	Goebels
Reith	#382	Brandt

SECRET SERVICE DIVISION.

Ciphers Used In
Confidential Reports
(Oct.1914 - Sept.1915)

---oOo---

5000 - - - - I. G. Embassy

7000 - - - - " " Military Attache

8000 - - - - " " Naval Attache

9000 - - - - " " Commercial Attache

7354 - - - - von Knorr

7371 - - - - Tomaseck

7379 - - - - Tokio

7381 - - - - Copenhagen

7600 - - - - Burns Agency

9001 - - - - Herbert Boas

SECRET SERVICE DIVISION.

SAFETY BLOCK SYSTEM

Operatives of the S. S. Division, when receiving instructions from me or through the medium of my secretary as to designating meeting places, will understand that such instructions must be translated as follows:

For week Nov.28 to Dec.4 (midnight)

A street number in Manhattan named over the telephone means that the meeting will take place 5 blocks further uptown than the street mentioned.
Pennsylvania R. R. Station means Grand Central Depot.
Kaiserhof means General Post Office, in front of P. O. Box 840.
Hotel Ansonia means Cafe in Hotel Manhattan (basement).
Hotel Belmont means at the Bar in Pabst' Columbus Circle.
Brooklyn Bridge means Bar in Unter den Linden.

For week Dec.5 to Dec.12 (midnight)

Code to remain the same as previous week.

For week Dec.12 to Dec.19 (midnight

A street number in Manhattan named over the telephone means that the meeting will take place 5 blocks further downtown than the street mentioned.

SECRET SERVICE DIVISION.
(Geheimdienst)

Rules and Regulations.
- 1915 -

#1. Beginning with November 6th, no blue copies are to be made of reports submitted in connection with D-Case #343, and the original reports will be sent to H.M.G. instead of the duplicates, as formerly.

#2. In order to accomplish better results in connection with D-Case #343, and to shorten the stay of the informing agent at the place of meeting, it has been decided to discontinue the former practice of dining with this agent prior to receiving his report. It will also be made a rule to refrain from working on other matters until the informant in this case has been fully heard; and all data taken down in shorthand. (11-11-15)

#3. Beginning with November 28th, 1915, all operations designated as D-Cases will be handled exclusively by the Secret Service Division, the Headquarters of which will not be at the Central Office, as heretofore. This change will result in discontinuing utilizing operatives or employees attached to the Central Office, Division for Special Detail and Pier Division. On the other hand, great

Four pages from Paul Koenig's notebook.

And Koenig refused to cooperate. He enjoyed Tom's fruitless struggle to make sense of his notebook. Despite his arrest, Koenig convinced himself that he was having the last victorious laugh.

Still, Tom was undeterred. He wanted to believe that among the D-cases was a record of the German germ warfare campaign, the secrets of von Steinmetz's mission. It would outline, he predicted with bitter conviction, the details of the new biological attack that von Rintelen had urged. These suspicions kept him focused on the D-cases with an urgent attention. He could not put the pages down.

But of all the many cases, it was D-Case 343 that day after day occupied his thoughts. It was so significant that Koenig, displaying a level of caution rare for even this most scrupulous of case officers, had given it its own set of rules: "Beginning with Nov. 6 no blue copies are to be made of reports submitted in connection with D-Case 343, and the original reports will be sent to H.M.G. instead of duplicates, as formerly."

H.M.G., Tom had managed to decipher, was von Papen. But what could have been so secret that the military attaché himself needed to keep the original reports?

Rule 2 was further testimony to the importance of the operation: "In order to accomplish better results in connection with D-Case 343, to shorten the stay of the informing agent at the place of the meeting, it has been decided to discontinue the former practice of dining with this agent prior to receiving his report. It will also be a rule to refrain from working on other matters until the informant in this case has been fully heard, and all the data taken down in shorthand."

Clearly, Tom was beginning to appreciate, these debriefings had been accorded a special operational significance. Security required that the agent not be allowed to linger. And Koenig would occupy himself with no other business until the agent had completed his report. Who was this agent? What was his secret mission? The more Tom pondered these questions, the more he grew convinced that the answers involved the germ warfare program. What else, he asked himself, would require such unprecedented secrecy and caution?

CHAPTER 57

——

With a renewed sense of urgency, Tom went back to the notebook. Koenig's alias in D-Case 343 was Woehler. As for the agent, his aliases kept changing. At first, he was identified as Operative #51. Then as Agent C.O. And still later as Agent B.I. Were they all the same person? Or were there a number of field agents in this operation? The mystery kept growing.

Backtracking through the notebook, Tom saw an earlier reference to Woehler's meeting with a Friedrich Schleindl. Tom read it slowly. Then, just to be certain, he read it again. When he'd finished, Tom knew he had it. Koenig had slipped up.

This was, he understood in a moment of sudden perception, a record of Koenig's initial meeting with his agent. He had, as good tradecraft required, used his work name, but he had not yet assigned an alias to his agent.

Why? Tom asked, and then excitedly answered his own question: because Koenig at this first sit-down didn't know if the new recruit's intelligence would be of any value. He didn't know if there'd be a subsequent meeting. Koenig had no inkling of the agent that Schleindl would become. And after the recruit had blossomed into a key operative, Koenig had never thought to thumb back through the notebook to edit his account of their first encounter.

Friedrich Schleindl, the bank clerk and German spy exposed in Koenig's notebooks.

By going backward, then reading forward, Tom found that the notebook revealed a clear trail: calling himself Woehler, Koenig had met Schleindl, and it was Woehler who continued as the handler of Operative #51, then Agent C.O., and finally Agent B.I.

Certain that he would soon have his first real intelligence about Germany's germ warfare program, he gave the order to find Friedrich Schleindl.

IT TOOK ONLY A CHECK of the city's telephone directories for the team to locate Schleindl. And after he was brought in, he did help solve a mystery. But it was not the one Tom had anticipated.

When the war started, according to the story Tom easily drew out of the terrified prisoner, Schleindl was a clerk in the City National Bank. He was also a German reservist, having been born in Bavaria, and he reported to the German consulate for duty. Months passed without further communication from the consulate, but then he received a call instructing him to meet a Herr Woehler at the Manhattan Hotel. "You'll find him in the bar," he was told.

Woehler—or, as Tom knew him, Koenig—bought the young man a beer and led him to a secluded table where they could talk. "Tell me more about yourself," Woehler said when they were seated.

It was more an interrogation than a casual conversation. As it continued, Woehler made an important discovery. Schleindl's job gave him access to daily cables from Allied governments to the bank, arranging the purchase and shipment of war supplies.

That first night, Woehler made his pitch. He offered Schleindl $25 a week to steal all the orders cabled by the Allies, together with copies of contracts showing when the goods would be delivered to the piers for shipment, as well as the detailed descriptions of the purchases. Schleindl agreed. He was a patriot, and, he added candidly to Tom, the extra $25 nearly doubled his clerk's salary.

A routine developed. Schleindl would wait until the end of the week, then gather up all the cables and contracts that had come in over the previous five days. On Friday night he'd meet with his control, and Woehler would have the documents copied in time for Schleindl to replace them early Monday morning before anyone knew they had been borrowed.

And Koenig would have crucial information to pass on to von Rintelen. The contracts and cargo manifests enabled cigar bombs to be placed on the ships where they would do the most damage to the Allies. Shipments to the Allies were closely guarded secrets, but the cigar bombs unerringly targeted the correct ships. Now Tom knew how this had been accomplished.

But as he diligently went back over the many documents that Schleindl had passed on to Koenig, something caught Tom's eye. And another, more momentous mystery began to unravel.

It was the shipping contract for several thousand magnetos needed to power the ignition systems of Allied trucks and automobiles at the front. They had been loaded into hold 2 of the steamship *Minnehaha*: the same steamship on which an explosion had erupted in the number 2 hold on July 7, 1915. The same date that Erich Muenter/ Frank Holt had told Tom an explosion would take place.

Ever since that blast, Tom had wondered how a Cornell professor knew to plant his bomb on the one ship in New York Harbor that day heading off with vital war matériel. Muenter had died before Tom had a chance to ask him. Perhaps, Tom had tried not very successfully to convince himself, Muenter had just made a lucky guess. After all, only the executives at the magneto factory and the officers of the bank would have seen the bill of lading.

Now Tom understood. Schleindl had passed the bill of lading to Koenig, who had given it to von Rintelen, who had passed the information on—there was no other logical explanation!—to Muenter.

His long, brooding suspicion that Muenter had not acted alone, he felt, was confirmed. Tom had no doubt that when Muenter placed the bomb in the U.S. Capitol Building and shot J. P. Morgan, he had been acting with the assistance of the German secret service.

BUT THIS REALIZATION GAVE TOM little comfort. Instead, it only served to remind him of the cruel nature of the enemy he was pursuing. Once a line has been crossed, Tom knew, anything becomes possible. Terror was very much a matter of habit. Tom had no doubt that the unprincipled adversary who had planted bombs and sent out assassins would not hesitate to attack America with germs.

CHAPTER 58

———

The man was dying. He was forty-seven years old and had previously enjoyed good health, but three weeks earlier he had entered Bellevue Hospital in New York complaining that he felt weak, tired, and feverish. Now he was in a coma. His organs were shutting down. The doctors did not understand why.

As they struggled to make a diagnosis, they kept returning to two possible clues. The first was his job. He worked on ships transporting warhorses to Europe, feeding the animals and mucking out the stalls. The other clue was on his body. His face was scarred with ugly sores, and inflamed nodules about the size of nickels covered his legs and feet.

Most of the doctors assumed the skin irritations were a rash caused by his work with horses, but they were not convinced these epidermal abrasions were directly connected to the disease that was killing him. Several of the physicians had an entirely different diagnosis. In his trips overseas, the patient had contracted a previously unknown strain of foreign measles; that would explain both his illness and the condition of his body.

The doctors went back and forth, and during the patient's second week of hospitalization, the nodules began to swell. They burst, and a dark yellow pus spewed out. The patient's fever rose precipitously. Then he became delirious.

Twenty-one days after admission, he fell into a coma. Two days later he was dead. The doctors still did not know the cause.

With the patient's death, the doctors intensified their investigation. A new theory held that it might have been a case of plague. If that were true, the entire city would need to be put on alert and rigorous precautions taken. So blood was taken from the corpse and injected into guinea pigs. The excreted pus was also applied to the lab animals.

Within days, the animals became ill. Soon they were dead. And the anxious doctors made a diagnosis. This was not plague, but glanders. The patient, it was now decided, most probably had come in contact with an infected horse, or had simply changed the sick animal's water or cleaned its stall. The autopsy confirmed this. "Glanders invasion of the liver and lungs" was listed as the cause of death.

Not until nine years after the war was over, as lawyers seeking reparations for Germany's sabotage activities in the United States conducted their investigations, would Dilger's culturing of the glanders pathogen in his basement become known. And then this death would take on a new significance. Doctors suspected it was ground zero: the first known human fatality in the contagion caused by Germany's germ warfare attack.

WEEKS AFTER THE DEATH IN New York, in Newport News, Virginia, John Grant, a stevedore from Baltimore, crouched outside the animal pens at the Breeze Point wharf. It was dark and cold, with a harsh December wind coming off the James River, but Grant did not hurry. He waited and watched.

His boss, Ed Felton, said he had paid the night watchman to stay in his office, but Grant still worried about the British remount officers. They normally left at the end of the day, yet if one happened to be around, he'd shoot an intruder on sight. Grant was getting paid $10 for his work. It was good money, and it was a lot easier than lifting crates on the docks. But he had no intention of risking his life.

He listened to the night sounds: distant voices coming off the transport ships anchored in the harbor; the whinnies and neighs of the animals in the pens; the steady shuffling of hooves. When he was satisfied there were no patrolling guards, Grant removed a pair of rubber gloves from his back pocket and pulled them on.

He made sure they fitted tightly, then turned his attention to the package lying by his feet. Grant removed the brown paper wrapping. Inside was a wooden container, and he unscrewed its top. There was a layer of cotton, and after he pushed it aside, he saw the two glass vials. They were about two inches long, and stoppered with pieces of cork.

Now came the dangerous part, he knew. If he wasn't careful, Felton had warned, he could die. Grant could not let the yellow liquid in the vials touch his skin.

He pulled the cork out very slowly. With two fingers, he grasped the steel-tipped syringe inside, and extracted it. Inadvertently, he let drops of the yellow liquid fall onto the ground, but, after a moment's panic, he decided that none had touched his clothes or his skin. With the syringe raised in his hand like a dagger, he hurried to the first mule corral.

He stabbed the needle deep into the haunch of a mule. The animal immediately went wild. It kicked and brayed savagely. As Grant struggled to pull the needle out of the mule's thick hide, the animal turned its neck and tried to bite him. Grant finally managed to remove it, but now all the animals in the pen were braying, snorting. In their collective fury, they banged into each other and kicked at the corral fence.

Alarmed, Grant grabbed his package and rushed toward a wooden storage shed. He leaned against it, hiding in the shadows, waiting for the animals to quiet. His instinct was to run, to throw the vials into the James River and escape before a British soldier came to see what was causing the commotion. But he knew Felton would be angry. And if Felton told Captain Hinsch that he'd run, the consequences would be as bad as being caught. No, he decided, they'd be worse.

After a while, when the mules had grown silent, Grant returned to the corral. He worked quickly, stabbing as many animals as he could. When there wasn't enough of the yellow liquid remaining in the vial to refill the syringe, he emptied the contents into water basins and food troughs.

He uncorked the second vial and moved on to the horse corral. As soon as he stabbed the first horse, the animals started neighing and racing about. But Grant was determined to complete his mission and get off the wharf. He did his best to calm the horses, and then, working rapidly, jabbed one animal after another.

His work completed, he went to the banks of the James River. He pulled off his gloves and tossed them one at a time into the shadowy, fast-moving water. He watched as the current took them downstream. He threw the vials into the water, too, and after a moment they sank. Then he hurried off the wharf. He was already looking forward to the morning when he'd take the train back to Baltimore.

As with the glanders case in New York, it would not be until years later, after the lawyers in the postwar reparations case had interviewed Grant and doctors had studied the transcripts, that the full significance of the stevedore's activities that night was understood.

Too many years had passed to allow the doctors to be sure when the ground-zero moment had occurred. It might have been when droplets of yellow liquid fell onto the ground outside the mule corral. Or when the gloves and vials were tossed into the James River. Or, as with the Bellevue patient, perhaps people had simply come in contact with the animals or their water and food. But they now believed with great certainty that they had found the cause of four mysterious deaths, accompanied by anthraxlike symptoms, during the winter of 1915–16 in Virginia. And they wondered how many more deaths caused by the German Secret Service's anthrax attack had gone undiagnosed.

TOM WORKED IN A VACUUM. He had no knowledge of the deaths in New York and Virginia. All he had driving him, goading him on, was his instincts. And his fears. He was certain Germany would launch a second germ attack.

Yet he might as well have been chasing after an elusive ghost; his pursuit was a hunt for intangibles. He had no suspects. No clues. The lethal weapon he so feared struck with deadly silence, leaving behind only hints of its terrible efficacy. He lay awake at night wondering if the attack had already begun and he didn't know it. Would the doctors, he asked himself anxiously, even be able to identify an outbreak? Would they be able to treat it? Facing such an invisible, powerful threat, what could he do?

Still, it was not in Tom's nature to surrender. He made sure the guards were doubled at the New York horse corrals. He sent his men up and down the waterfront to warn about enemy agents intent on poisoning animals. And he implored Woods and Scull to reiterate to their many friends in Washington that the threat of a germ attack was very real.

Tom was attempting something he had never done before in his career. He was no longer the indefatigable detective tracking down the culprits. Instead, he was trying to prevent a crime. And although he would not know all that happened until years later, he succeeded.

CHAPTER 59

In the cruel winter months, the Jersey shore was a cold and lonely destination. Waves swelled, gusts blew, and the beachfront cottages remained shuttered. But it was precisely this isolation, Hilken decided, that made it the ideal location for an emergency meeting. He ordered the two main conspirators in his operation to meet him at a beachfront bungalow he had hastily rented not too far from Atlantic City. And he warned them to make sure they were not followed.

Hinsch drove his Model T; Dilger took the train and then a taxi. Hilken was waiting when they arrived. He greeted them warmly, hospitably served beers, but it was clear to Dilger that the young man was out of sorts. He was nervous, trying to hide his anxiety but not succeeding.

Hilken did not possess the spy's special courage, the ability to stand up to what his imagination was shouting was about to happen and still find the nerve to go on as if nothing at all was wrong. Hilken had bad news to deliver, and its implications had left him undone.

"They're on to us," he announced flatly. He had been contacted by Koenig, now free on $50,000 bail after his arrest. Koenig said that New York police were swarming about the harbor, asking questions about plots to poison the horses awaiting shipment to the Allies. Koenig had also learned that there were more guards at the corrals. They're on alert, waiting to catch someone, he said.

Hilken continued, now edging dangerously close to panic. He had been summoned to meet with Wolf von Igel, the German diplomat who had replaced Captain von Papen in New York. Von Igel had delivered a message from von Bernstorff. The ambassador, Hilken said, was furious with them.

"Don't those imbeciles understand the potential consequences of their actions?" the ambassador had demanded, according to the report von Igel gave to Hilken. Von Bernstorff had already been informed that the authorities suspected Germany was engaged in germ warfare. But if the Americans could prove it, the ambassador had lectured, it would be the final outrage that would push the country into the war. Any tactical advantage gained by poisoning animals would be more than outweighed by American troops being sent to Europe. The ambassador wanted the operation to stop immediately.

Dilger objected. He didn't take his orders from von Bernstorff, he said; he was assigned to Abteilung IIIB, and he received his orders from them.

As if on cue, Hilken handed him a cable. He was to return to Berlin as soon as possible "for discussions." It was signed, Dilger recognized, with one of Nicolai's work names.

On January 29, 1916, using a new passport that the State Department had issued so that he could work, or so he had claimed, as a surgeon at a German Red Cross hospital in Heidelberg, Dilger boarded the Norwegian passenger liner *Kristianiafjord*. As the ship crossed the Atlantic, Hinsch, who would continue to participate in sabotage operations until he fled to Germany, dismantled "Tony's lab."

Dilger would never return to America. After being briefed in Berlin, he was sent on a secret mission to Spain. In Madrid, he was infected by the Spanish influenza virus sweeping through the world's population, and died. The doctor who had propagated germs had become their victim.

Tom, without at the time realizing the effectiveness of his actions or the lives he'd saved, had won a great victory. Over the past two years, he had slowly come to learn that he was engaged in an entirely new sort of conflict, one where the action took place in the shadows, where the investigative goal often was to prevent crimes before they happened. However, he had not yet begun to appreciate the hard wisdom that drove counterintelligence work: triumphs often went unheralded or even unrecognized, while defeats always made headlines.

AS FOR HILKEN, DESPITE HIS tightly wound nerves, the secret life continued to pull him back in. The thrill of being a clandestine actor with the power to influence world historical events was too grand an experience to abandon. He could not return to a life lived only as his father's dutiful son. He had discovered that he enjoyed performing on a bigger stage.

He would be involved with other plots, his role in which would not be uncovered until after the war. Working once again with Hinsch, he helped plan and then finalize a mission code-named Jersey.

The idea had originated with von Rintelen, who first decided to give Black Tom, the largest munitions and gunpowder shipping center in America, "a sound knock on the head." He'd diagrammed where the saboteurs should land their boats and the barges they should target, only to receive the telegram ordering him back to Germany. Hilken and Hinsch inherited the mission.

Since the target was across the Hudson, most of the final planning was done in New York in the boozy, good-time safety of Martha Held's town house. Sitting there, the easy friendship of Martha's pretty women available to him, surrounded by his fellow conspirators, Hilken felt he had at last become the equal of the man who had recruited him. Like von Rintelen, he was a master spy. Like the cause he worked for, he was invincible.

ON SUNDAY, JULY 30, 1916, at 12:24 a.m., the first fire started at the terminal. Two hours later, Black Tom had become a great white light illuminating the night sky. Stockpiled shells exploded, and stored bullets flew about wildly. There was a tremendous, awful, sustained boom, powerful enough, it seemed, to shake the planet down to its core.

Far across the river in Manhattan the windows in the library at Forty-Second Street were blown out, water mains broke, downtown streets flooded, and people, certain that the world was coming to an end, rushed from their apartments and hotel rooms and into the street. By the end of the week, newspapers estimated the damage to New York and New Jersey warehouses, railroads, and businesses at a staggering $20 million. And the bodies of five victims were recovered.

In Brooklyn that evening, Tom was pulled from his sleep and hurried to his window. The sky was lit with an unnatural glow: high noon in the middle of the night. Although he did not yet know the cause (and it would be litigious decades before the blame was officially resolved), he had no doubts about the perpetrators, or the consequences. Other people might not be certain whether the explosion was an accident or sabotage, but he was. Germany had gone too far. The nation would demand revenge.

At that moment, the nighttime quiet destroyed, the wooden planks in his bedroom floor shaking beneath his feet, Tom knew that his long, solitary war was about to come to an end. A new fight would soon begin. He'd battle on, but he'd no longer be wearing a policeman's blue uniform. He'd be marching off alongside tens of thousands of other Americans on a common mission.

Workers sorting shells at the Black Tom munitions
plant in Jersey City, New Jersey.

View of the aftermath of a series of massive explosions at the Black
Tom munitions facility on July 30, 1916. The explosion, which
resulted from the detonation of a train car full of dynamite and
subsequent explosions of other munitions, leveled the facility.

CHAPTER 60

Moored German submarines, circa 1914–1915. Second from left
in the front row is U-20, which sank the RMS *Lusitania*.

At last, Woodrow Wilson gave in to his long-building fury. With a statesman's lofty philosophy and the patience of a would-be saint, he had tried to ignore or, when that was not possible, rationalize all of Germany's many provocations. Then, with the nation's anger already ratcheted up by the catastrophic Black Tom explosion, the conduct of the kaiser's government toward the United States became even more intolerable.

On February 1, 1917, Germany announced a policy of unrestricted submarine warfare. Its U-boats would sink without warning any neutral ships in a designated zone around Great Britain, France, and Italy.

The United States was told to surrender its sovereign right to trade and travel across the high seas, or its ships would be torpedoed. As one indignant paper huffed, the kaiser had declared that henceforth freedom of the seas would exist only for "icebergs and fish."

His resolve inching closer to a once unthinkable decision, the president responded by severing diplomatic relations with Germany. Von Bernstorff, the German ambassador and head of the Abteilung IIIB network in America, was ordered home along with Albert and the rest of the embassy's officials.

Guy Gaunt sent his superiors a triumphant telegram: "Bernstorff goes home. I get drunk tonight." And then he did just that, with Tom, Woods, and Scull in the Harvard Club bar.

British intelligence, however, was too busy plotting its next move to celebrate. The team of wranglers in Room 40 had decoded an intercepted cable signed by Arthur Zimmermann, the German foreign secretary, to Heinrich von Eckhardt, the imperial minister in Mexico.

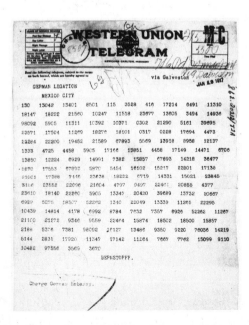

The Zimmermann telegram as received by the German ambassador to Mexico.

The Zimmermann telegram, decoded.

TELEGRAM RECEIVED.

FROM 2nd from London # 5747.

"We intend to begin on the first of February
unrestricted submarine warfare. We shall endeavor
in spite of this to keep the United States of
America neutral. In the event of this not succeeding, we make Mexico a proposal of alliance on the
following basis: make war together, make peace
together, generous financial support and an understanding on our part that Mexico is to reconquer
the lost territory in Texas, New Mexico, and
Arizona. The settlement in detail is left to you.
You will inform the President of the above most
secretly as soon as the outbreak of war with the
United States of America is certain and add the
suggestion that he should, on his own initiative,
invite Japan to immediate adherence and at the same
time mediate between Japan and ourselves. Please
call the President's attention to the fact that
the ruthless employment of our submarines now
offers the prospect of compelling England in a
few months to make peace." Signed, ZIMMERMANN.

The receipt of this information has so
greatly exercised the British Government that they
have lost no time in communicating it to me to
transmit to you, in order that our Government may
be able without delay to make such disposition as
may

Von Rintelen's sly scheming with Huerta, and von Papen's reconnaissance trips to Mexico, had offered tantalizing hints of Germany's
intentions. But this telegram was solid, undeniable proof of official
imperial government policy. It proposed an alliance with Mexico and
Japan in a joint war against the United States, and solemnly promised
to help Mexico "regain by conquest her lost territory in Texas, Arizona, and New Mexico."

Once again managing to protect the powerful secret that the team
in Room 40 had broken the German diplomatic code, the British had a
copy of the bombshell telegram delivered to Wilson. This time it was the
president who instructed that the cable be shared with the press.

Eight-column headlines stretched across newspapers all over the
country on the morning of March 1, 1917. The *Washington Post*
shouted: "German Plot to Conquer United States with Aid of Japan
and Mexico Revealed." The *New York Times* trumpeted: "Germany
Seeks Alliance Against U.S., Asks Japan and Mexico to Join Her."

Over the days that followed, the president wrote his speech himself, typing out the words in the Oval Office. Then, on the rainy evening of April 2, an army cavalry unit riding alongside his car, Wilson drove down Pennsylvania Avenue to the Capitol Building. As he stood at the lectern in the crowded House chamber and prepared to begin his address to a joint session of Congress, an unprecedented ovation broke out. It lasted a full two minutes. Then President Woodrow Wilson asked Congress to declare war against Germany.

What prompted this irrevocable decision by a president who only three months earlier had agonized that going to war would be a "crime against civilization"? It would be a brash conceit to assign a single motive to such a complicated, thoughtful man. And it would be no less of a mistake to identify a single event as the final straw that broke an indomitable patience.

President Woodrow Wilson asks Congress to declare war on April 2, 1917.

Rather, more than anything else, a fundamental change of heart had gripped this most idealistic of men. It had come slowly, gradually. With his growing awareness of Germany's extensive secret operations against America, Wilson had been forced to rethink how he looked at the world.

He had become president believing that both men and nations were required to act in certain well-understood, honorable ways. With a naïveté fostered as much by wishful thinking as by moral doctrine, he found it difficult to accept that a state would knowingly flout these standards of behavior. So he had been puzzled. He could not fully believe the reports that were being passed on by the New York police. Bomb plots, assassinations, germ warfare, subversion—all of it seemed quite impossible, even as, at the same time, he knew the evidence was undeniable.

It took time for his benevolent, hopeful notions to wear thin. A fierce internal struggle had raged inside him. Yet as the unnatural became undeniable, his shock hardened into the resigned anger of someone who now understood he had been coldly deceived.

As the nation prepared to go to war, Wilson's Flag Day speech of June 1917 made it clear that a more distrustful worldview had become anchored in his mind. "It is plain enough how we were forced into the war," he said, with the firm confidence of a convert who had permanently turned his back on false gods. "They filled our unsuspecting communities with vicious spies and conspirators and sought to corrupt the opinion of our people in their own behalf. When they found they could not do that, their agents diligently spread sedition amongst us and sought to draw our own citizens from their allegiance—and some of these agents were men connected with the official embassy of the German government itself here in our own capital. They sought by violence to destroy our industries and arrest our commerce. . . . What great nation in such circumstance would not have taken up arms?"

For three years, Abteilung IIIB's relentless operations in America had kept banging and banging against Wilson's faith until finally all his heartfelt beliefs were shattered. Stripped of his illusions and his innocence, a different man from the one who'd taken office five years ago, the president led the nation into war.

TOM HAD NO ILLUSIONS, AND certainly no innocence, about the nature of the enemy. His concerns centered on his own country.

Paradoxically, these troubling thoughts occurred to him at a time when he should have been enjoying his accolades and celebrating his triumphs. Just weeks after Congress voted to declare war, Commissioner Woods had rewarded the squad's work by promoting him to inspector and the loyal Barnitz to lieutenant. Yet today, December 17, 1917, he felt troubled by the *Times* report on the next giant step in his career. "City's Bomb Squad Goes to the Army," read the tiered headline. "Tunney, Head of Noted Organization, Will Be a Major—Men to Enlist. Will Pursue Plotters."

The article below was no less flattering:

The famous Bomb Squad of the New York Police Department, which, under the command of Inspector Thomas Tunney, has won for itself a national reputation in bringing to justice German spies, has been taken over by the War Department. . . . The entire squad will be assigned to duty with the Army Intelligence Service in the New York district.

The new step taken by the Government was characterized by Federal officials as of far-reaching importance, and was cited as proof of the intention of the authorities to handle the Teuton spy and plot situation vigorously.

Tom, though, reading the newspaper report, found that he was unable to summon up any of its optimism. The nation, he knew only too well, had shown little inclination to deal with espionage "vigorously." In the course of his three-year hunt, he had grown convinced that the United States was dangerously unprepared for the injuries a clandestine enemy could inflict on the homeland. We are a trusting nation, and that has made us a vulnerable one, he decided. A complacent America has developed neither the intelligence capabilities to collect information on our adversaries' plans nor the resources to stop terrorist attacks from happening.

The well-funded German secret service had destroyed, Tom knew, over $150 million in property during the past three years. Ships had foundered at sea. Factories had gone up in flames. Munitions depots had exploded. Assassins had been deployed. Germs had been spread. The sabotage had caused more than one hundred deaths.

The Bureau of Investigation, the Secret Service, Military Intelligence— all the supposedly vigilant resources the republic had assembled to guard its towns and cities—were feuding, disorganized, and ineffective. They did not gather information about the enemy agents quietly prowling the nation's streets. They were ignorant of the sinister aspirations of the forces preparing to attack, and of their frightful weapons.

In the end, it had been left to Tom and his small group of men to protect the homeland. Thrown into a war for which they were largely unprepared, in the course of its many battles they had succeeded in acquiring the ingenuity, tenacity, and self-sacrifice that this invisible conflict required of its secret soldiers. Their victories made the nation safer.

Still, this achievement was insufficient. Tom feared for the future. The nation had been exposed: it was a land of targets. Already the Capitol Building had been bombed, and anthrax deployed. Grim precedents had been established. In the years to come, what new terrors would strike his city, his country? Just as the saboteur's cigar bomb had been superseded by the ingenuity of the explosive rudder device, it was in the cruel nature of man to fabricate more destructive weapons, to perfect more effective ways to disseminate germs.

And then what?

Tom could only wonder.

A NOTE ON SOURCES

On the fourteenth floor of the redbrick police headquarters building in lower Manhattan, the commissioner meets every morning just after nine with the deputy commissioner for counterterrorism and the deputy commissioner for intelligence. The sessions take place in the Executive Command Center, a big room whose walls display video screens showing news broadcasts from all over the world, live videocasts of traffic from streets and highways, images from helicopters outfitted with radiation detection devices (RDDs) hovering above the piers and harbors, and recent crime reports from precincts.

The purpose of the meetings is to discuss any terrorist threats that have developed over the past twenty-four hours. As soon as the two commissioners are seated at the long table in the center of the room, they address what Police Chief Raymond Kelly, a flinty, hard-minded former street cop and marine, has called "the New York question." The commissioner wants to know what is happening anywhere in the world that could affect the safety of the city and its people.

I have been allowed to attend one of these Command Center briefings, given a seat in a straight-backed plastic chair against the wall underneath a video showing a live feed of Wall Street traffic. With rapt attention, I hear a chilling inventory of concerns: a possible bomb attack on a Port Authority train or tunnel at rush hour; a suspect in Virginia who may or may not be developing a biological weapon to use on subways; a cell in Jordan that quite possibly has ties to a group in Queens that has been taking photographs of the Brooklyn and Manhattan Bridges; and an al-Qaeda website that promises an attack on New York will come soon.

Yet as I listen, in my mind I find myself stripping away all the technology and nonessentials, and I realize that what is happening in this cloistered tower room is not all that different from what occurred nearly a century ago when Tom would take the private elevator up into the commissioner's mahogany-paneled office. Those meetings, too, were driven by brooding suspicions and gnawing fears.

And as I sit in this command post, it becomes clearer to me that in one large and affecting way, little has changed over the past one hundred years for the officers who are responsible for defending our sprawling republic. Like Tom with his victories over the ship bombers, von Rintelen, Fay, and Koenig, the homeland's new protectors have slain their dragons and made the country a safer place. Yet for them too there is always tomorrow, and with it comes the dread that someone is out there plotting, preparing, getting closer and closer to striking.

It was these thoughts that stayed prominent in my mind as I researched and wrote this book. The relevance of Tom Tunney's activities to today's headlines was a constant reminder to me that, as Faulkner observed, "the past is never past." It is one reason why I am drawn to history, and why I wanted to tell this story.

At the same time, my writing of this book was also influenced and inspired by the two other nonfiction tales I published immediately preceding this one. *American Lightning*, an account of the 1910 bombing of the Los Angeles Times Building that left twenty-one people dead, was at its dramatic core a story about the war between labor and capital that gripped the nation at the turn of the century. *The Floor of Heaven* was another story about the country at a turning point as the nineteenth century came to a close: with the West won, intrepid cowboys and pioneers set off to find new frontiers to conquer. And *Dark Invasion* is a story of the United States finding the will, the commitment, and the strength to become a world power.

Each of these three books tells an independent story, propelled by its own cast of real-life characters. However, together they form a sort of trilogy. And although the first book's narrative is shaped as a detective story, the next as a western, and this one as a spy tale, a bold central character unites and dominates these three self-contained histories: turn-of-the-century America. Each of these books focuses on a different and transforming aspect of the story of a young country struggling to come of age and assume its place in the world.

These are true stories. There are no inventions in my accounts. I have tried to re-create events as they happened, and with as much objectivity as possible. I have searched for intersecting circumstances and ideas, and then presented them in a way that made informed sense to me.

In order to write what the heroes and villains in this spy story were saying, doing, feeling, and even thinking accurately as well as vividly, I have relied on firsthand accounts and memoirs, in addition to contemporaneous newspaper stories, government documents, legal papers, and a tall stack of histories. Therefore, when quotation marks bracket any dialogue, this is an indication that at least one of the principals was the source. Further, when a character reveals what he is thinking or feeling, I found this too in a memoir, a letter, or a previously published interview.

Particularly valuable, then, in putting together this determinedly firsthand account were the papers and documents—1,032 cubic feet of them!—stored at the Foreign Affairs Branch of the National Archives in Washington. These archives contain the extensive files compiled by the Mixed Claims Commission of the United States and Germany, investigating the Black Tom explosion and the activities of the German spy network in the United States in the years preceding America's entry into the war, including testimony about

Abteilung IIIB's germ warfare program; transcripts of German government messages intercepted by the British; papers relating to the workings of British intelligence in America prior to the United States' entry into the war; testimony of witnesses and members of the German secret service; and biographies of the saboteurs.

A roughly equivalent resource, providing German documents and testimony by government officials, was published in two volumes by the Carnegie Endowment for International Peace in 1923: *Official German Documents Relating to the World War: The Report of the First and Second Subcommittee of the Committee Appointed by the National Constituent Assembly to Inquire into the Responsibility for the War.*

My understanding of President Wilson's evolving mind-set (as well as the government's mercurial positions regarding neutrality) was facilitated by the State Department's *Papers Relating to the Foreign Relations of the United States*, and *Supplements, World War, 1914–1918*, published by the Government Printing Office.

Similarly, Tom Tunney's candid postwar testimony to the Senate Judiciary Committee provided insight into his nascent role in counterintelligence: *Report and Hearings Before the Senate Subcommittee on the Judiciary*, 66th Cong., 1st sess., doc. 62 (1919). And a good overview of the entire fledgling American intelligence operation is provided by the many officials who testified in *Espionage and Interference with Neutrality: Hearings on H.R. 291 Before the Committee on the Judiciary*, 65th Cong., 1st sess. (1917).

I got an informed sense of the efficacy of J. P. Morgan Jr.'s. extensive machinations to influence aid for the Allies from reading the often acerbic testimony in *Investigation Relative to the Treaty of Peace with Germany: Hearings Before the U.S. State Senate Committee on Foreign Relations*, 66th Cong., 1st sess. (1919), as well as *Hearings Before the Special U.S. Senate Committee Investigating the Munitions Industry*, 74th Cong., 2nd sess. (1937).

I frequently consulted the myriad official government position papers and presidential speeches issued during the years leading to America's joining the Allies. The complete text of these was found at Brigham Young University's World War I Document Archive, available online at http://wwi.lib.byu.edu/index.

Books about World War I fill entire libraries, and over the four years I spent researching this book, my workroom became a daunting obstacle course littered with waist-high stacks of several hundred volumes. But rather than listing all the titles I consulted, as one would in an academic history, let me point the way for the curious general reader to those books that I found most valuable in telling this story.

Throttled! The Detection of the German and Anarchist Bomb Plotters, by Inspector Thomas J. Tunney with Paul Merrick Hollister, is a lively and very personal account of the investigations conducted by the man who, while he didn't have the title, was the nation's first head of homeland security. And reading Tunney's story in conjunction with Franz von Rintelen's two-volume memoir, *The Dark Invader* and *Return of the Dark Invader*, conveys a gripping sense of the cat-and-mouse game the two men were playing. Additionally, my knowledge of Tunney's career was greatly facilitated by photostats of his original New York Police Department service records, made available to me by Paul Browne, deputy commissioner of public information, NYPD, who also made it possible for me to attend the commissioner's daily intelligence briefing.

Other memoirs that effectively detail—although too often with melodramatic embellishments that strain credulity—what it was like to be a German agent behind the lines in enemy territory include the anonymously written *German Spy System from Within, by an Ex-Intelligence Officer*; Armgaard Karl Graves, *The Secrets of the German War Office*; "M.," *My Experiences in the German Espionage*; Edward Myers, *Adventures of a Former Agent of the Kaiser's Secret Service*; Horst von der Goltz, *My Adventures as a German Secret Agent*; and Eric Fisher Wood, *The Note-Book of an Intelligence Officer*.

Memoirs by diplomats are frequently more self-serving rewritings of history than factual accounts. Nevertheless, for the way they helped to evoke the frantic hustling through the corridors of power in Washington, New York, and Berlin as the war raged in Europe and was fought more covertly in America, I found useful the memoirs by James W. Gerard, *My Four Years in Germany* and *Face to Face with Kaiserism*; Robert Lansing, *War Memoirs*; Walter Nicolai, *The German Secret Service*; Johann von Bernstorff, *My Three Years in America* and *Memoirs of Count Bernstorff*; and Franz von Papen, *Memoirs*.

Additionally, while they are neither memoirs nor full-blown biographies, two affectionate histories give unique insight into two complicated men (and, in Case's book, reveal a bit about Tom Tunney too): Henry Jay Case, *Guy Hamilton Scull*; and Joseph P. Tumulty, *Woodrow Wilson as I Know Him*.

In piecing together the full scope of the German spy network's attack on America, I found some journalistic book-length accounts written in the aftermath of the initial revelations of the enemy operations to be essential models of detailed, if not always objective, reporting: George Barton, *Celebrated Spies and Famous Mysteries of the Great War*; John Price Jones and Paul Merrick Hollister, *The German Secret Service in America, 1914–1918*; Henry Landau, *The Enemy Within*; and French Strother, *Fighting Germany's Spies*.

This is territory that has been covered in more recent histories too. Jules Witcover's *Sabotage at Black Tom* is an important and very readable account of Germany's secret war in America. In *The Fourth Horseman*, Robert Koenig does groundbreaking original research into the first biowar against the nation; my account of Dilger and his activities is greatly indebted to Koenig's inventive and tenacious work. Chad Millman's well-documented and absorbing tale *The Detonators* puts particular emphasis on the Black Tom explosion. Barbara W. Tuchman's elegantly written *Zimmermann Telegram* provides insights into both the British and German spy operations in America. And the most comprehensive accounts of how both the federal government and the New York Police Department attempted to deal with enemy operatives in the years leading up to the war are Thomas A. Reppetto's *Battleground, New York City* and, written with James Lardner, *NYPD: A City and Its Police*. Mr. Reppetto is the foremost authority on the history of the New York Police Department, and he graciously supplemented the information in his books during the course of several spirited and entertaining conversations.

The books to which I most often turned to provide context on the world historical events that swirled around and influenced Tom Tunney's very personal quest included Herbert J. Bass, ed., *America's Entry into World War I*; Justin D. Doenecke, *Nothing Less Than War: A New History of America's Entry into World War I*; Richard Holmes, *The Oxford Companion to Military History*; John Keegan, *A History of Warfare* and *The First World War*; the first volume of John Bach McMaster, *United States in the World War*; Marc B. Powe, *The Emergence of the War Department Intelligence Agency, 1885–1918*; Charles Seymour, *Woodrow Wilson and the World War*; David Stevenson, *Cataclysm: The First World War as Political Tragedy*; and A. Willert, *The Road to Safety: A Study in Anglo-American Relations*.

Finally, I kept rereading several monographs, linchpins that both grounded and shaped my narrative. The ones I consulted most frequently included Tom Montalbano, "The Station Agent and the Anarchist," *Syosset Jericho Tribune*, March 19, 2010; Frank J. Rafalko, "Imperial Germany's Sabotage Operations in the U.S.," in *A Counterintelligence Reader: American Revolution to World War II*; Richard Spence, "Englishmen in New York: The SIS American Station, 1915–21," *Intelligence and National Security*; Michael Warner, "The Kaiser Sows Destruction: Protecting the Homeland the First Time Around," in *Studies in Intelligence*; Douglas Wheeler, "A Guide to the History of Intelligence, 1800–1918," *Intelligencer: Journal of U.S.*

Intelligence Studies; and, indispensably, Daniel E. Russell, *The Day Morgan Was Shot*.

The primary sources for each chapter of this book follow.

Prologue

Tunney, *Throttled!*; Russell, *Day Morgan Was Shot*; "Muenter, Once German Teacher Here," *Harvard Crimson*, February 14, 1942; "Invents Machines for 'Cure of Liars,'" *New York Times*, September 11, 1907; David J. Krajicek, "The Nutty Professor," *New York Daily News*, June 21, 1909; Harvard College German Club interviews and archives; Hugo Munsterberg, *On the Witness Stand: Essays on Psychology and Crime* (New York: Doubleday, Page, 1908) and *Psychology of the Teacher* (New York: Doubleday, Page, 1909); Matthew Hale Jr., *Hugo Munsterberg and the Origins of Applied Psychology* (Philadelphia: Temple University Press, 1980); Gregory Kimble et al., *Portraits of Pioneers of Psychology* (Washington, DC: American Psychological Association, 1991); "Seek Harvard Teacher," *New York Times*, May 26, 2008; interviews with Cambridge police; "No Trace of Muenter," *New York Times*, April 29, 1906; "Muenter Not Yet Found," *New York Times*, April 30, 1906.

Chapter 1

Tunney, *Throttled!*; "Trap Bomb Layer in Cathedral," *New York Times*, March 5, 1915; NYPD service records; "Fireman's Athletic Meet," *New York Times*, September 14, 1898; "Restores Shoo-Fly Squad," *New York Times*, September 16, 1910; "Catch Autoist Who Killed Dr. Bender," *New York Times*, August 16, 1911; "Find Where Crones Once Resided Here," *New York Times*, February 20, 1908; "Hartigan Facing Sentence Today," *New York Times*, March 26, 1913; "New York's IED Task Force, 1905–1919," *New York Times*, January 17, 1912, and "The EOD Operator Who Dealt with More IEDs Than Anyone Else," January 14, 1912, http://www.standingwellback.com/home/2012/1/14/the-eod-operator-who-dealt-with-more-ieds-than-anyone-else.html; Reppetto, *Battleground, New York City*; Reppetto and Lardner, *NYPD*; "T. J. Tunney Dead," *New York Times*, January 27, 1952.

Chapter 2

Tunney, *Throttled!*; Tresca and Pernicone, *The Autobiography of Carlo Tresca*; Case, *Guy Hamilton Scull*; Reppetto, *Battleground, New York City*; Reppetto and Lardner, *NYPD*; *New York Times*, March 15, 1915; Millman, *Detonators*.

Chapter 3

Tuchman, *Zimmermann*; Tuchman, *Guns*; von Bernstorff, *Three Years*; von Bernstorff, *Memoirs*; Doerries, *Imperial Challenge*; Carnegie Endowment, *Official German Documents*; *Foreign Affairs Documents*, National Archives; Gerard, *Four Years*; Millman, *Detonators*; Witcover, *Sabotage*; Jones and Hollister, *German Secret Service*; Landau, *Enemy Within*; Wheeler, "History of Intelligence"; Frank Harris, *Latest Contemporary Portraits* (New York: Macaulay, 1927).

Chapter 4

Nicolai, *German Secret Service*; Richelson, *Century of Spies*; von der Goltz, *My Adventures*; Jones and Hollister, *German Secret Service*; Landau, *Enemy Within*; Strother, *Fighting Germany's Spies*; Anonymous, *German Spy System*; Graves, *Secrets*; M, *My Experiences*; Richard B. Spence, "K. A. Jahnke and the German Sabotage Campaign in the United States and Mexico, 1914–1918," *Historian* 59, no. 1 (1996): 89–112; Millman, *Detonators*; Witcover, *Sabotage*; Carnegie Endowment, *Official German Documents*; Gerard, *Four Years*.

Chapter 5

Tunney, *Throttled!*; Case, *Guy Hamilton Scull*; *New York Times*, March 5, 1915; Tresca and Pernicone, *The Autobiography of Carlo Tresca*; Millman, *Detonators*; Reppetto, *Battleground, New York City*; Reppetto and Lardner, *NYPD*.

Chapter 6

Tuchman, *Guns*; Millman, *Detonators*; Jones and Hollister, *German Secret Service*; Landau, *Enemy Within*; Strother, *Fighting Germany's Spies*; Nicolai, *German Secret Service*; von Bernstorff, *Three Years*; von Bernstorff, *Memoirs*; Doerries, *Imperial Challenge*; Carnegie Endowment, *Official German Documents*; Witcover, *Sabotage*; Seymour, *Woodrow Wilson*; Bass, *America's Entry*; Doenecke, *Nothing Less*; McMaster, *United States in the World War*; Stevenson, *Cataclysm*.

Chapter 7

Tunney, *Throttled!*; Reppetto, *Battleground, New York City*; Reppetto and Lardner, *NYPD*; *New York Times*, March 5, 1915; Case, *Guy Hamilton Scull*.

Chapter 8

Von Bernstorff, *Three Years*; von Bernstorff, *Memoirs*; Witcover, *Sabotage*; Millman, *Detonators*; Tunney, *Throttled!*; New York Police Department service records; New York City real estate records; interviews with Fuller Place residents; Case, *Guy Hamilton Scull*.

Chapter 9

"Harvard Teacher Still at Large," *New York Times*, April 30, 1906; Russell, *Day Morgan Was Shot*; Tunney, *Throttled!*; Montalbano, "The Station Agent"; "Knew Muenter in Mexico," *New York Times*, July 10, 1915; "Muenter Letters Rational," *New York Times*, July 10, 1915; "Holt Is Muenter, Say Associates," *New York Times*, July 5, 1915.

Chapter 10

Von Bernstorff, *Memoirs*; Tuchman, *Zimmermann*; von Bernstorff, *Three Years*; Landau, *Enemy Within*; Millman, *Detonators*; Strother, *Fighting Germany's Spies*; Jones and Hollister, *German Secret Service*; Carnegie Endowment, *Official German Documents*; National Archives; Witcover, *Sabotage*; von der Goltz, *My Adventures*; Barton, *Celebrated Spies*; Wheeler, "History of Intelligence"; von Papen, *Memoirs*; Koeves, *Satan in Top Hat*; Doenecke, *Nothing Less*; McMaster, *United States in the World War*; Stevenson, *Cataclysm*; Tuchman, *Guns*.

Chapter 11

Von der Goltz, *My Adventures*; Witcover, *Sabotage*; Millman, *Detonators*; National Archives; Douglas L. Wheeler, "Spy Mania and the Information War: The Hour of the Counterspy, 1914/15," *American Intelligence Journal* 14, no. 1 (1993): 41–45; Wheeler, "History of Intelligence"; von Papen, *Memoirs*; Nicolai, *German Secret Service*.

Chapter 12

Carnegie Endowment, *Official German Documents*; National Archives; Tuchman, *Zimmermann*; Stevenson, *Cataclysm*; Witcover, *Sabotage*; Millman, *Detonators*; Landau, *Enemy Within*; Jones and Hollister, *German Secret Service*; Wheeler, "History of Intelligence"; "A Decent Bed," Streetscapes, *New York Times*, January 14, 2000.

Chapter 13

National Archives; Tuchman, *Zimmermann*; Tunney, *Throttled!*; Landau, *Enemy Within*; Jones and Hollister, *German Secret Service*; Warner, "Kaiser Sows Destruction"; Wheeler, "History of Intelligence."

Chapter 14

Tunney, *Throttled!*; Reppetto, *Battleground, New York City*; Reppetto and Lardner, *NYPD*; Case, *Guy Hamilton Scull*; Harvard College Alumni Directory; "Guy H. Scull Dies," *New York Times*, October 20, 1920; New York Police Department Museum; Tuchman, *Zimmermann*; Spence, "Englishmen in New York."

Chapter 15

Tuchman, *Zimmermann*; von der Goltz, *My Adventures*; Nicolai, *German Secret Service*; Carnegie Endowment, *Official German Documents*; National Archives, Hall's affidavit, Mixed Claims Commission; Landau, *Enemy Within*; Jones and Hollister, *German Secret Service*; James, *Eyes of the Navy*; Ewing, *Man of Room 40*; Willert, *Road to Safety*; Witcover, *Sabotage*; Millman, *Detonators*; Andrew, *Her Majesty's Secret Service*; Beesley, *Room 40*; Gannon, *Inside Room 40*.

Chapter 16

Tuchman, *Zimmermann*; Case, *Guy Hamilton Scull*; Tunney, *Throttled!*; Andrew, *Her Majesty's Secret Service*; Beesley, *Room 40*; Gannon, *Inside Room 40*; Warner, "Kaiser Sows Destruction"; Wheeler, "History of Intelligence"; National Archives; Spence, "Englishmen in New York"; Russell, *True Adventures*; George G. Aston, *Secret Service* (New York: Cosmopolitan, 1930);

Millman, *Detonators*; Witcover, *Sabotage*; Jeffrey M. Dorwart, *The Office of Naval Intelligence: The Birth of America's First Intelligence Agency, 1865–1918* (Annapolis, MD: Naval Institute Press, 1979); Jones and Hollister, *German Secret Service*; Powe, *War Department Intelligence Agency*; Willert, *Road to Safety*; *Report and Hearings Before the Senate Subcommittee on the Judiciary*, 65th Cong., 1st sess., doc. 62 (1919); *Espionage and Interference with Neutrality: Hearings on H.R. 291 Before the Committee on the Judiciary*, 65th Cong., 1st sess. (1917).

Chapter 17
Arthur Woods, "The Policeman of Today," *Journal of the National Institute of Social Science* 3 (1917); Tunney, *Throttled!*; Reppetto, *Battleground, New York City*; Reppetto and Lardner, *NYPD*; "Ex-Detective Barnitz Buried," *New York Times*, June 8, 1927; New York Police Department service records.

Chapter 18
Witcover, *Sabotage*; Millman, *Detonators*; Tunney, *Throttled!*; Lopate, *Waterfront*; Case, *Guy Hamilton Scull*.

Chapter 19
Witcover, *Sabotage*; Millman, *Detonators*; Tunney, *Throttled!*; Case, *Guy Hamilton Scull*; Landau, *Enemy Within*; Jones and Hollister, *German Secret Service*; Wheeler, "History of Intelligence"; R. B. Hill, "The Early Years of the Strowger System" and "Early Work on Dial System," *Bell Laboratories Record*, March 1953 and January 1953; Bob Stoffels, "Almon Brown Strowger and Patent No. 447,918," *OSP Magazine*, January 2010.

Chapter 20
Carnegie Endowment, *Official German Documents*; National Archives; Doenecke, *Nothing Less*; Stevenson, *Cataclysm*; Tuchman, *Zimmermann*; Millman, *Detonators*; Witcover, *Sabotage*; McMaster, *United States in the World War*; Chernow, *House of Morgan*; Forbes, *J. P. Morgan*; *Hearings Before the Special U.S. Senate Committee Investigating the Munitions Industry*, 74th Cong., 2nd sess. (1937); Willert, *Road to Safety*; Keegan, *First World War*; Tumulty, *Wilson*

as I Know Him; Daniels, *Years of Peace*; Dearle, *Economic Chronicle of the Great War*; Lansing, *War Memoirs*; "Wilson's Change of Attitude on War Loans" and "U.S. Policy on War Loans to Belligerents," Brigham Young University World War I Document Archive.

Chapter 21

Von Rintelen, *Dark Invader*; Millman, *Detonators*; Witcover, *Sabotage*; Nicolai, *German Secret Service*; Holmes, *Oxford Companion to Military History*; Tuchman, *Zimmermann*; Wheeler, "History of Intelligence"; Jones and Hollister, *German Secret Service*; Strother, *Fighting Germany's Spies*; Landau, *Enemy Within*; Keegan, *First World War*; Tuchman, *Guns*; Willert, *Road to Safety*; Tunney, *Throttled!*

Chapter 22

Russell, *Day Morgan Was Shot*; Montalbano, "Station Agent"; Tunney, *Throttled!*; *New York Times*, July 5, 1915; "Muenter Sang of Death," *New York Times*, July 8, 1915.

Chapter 23

Tunney, *Throttled!*; Carnegie Endowment, *Official German Documents*; National Archives; Witcover, *Sabotage*; Millman, *Detonators*; Wheeler, "History of Intelligence"; Jones and Hollister, *German Secret Service*; Strother, *Fighting Germany's Spies*; Landau, *Enemy Within*; von der Goltz, *My Adventures*; Case, *Guy Hamilton Scull*.

Chapter 24

Von Rintelen, *Dark Invader*; Nicolai, *German Secret Service*; Jones and Hollister, *German Secret Service*; Landau, *Enemy Within*; Millman, *Detonators*; Witcover, *Sabotage*; Tunney, *Throttled!*; von Papen, *Memoirs*; von Bernstorff, *Three Years*.

Chapter 25

Von Rintelen, *Dark Invader*; Witcover, *Sabotage*; Millman, *Detonators*; Tunney, *Throttled!*; National Archives; Tuchman, *Zimmermann*.

Chapter 26

Von Rintelen, *Dark Invader*; Tunney, *Throttled!*; Witcover, *Sabotage*; Millman, *Detonators*; Landau, *Enemy Within*; Strother, *Fighting Germany's Spies*; Wheeler, "History of Intelligence"; Willert, *Road to Safety*; National Archives, particularly Mixed Claims Commission files, Exhibit 320; *New York World*, May 1917 (several articles on von Rintelen's career); von Papen, *Memoirs*; Warner, "Kaiser Sows Destruction"; Keegan, *First World War*.

Chapter 27

Von Rintelen, *Dark Invader*; Witcover, *Sabotage*; Millman, *Detonators*; Tunney, *Throttled!*; National Archives, particularly Exhibit 320; Landau, *Enemy Within*; Jones and Hollister, *German Secret Service*; Strother, *Fighting Germany's Spies*; Tuchman, *Zimmermann*.

Chapter 28

Tunney, *Throttled!*; Case, *Guy Hamilton Scull*; Landau, *Enemy Within*; Jones and Hollister, *German Secret Service*; Strother, *Fighting Germany's Spies*; Wheeler, "History of Intelligence"; Willert, *Road to Safety*; Barton, *Celebrated Spies*.

Chapter 29

Tunney, *Throttled!*; Witcover, *Sabotage*; Millman, *Detonators*; Jones and Hollister, *German Secret Service*; Landau, *Enemy Within*; *Espionage and Interference with Neutrality: Hearings on H.R. 291 Before the Committee on the Judiciary*, 65th Cong., 1st sess. (1917); *Report and Hearings Before the Senate Subcommittee on the Judiciary*, 65th Cong., 1st sess., doc. 62 (1919).

Chapter 30

Tunney, *Throttled!*; Case, *Guy Hamilton Scull*; South Street Seaport Museum; Lopate, *Waterfront*; Barton, *Celebrated Spies*.

Chapter 31

Tunney, *Throttled!*; Jones and Hollister, *German Secret Service*; Landau, *Enemy Within*; Strother, *Fighting Germany's Spies*; Wheeler, "History of Intelligence"; Willert, *Road to Safety*; National Archives.

Chapter 32

Tunney, *Throttled!*; Witcover, *Sabotage*; Millman, *Detonators*; Landau, *Enemy Within*; Strother, *Fighting Germany's Spies*; Jones and Hollister, *German Secret Service*; New York Police Department service records; National Archives; George MacAdam, "Spies, Plotters, and Hysteria," *New York Times*, February 17, 1918; "Arrest Three More in Ship Bomb Plot," *New York Times*, November 1, 1915; "Von Papen Named in Plot," *New York Times*, April 12, 1918.

Chapter 33

Von Rintelen, *Dark Invader*; National Archives; Tunney, *Throttled!*; Landau, *Enemy Within*; Jones and Hollister, *German Secret Service*; Wheeler, "History of Intelligence"; Willert, *Road to Safety*; Witcover, *Sabotage*; Millman, *Detonators*.

Chapter 34

Von Rintelen, *Dark Invader*; *Official German Documents*; Tuchman, *Zimmermann*; Tunney, *Throttled!*; Spence, "Englishmen in New York"; *Espionage and Interference with Neutrality: Hearings on H.R. 291 Before the Committee on the Judiciary*, 65th Cong., 1st sess. (1917); "See Lamar's Hand in 'Labor' Peace Move," *New York Times*, June 26, 1915; *New York Times* articles on Lamar, 1913–18, passim; "The Wolf of Wall Street," *Nation* 97 (1917).

Chapter 35

Von Rintelen, *Dark Invader*; Tuchman, *Zimmermann*; Spence, "Englishmen in New York"; Willert, *Road to Safety*; Witcover, *Sabotage*; Millman, *Detonators*; Jones and Hollister, *German Secret Service*; Landau, *Enemy Within*; National Archives, particularly file 812.001 on Huerta; Report of House of Representatives Committee on Foreign Affairs, "German Community in Mexico," *Congressional Record* 55, no. 4; Voska and Irwin, *Spy and Counterspy*; *Report and Hearings Before the Senate Subcommittee on the Judiciary*, 65th Cong., 1st sess., doc. 62 (1919); *New York Times* articles on plot, August, November, and December 1915, passim.

Chapter 36

Von Rintelen, *Dark Invader*; Landau, *Enemy Within*; National Archives, particularly Mixed Claims Commission files; Witcover, *Sabotage*; Millman, *Detonators*; Tunney, *Throttled!*; Nicolai, *German Secret Service*; Wheeler, "History of Intelligence"; Willert, *Road to Safety*.

Chapter 37

Russell, *Day Morgan Was Shot*; Montalbano, "Station Agent"; Tunney, *Throttled!*; "Critics Silence Prof. Gould," *New York Times*, July 8, 1915; "Point of Ethics" (editorial), *Chicago Herald*, July 9, 1915; "Glad He Shielded Muenter," *New York Times*, July 9, 1915; "Schiff Foundation Purpose to Be Changed," *New York Times*, June 25, 1918.

Chapter 38

Tunney, *Throttled!*; Spence, "Englishmen in New York"; von Rintelen, *Dark Invader*; Case, *Guy Hamilton Scull*; Millman, *Detonators*; Witcover, *Sabotage*; Landau, *Enemy Within*; Jones and Hollister, *German Secret Service*; Willert, *Road to Safety*; National Archives, particularly Mixed Claims Commission files; Reppetto, *Battleground, New York City*.

Chapter 39

Tunney, *Throttled!*; Landau, *Enemy Within*; Strother, *Fighting Germany's Spies*; Jones and Hollister, *German Secret Service*; Willert, *Road to Safety*; Wheeler, "History of Intelligence"; National Archives; Witcover, *Sabotage*; Millman, *Detonators*.

Chapter 40

Tunney, *Throttled!*; Reppetto, *Battleground, New York City*; Reppetto and Lardner, *NYPD*; Landau, *Enemy Within*; National Archives, particularly Mixed Claims Commission files; Jones and Hollister, *German Secret Service*; Wheeler, "History of Intelligence"; von Rintelen, *Dark Invader*.

Chapter 41

National Archives, particularly Mixed Claims Commission files; Tunney,

Throttled!; Witcover, *Sabotage*; Millman, *Detonators*; Jones and Hollister, *German Secret Service*; Landau, *Enemy Within*; Strother, *Fighting Germany's Spies*; Koenig, *Fourth Horseman*; Jamie Bisher, "During World War, Terrorists Schemed to Use Anthrax in the Cause of Finnish Independence," *Military History*, August 2003; Basil Clarke, "The Story of the British War-Horse from Prairie to Battlefield," in *The Great War* (London: Amalgamated Press, 1917); Cooper, *Animals in War*; Witcover, *Sabotage*; Millman, *Detonators*; Geissler, *Biological and Toxin Weapons*; Livingston and Roberts, *War Horse*; Miller, Engleberg, and Broad, *Germs*; Marchisio and Noreisch, "Chemical Warfare"; "Glanders," Center for Food Security and Public Health, Iowa State University, 2008; "Glanders," Centers for Disease Control, http://www.cdc.gov/glanders/; "Technical Fact Sheet on Glanders," Louisiana State University.

Chapter 42
Russell, *Day Morgan Was Shot*; Montalbano, "Station Agent"; Tunney, *Throttled!*; Munsterberg, *War and America*; unsigned review of *The War and America*, *New York Times*, September 20, 1914.

Chapter 43
Interview with Thomas Twetten, former director of operations, CIA; Tunney, *Throttled!*; Russell, *Day Morgan Was Shot*; Montalbano, "Station Agent"; Voska and Irwin, *Spy and Counterspy*.

Chapter 44
Russell, *Day Morgan Was Shot*; Montalbano, "Station Agent"; Tunney, *Throttled!*; Witcover, *Sabotage*; Landau, *Enemy Within*; *New York Times*, July 1915, passim; New York Police Department service records; Glen Cove Historical Society; Chernow, *House of Morgan*; Forbes, *J. P. Morgan*.

Chapter 45
U.S. Capitol Visitor Center Guide, U.S. Printing Office; Tour of Capitol Building, Capitol Guide Service; Tunney, *Throttled!*; Russell, *Day Morgan Was Shot*; Montalbano, "Station Agent"; *New York Times*, July 1915, passim.

Chapter 46

Russell, *Day Morgan Was Shot*; Forbes, *J. P. Morgan*; Chernow, *House of Morgan*; Tunney, *Throttled!*; Montalbano, "Station Agent"; *New York Times*, July 1915, passim; Glen Cove Historical Society.

Chapter 47

Tunney, *Throttled!*; visit to Gravesend Park; New York Police Department service records; Russell, *Day Morgan Was Shot*; Montalbano, "Station Agent"; *New York Times* articles on Muenter and Morgan, July 1915, passim, and particularly "Prominent Oyster Bay Residents Want Better Protection," July 10, 1915.

Chapter 48

Russell, *Day Morgan Was Shot*; Tunney, *Throttled!*; Montalbano, "Station Agent"; *New York Times*, July 1915, passim, and particularly "Holt Is Muenter, Say Associates," July 15, 1915; City of Cambridge Police Department, website and interviews.

Chapter 49

Russell, *Day Morgan Was Shot*; Tunney, *Throttled!*; Montalbano, "Station Agent"; *New York Times*, July 1915, passim, particularly "Seek Dynamite Muenter Hid," July 8, 1915, "Muenter's Acid Bomb Myth," July 8, 1915, "Dynamite Buyer Had Holt's Alias," July 6, 1915, "Holt's Past Dark to Wife," July 6, 1915, and "Muenter's Brain Held for Alienist," July 9, 1915; Spence, "Englishmen in New York"; Tuchman, *Zimmermann*; von Rintelen, *Dark Invader*; *New York Times* interviews with Rintelen, October 4, 1939, and January 3, 1940, in which he concludes his recall was "a trick"; Millman, *Detonators*.

Chapter 50

Ernest W. Henberg, "The Thrifty Spy on the Sixth Ave El," *American Heritage* 17, no. 1 (1965); McAdoo, *Crowded Years*; Russell, *True Adventures*; Jones and Hollister, *German Secret Service*; Landau, *Enemy Within*; Wheeler, "History of Intelligence"; Willert, *Road to Safety*; Strother, *Fighting Germany's Spies*; Warner, "Kaiser Sows Destruction"; Tuchman, *Zimmermann*; Tunney, *Throttled!*;

Witcover, *Sabotage*; Millman, *Detonators*; "U.S. Protests Against Maritime Warfare," Brigham Young University documents archives; Doenecke, *Nothing Less*; von Rintelen, *Dark Invader*; National Archives; Committee on the Judiciary, House of Representatives, 1917; Stevenson, *Cataclysm*; Senate hearing on munitions industry, 1937; *New York World*, August 15, 1915; Spence, "Englishmen in New York"; William J. Flynn, "Trapped Wires," *Liberty*, June 2, 1928; Thwaites, *Velvet and Vinegar*; Tumulty, *Wilson as I Know Him*.

Chapter 51

Koenig, *The Fourth Horseman*; National Archives, particularly Mixed Claims Commission files; Millman, *Detonators*; Witcover, *Sabotage*; Miller, Engleberg, and Broad, *Germs*; Geissler, *Biological and Toxin Weapons*; Jones and Hollister, *German Secret Service*; Landau, *Enemy Within*; Wheeler, "History of Intelligence"; Warner, "Kaiser Sows Destruction."

Chapter 52

Clint Padgitt, "German Seamen's Mission of New York, 1907–2001," *Newsletter of the International Association for the Study of Maritime Mission*, Spring/Summer 2001; Tunney, *Throttled!*; New York Police Department service records; National Archives; Jones and Hollister, *German Secret Service*; Landau, *Enemy Within*; Wheeler, "History of Intelligence"; Warner, "Kaiser Sows Destruction"; Millman, *Detonators*; Witcover, *Sabotage*.

Chapter 53

Tunney, *Throttled!*; Landau, *Enemy Within*; Jones and Hollister, *German Secret Service*; Wheeler, "History of Intelligence"; Warner, "Kaiser Sows Destruction"; von Rintelen, *Dark Invader*; National Archives, particularly Mixed Claims Commission files.

Chapter 54

Koenig, *Fourth Horseman*; von Rintelen, *Dark Invader*; National Archives, particularly Mixed Claims Commission files; Jones and Hollister, *German Secret Service*; Landau, *Enemy Within*; Carnegie Endowment, *Official German Documents*.

Chapter 55

Tunney, *Throttled!*; Case, *Guy Hamilton Scull*; Keegan, *First World War*; New York City subway official history, www.mta.info/nyct/facts/ffhist.htm and www.nycsubway.org; Millman, *Detonators*; Witcover, *Sabotage*; Doenecke, *Nothing Less*; Jones and Hollister, *German Secret Service*; Landau, *Enemy Within*; Strother, *Fighting Germany's Spies*; Wheeler, "History of Intelligence"; Willert, *Road to Safety*; McMaster, *United States in the World War*; Tuchman, *Zimmermann*; Seymour, *Intimate Papers of Colonel House*.

Chapter 56

Tunney, *Throttled!*; Jones and Hollister, *German Secret Service*; Landau, *Enemy Within*; Wheeler, "History of Intelligence"; Warner, "Kaiser Sows Destruction"; Strother, *Fighting Germany's Spies*; National Archives.

Chapter 57

Koenig, *Fourth Horseman*; National Archives, particularly Mixed Claims Commission files; Millman, *Detonators*; Witcover, *Sabotage*; Miller, Engleberg, and Broad, *Germs*; Geissler, *Biological and Toxin Weapons*; Landau, *Enemy Within*; Jones and Hollister, *German Secret Service*; Tunney, *Throttled!*; Marchisio and Noreisch, "Chemical Warfare."

Chapter 58

Koenig, *Fourth Horseman*; National Archives, particularly Mixed Claims Commission files; Miller, Engleberg, and Broad, *Germs*; Geissler, *Biological and Toxin Weapons*; Marchisio and Noreisch, "Chemical Warfare"; Nathaniel Potter, "Human Glanders: A Report of Three Cases, One of Which Was Unsuccessfully Treated with Large Doses of Autogenous Vaccines," *Bulletin of the Department of Public Charities* 1, no. 1 (1916): 5–30; Bellevue Hospital records; Johns Hopkins Hospital records and interviews with Immunology Department physicians; Tunney, *Throttled!*

Chapter 59

Koenig, *Fourth Horseman*; Nicolai, *German Secret Service*; Millman, *Detonators*; Witcover, *Sabotage*; Landau, *Enemy Within*; Jones and Hollister, *German*

Secret Service; Strother, *Fighting Germany's Spies*; Warner, "Kaiser Sows Destruction"; von Rintelen, *Dark Invader*; Tunney, *Throttled!*

Chapter 60

"U.S. Protests Against Maritime Warfare," Brigham Young University archives; Tuchman, *Zimmermann*; Spence, "Englishmen in New York"; Witcover, *Sabotage*; Millman, *Detonators*; Landau, *Enemy Within*; Wheeler, "History of Intelligence"; Warner, "Kaiser Sows Destruction"; Doenecke, *Nothing Less*; McMaster, *United States in the World War*; von Berstorff, *Three Years*; Tumulty, *Wilson as I Know Him*; *New York Times*, February–March 1917, passim; Tunney, *Throttled!*; "City's Bomb Squad Goes to the Army," *New York Times*, December 10, 1917; Jones and Hollister, *German Secret Service*; New York Police Department service records; Reppetto, *Battleground, New York City*.

BIBLIOGRAPHY

Andrew, Christopher. *Her Majesty's Secret Service: The Making of British Intelligence*. New York: Viking, 1986.

Anonymous. *The German Spy System from Within, by an Ex–Intelligence Officer*. London: Hodder & Stoughton, 1915.

Barton, George. *Celebrated Spies and Famous Mysteries of the Great War*. Boston: Page, 1919.

Bass, Herbert J., ed. *America's Entry into World War I*. New York: Dryden Press, 1964.

Beesley, Patrick. *Room 40: British Naval Intelligence, 1914–18*. London: Hamish Hamilton, 1982.

Carnegie Endowment for International Peace. *Official German Documents Relating to the World War: The Report of the First and Second Subcommittee of the Committee Appointed by the National Constituent Assembly to Inquire into the Responsibility for the War*. 2 vols. New York: Oxford University Press, 1965.

Case, Henry Jay. *Guy Hamilton Scull*. New York: Duffield, 1922.

Chernow, Ron. *The House of Morgan: An American Banking Dynasty and the Rise of Modern Finance*. New York: Grove Press, 2010.

Cooper, Jilly. *Animals in War*. New York: Lyons Press, 2003.

Daniels, Josephus. *The Years of Peace, 1910–1917*. Vol. 1 of *The Wilson Era*. Chapel Hill: University of North Carolina Press, 1946.

Dearle, N. B. *An Economic Chronicle of the Great War for Great Britain and Ireland*. Oxford: Oxford University Press, 1929.

Doenecke, Justin D. *Nothing Less Than War: A New History of America's Entry into World War I*. Lexington: University Press of Kentucky, 2011.

Doerries, Reinhard R. *Imperial Challenge: Ambassador Count von Bernstorff and German-American Relations, 1908–1917*. Chapel Hill: University of North Carolina Press, 1989.

Ewing, Alfred, Jr. *The Man of Room 40: The Life of Sir Alfred Ewing*. London: Hutchinson, 1939.

Forbes, John Douglas. *J. P. Morgan, Jr., 1867–1943*. Charlottesville: University of Virginia Press, 1988.

Gannon, Paul. *Inside Room 40*. London: Ian Allen, 2011.

Geissler, Erhard, ed. *Biological and Toxin Weapons: Research, Development and Use from the Middle Ages to 1943*. Oxford: Oxford University Press, 1999.

Gerard, James W. *My Four Years in Germany*. New York: G. H. Doran, 1917.

———. *Face to Face with Kaiserism*. New York: G. H. Doran, 1918.

Graves, Armgaard Karl. *The Secrets of the German War Office*. New York: McBride, Nast, 1914.

Holmes, Richard. *The Oxford Companion to Military History*. Oxford: Oxford University Press, 2001.

James, Sir William. *The Eyes of the Navy: A Biographical Study of Admiral Sir Reginald Hall*. London: Methuen, 1956.

Jones, John Price, and Paul Merrick Hollister. *The German Secret Service in America, 1914–1918*. Boston: Small, Maynard, 1918.

Keegan, John. *A History of Warfare*. New York: Vintage Books, 1994.

———. *The First World War*. New York: Alfred A. Knopf, 1998.

Koenig, Robert. *The Fourth Horseman*. New York: PublicAffairs, 2006.

Koeves, Tibor. *Satan in Top Hat*. New York: Alliance, 1941.

Landau, Henry. *The Enemy Within*. New York: Putnam, 1937.

Lansing, Robert. *War Memoirs*. Indianapolis: Bobbs-Merrill, 1935.

Livingston, Phil, and Ed Roberts. *War Horse: Mounting the Cavalry with America's Finest Horses*. New York: Black Sky Press, 2003.

Lopate, Phillip. *Waterfront: A Journey Around Manhattan*. New York: Crown, 2004.

M. *My Experiences in the German Espionage*. New York: BiblioBazaar, 2010.

Marchisio, M., and W. Noreisch. "Chemical Warfare During World War One (1914–1918): Remarks Related to the Horses Employed in the Main Armies." Paper presented at the 35th International Conference of the World Association for the History of Veterinary Medicine, Turin, 2004. http://documenti.fondiz.it/59.pdf.

McAdoo, William Gibbs. *Crowded Years*. Boston: Houghton-Mifflin, 1931.

McMaster, John Bach. *United States in the World War*. Vol. 1. New York: D. Appleton, 1918.

Miller, Judith, Stephen Engleberg, and William Broad. *Germs: Biological Weapons and America's Secret War.* New York: Simon & Schuster, 2001.

Millman, Chad. *The Detonators.* New York: Little, Brown, 2006.

Montalbano, Tom. "The Station Agent and the Anarchist." *Syosset Jericho Tribune*, March 19, 2010.

Munsterberg, Hugo. *The War and America.* New York: D. Appleton, 1914.

Myers, Edward. *Adventures of a Former Agent of the Kaiser's Secret Service.* London: Hodder & Stoughton, 1914.

Nicolai, Walter. *The German Secret Service.* London: Stanley Paul, 1924.

Powe, Marc B. *The Emergence of the War Department Intelligence Agency, 1885–1918.* Manhattan, KS: Military Affairs, 1975.

Rafalko, Frank J. "Imperial Germany's Sabotage Operations in the U.S." Chap. 3 in *A Counterintelligence Reader: American Revolution to World War II*, vol. 1. Washington, DC: National Counterintelligence Center, 2006. www.fas.org/irp/ops/ci/docs/ci1/ch3c.htm.

Reppetto, Thomas A. *Battleground, New York City.* Washington, DC: Potomac Books, 2012.

Reppetto, Thomas A., with James Lardner. *NYPD: A City and Its Police.* New York: Macmillan, 2001.

Richelson, Jeffrey T. *A Century of Spies: Intelligence in the Twentieth Century.* New York: Oxford University Press, 1997.

Russell, Charles Edmund. *True Adventures of the Secret Service.* New York: Burt, 1923.

Russell, Daniel E. *The Day Morgan Was Shot.* Glen Cove: Privately printed, 2004.

Seymour, Charles. *Woodrow Wilson and the World War.* New Haven, CT: Yale University Press, 1921.

———. *The Intimate Papers of Colonel House.* 4 vols. Boston: Houghton Mifflin, 1926–28.

Spence, Richard. "Englishmen in New York: The SIS American Station, 1915–21." *Intelligence and National Security* (London), 2004.

Stevenson, David. *Cataclysm: The First World War as Political Tragedy.* New York: Basic Books, 2004.

Strother, French. *Fighting Germany's Spies.* New York: Doubleday, Page, 1918.

Thwaites, Norman. *Velvet and Vinegar.* London: Grayson and Grayson, 1932.

Tresca, Carlo, and Nunzio Pernicone. *The Autobiography of Carlo Tresca.* New

York: John D. Calandra Italian American Institute, Queens College, City University of New York, 2003.

Tuchman, Barbara W. *The Guns of August*. New York: Ballantine Books, 1962.

———. *The Zimmermann Telegram*. New York: Ballantine Books, 1979.

Tumulty, Joseph P. *Woodrow Wilson as I Know Him*. New York: Doubleday, Page, 1921.

Tunney, Thomas J., with Paul Merrick Hollister. *Throttled! The Detection of the German and Anarchist Bomb Plotters*. Boston: Small, Maynard, 1919.

Von Bernstorff, Johann. *My Three Years in America*. New York: Scribner's, 1920.

———. *Memoirs of Count Bernstorff*. New York: Random House, 1936.

Von der Goltz, Horst. *My Adventures as a German Secret Agent*. New York: Robert M. McBride, 1917.

Von Papen, Franz. *Memoirs*. London: A. Deutsch, 1932.

Von Rintelen, Franz. *The Dark Invader: Wartime Reminiscences of a German Naval Intelligence Officer*. London: Lovat Dickson, 1933.

———. *Return of the Dark Invader*. London: Dickson & Thompson, 1935.

Voska, Emanuel Victor, and Will Irwin. *Spy and Counterspy*. New York: Doubleday, 1940.

Warner, Michael. "The Kaiser Sows Destruction: Protecting the Homeland the First Time Around." *Studies in Intelligence* (CIA Center for the Study of Intelligence) 46, no. 1 (2002): 3–9.

Wheeler, Douglas. "A Guide to the History of Intelligence, 1800–1918." *Intelligencer: Journal of U.S. Intelligence Studies* 19, no. 1 (2012): 47–50.

Willert, A. *The Road to Safety: A Study in Anglo-American Relations*. London: Derek Verchoyle, 1952.

Witcover, Jules. *Sabotage at Black Tom*. Chapel Hill, NC: Algonquin Books, 1989.

Wood, Eric Fisher. *The Note-Book of an Intelligence Officer*. New York: Century, 1917.

ACKNOWLEDGMENTS

I've put in enough days at my desk staring at a computer screen to come to realize that setting off to write a book, like embarking on any new love affair, can lead to some pretty rocky times. And, providentially, to days that zip by like a joyride, too. In writing this book I was particularly fortunate to be able to reach out, in both stormy and sunny weather, to a lot of people for support, advice, and comfort.

Lynn Nesbit has been my agent forever (or so it seems), and her friendship and wisdom are pillars I lean on. And in her office, I could always depend on Stephanie Koven, Lenore Hoffman, Tina Simms, and Hannah Davey.

At HarperCollins, I benefited from Jonathan Burnham's enthusiasm, Claire Wachtel's precise and authoritative editing, and Hannah Wood's many kindnesses.

I was also encouraged and guided in my work on this book by Rick Horgan and Nathan Roberson, who gave the manuscript several insightful reads. I owe both Rick and Nate large debts.

Bob Bookman, as he has for so many of my previous books, took the manuscript in hand and smartly guided it through the perils of Hollywood. It was Bob who brought this story to the attention of Warner Brothers, Bradley Cooper, and John Lesher, who will be producing the film based on this book. And now I can look forward to seeing Bradley's portrayal of Tom Tunney. Alan Hergott, still the wisest man I know, and Cindy Granta were also there to help in this complicated process.

At *Vanity Fair*, both Graydon Carter and Dana Brown were kind enough to read early versions of the manuscript and offer support.

And throughout the long process of writing, I leaned on my generous sister Marcy as well as a lot of friends who were there to rush to the rescue when things got sticky: Ken Lipper, Beth DeWoody, Susan and David Rich, Irene and Phil Werber, Sarah and Bill Rauch, Ed Koch, John Leventhal, Bruce Taub, Scott Silver, Pat and Bob Lusthaus, Bob Mitchell, Betsey and Len Rappoport, and Claudie and Andrew Skonka.

My children were another blessing. I'm immensely proud of Tony, Anna, and Dani and all they've accomplished. And, not least, I'm so very grateful to Daisy and Ivana.

CREDITS

———

Grateful acknowledgment is made for permission to reprint the following:

iv   *Chronicling America: Historic American Newspapers,* Library of Congress (http://chroniclingamerica.loc.gov/lccn/sn84026749/1915-07-04/ed-1/seq-1/)

7   © Bettmann/Corbis

16   Thomas J. Tunney, *Throttled!*

17   Thomas J. Tunney, *Throttled!*

20   George Grantham Bain Collection, Library of Congress

29   Harris & Ewing Collection, Library of Congress

33   akg-images / Imagno

44   George P. Hall and Son / Museum of the City of New York

47   George Grantham Bain Collection, Library of Congress

49   ullstein bild / The Granger Collection, NYC

61   George Grantham Bain Collection, Library of Congress

71   George Grantham Bain Collection, Library of Congress

72   Harris & Ewing Collection, Library of Congress

74   Harris & Ewing Collection, Library of Congress

76   Getty Images

87   John Price Jones and Paul Merrick Hollister, *The German Secret Service in America*

93   Thomas J. Tunney, *Throttled!*

107   Reproduced by permission of the National Library of Scotland

110   Courtesy Federal Bureau of Investigation

INDEX

Page numbers in *italics* refer to illustrations.

ABOUT THE AUTHOR

―――――

Howard Blum is the author of the *New York Times* bestseller and Edgar Award winner *American Lightning*, as well as *Wanted!*, *The Gold Exodus*, *Gangland*, and, most recently, *The Floor of Heaven*. Blum is a contributing editor at *Vanity Fair*. While at the *New York Times*, he was twice nominated for a Pulitzer Prize for investigative reporting. He lives in Connecticut and is the father of three children.

BOOKS BY HOWARD BLUM

DARK INVASION
1915: Germany's Secret War and the Hunt for the First Terrorist Cell in America
Available in Paperback and eBook

At the page-turning pace of a spy thriller, *Dark Invasion* tells the remarkable true story of Tunney and his pivotal role in discovering, and delivering to justice, a ruthless ring of German terrorists determined to annihilate the United States. As explosions leveled munitions plants and destroyed cargo ships, particularly in and around New York City, panicked officials talked about rogue activists and anarchists—but it was Tunney who suspected that these incidents were part of something bigger and became determined to bring down the culprits.

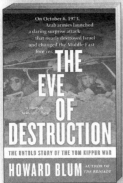

THE EVE OF DESTRUCTION
The Untold Story of the Yom Kippur War
Available in Paperback and eBook

In *Eve of Destruction*, the thrilling sequel to *New York Times* bestselling author Patrick Carman's *Dark Eden*, the seven teens who were "cured" by Rainsford reunite to find relief from their ailments . . . and realize they may have the power to stop Rainsford's ghoulish reign once and for all. Ensnared in a dangerous and ever-deepening mystery, Will Besting must lead his friends through a perilous underground trap masterminded by two devious souls at war with one another. It's a game of cat-and-mouse, and not everyone will be alive when it's over.

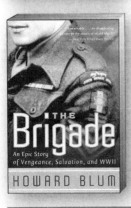

THE BRIGADE
An Epic Story of Vengeance, Salvation, and WWII
Available in Paperback and eBook

November 1944. The British government finally agrees to send a brigade of 5,000 Jewish volunteers from Palestine to Europe to fight the German army. But when the war ends and the soldiers witness firsthand the horrors their people have suffered in the concentration camps, the men launch a brutal and calculating campaign of vengeance. Their own ferocity threatens to overwhelm them until a fortuitous encounter with an orphaned girl sets the men on a course of action—rescuing Jewish war orphans and transporting them to Palestine—that will not only change their lives but also help create a nation and forever alter the course of world history.